OUR MOTHERS

OUR MOTHERS' SPIRITS

*Great Writers on the Death of Mothers
and the Grief of Men*

An Anthology

EDITED BY
BOB BLAUNER

ReganBooks
An Imprint of HarperPerennial
A Division of HarperCollins*Publishers*

First ReganBooks/HarperPerennial edition published 1999

Designed by Laura Lindgren

ISBN 0-06-098731-6

97 98 99 00 01 ❖/RRD 10 9 8 7 6 5 4 3 2 1

To Karina

CONTENTS

My deepest appreciation goes to all the writers of original articles, those I was able to include and those I wasn't, writers who had the courage to tackle a most difficult subject for a man, that of our relationship with our mothers. Then I want to specifically thank Peter Najarian for referring John Boe to me, Fred Moramarco for suggesting I get in touch with Gary Young, and Harry Brod for recommending Norman Sasowsky. Opal Palmer Adisa directed me to Juan Felipe Herrera, and Steve Masover came to my attention through Candace Falk.

Ideas for the previously published writers came from all quarters, but I found the fourth-floor stacks of the Berkeley Public Library's downtown branch—the 920 section for memoir and autobiography—to be the richest mine of usable material. Long live public libraries, they need our support.

This book is limited to the writings of men; we get the perspectives of women and mothers only indirectly. It was painful not to include Adrienne Rich's poem about one of her sons, "This." So it is important to acknowledge that such a book as *Our Mothers' Spirits* could not have been written without the pioneering work of women writers, some, but not all, feminists. I was influenced and inspired by Rich's *Of Woman Born.* Nancy Chodorow's *The Reproduction of Mothering* is another classic work of the late 1970s. Three pathbreaking books appeared in the early 1980s: Carole Klein's *Mothers and Sons,* Judith Arcana's *Every Mother's Son,* and Paul Olsen's moving and insightful *Sons and Mothers.* In the 1990s, also, women have been more likely than men to address the son-mother relationship. I think of

Olga Silverstein's *The Courage to Raise Good Men,* among a number of general works.

I am indebted to Judith Regan for seeing the potential of my subject matter and to some very helpful editors at Regan-Books/HarperCollins: Todd Silverstein, Emily Sklar, Andrew Albanese, and, above all, Dana Isaacson, who has so competently guided this book toward publication. I also want to thank Greg Villepique for his excellent copyediting. Jim Fox, of Harper-Collins's legal department, gave me good advice on permissions matters.

I am grateful to Dan Zola for his reading of the manuscript and to Stanley Marcus for some important legwork in finding books and photos. For submitting photos I want to thank, in addition to all the "original" essayists, Hilton Als and his photographer, Darryl Turner; T. George Harris; Paul Matthews; Andrew Solomon; Mary Stegner; and John Updike. Two artist-writers, Peter Najarian and Daniel Oberti, also contributed original line drawings.

My agent, Andrew Blauner of Blauner Books, has to be the best agent in the country. His enthusiasm for the project never wavered. And even when the book in a much earlier incarnation was probably setting records for rejection notices, Andrew always seemed to know more editors and more publishing houses to submit it to. His good advice has been indispensable and his positive attitude has sustained me.

Karina Epperlein provided much more than her daily offerings of love and encouragement. She read the essays as they came in and provided critical suggestions that improved many of the pieces. With an artist's eye she envisioned the project as a whole, and it was she who first thought of framing it on death and dying. Without her my life would be infinitely less rich and the present book might not exist at all.

The older I get, the more I look like my mother. Peering at my face in the mirror, I recognize many of her features, a resemblance I could not notice when I was younger. Had someone pointed it out to me then, I would have protested vigorously. My mother, Esther Shapiro Blauner, has been dead ten years now. I still miss her. When a mother dies at a ripe old age — mine was eighty-seven — it is one of life's natural events. "No big deal," we are led to believe, not like the death of a young mother who leaves children who are not yet grown. Not as momentous a disorientation to our lives as the death of a spouse or a partner. After all, we no longer live with our mothers, nor are we supposedly dependent on them. Nor as tragic and heart-rending as the death of a child to his or her parents. That kind of death violates the order of the universe. So it is no wonder that most of the academic studies and even the personal narratives about grief and loss focus on the deaths of children and of spouses, and not on our old gray parents.

Yet the deaths of our parents *are* momentous events. No matter if we are already in our forties, fifties, or even sixties when we lose a mother, her death still orphans us, as Marc Angel argues in his book *The Adult Orphan*. We are disoriented, thrown into a situation of loss that is something like being "shipwrecked," to borrow Angel's use of Ortega y Gasset's metaphor. The gravity of a mother's death for her son is a central theme of the essays now sprawled on my desk. I read them over and over preparing to write this introduction and ask myself what these stories say about men and their mothers, about the death of parents, about loss and grief, about generational ties and conflicts, about the human spirit, and the spirit, above all, of mothers.

Our Mothers' Spirits is a collection of personal narratives in which men tell the stories of their mothers' lives and deaths. I have chosen a mother's final illness and death as my focal point for a number of reasons. First, it is death that sets off a life so that we can see it whole. A mother's passing, for many of our writers, became the spur to make her spirit manifest to the world, to evoke her being in print. And no matter how advanced we are in age or development, the death of a parent will stir powerful emotions within us. It can cause us to question our lives, our values, our reasons for existence. A mother's dying does not end our relationship with her. Rather it throws that relationship into relief and often is the impetus for a man to reassess and transform it, internally at least. The death of a loved one asks us, finally, to mourn. We see in this book the various ways men grieve—and sometimes fail to grieve—the loss of their mothers, and how a mother's death can be a kind of "initiatory experience" (to use Michael Meade's term), changing a man forever.

For most men, the recognition that we carry forward our mother's spirit will come only in their middle years or in their old age—if at all.

Our mothers' spirits. What do I mean by *spirit*, that word at once vague and bandied about, used and misused?

First, I am struck by how *spirited* these mothers are. Almost without exception they are spunky, feisty, strong, larger than life—even and especially when they are short physically! (My mother, as well as Lucia Herrera and Peggy Wellman, powerful women all, were each under five feet.) Even some of the women who are hard to like, portrayed in these pages as obnoxious and miserable by their sons, are nevertheless in their own ways quite courageous.

For many of the writer-sons in this book, such a spirited mother becomes a model. Some men like John Updike and

Peter Najarian recognize this when their mothers are still alive. For others it is their death and dying that becomes a source of inspiration.

Many of our mothers impressed their sons by dying without apparent fear or anxiety, a fearlessness that was astonishing, even heroic to their sons. The mother of Kirk Douglas, on her hospital deathbed, catches the fear in her actor son's eyes and tells him: "Don't be scared, Issur, it happens to all of us." Douglas contrasts his mother's attitude with his father's fear in the face of death; a similar comparison is made by T. S. Matthews.

By her mid-seventies, my own mother, who I had thought could never directly face any of life's unpleasantnesses, began talking openly and without discomfort about her death in a series of conversations that I, her "enlightened" son, was by no means ready for. Perhaps the most striking model of dying in *Our Mothers' Spirits* is that of Andrew Solomon's mother. She chose to die by taking pills, helped and supported by her family. Inspired by her clarity, her love for them, and her utter fearlessness in the face of death, each of her survivors—husband and two sons—independently resolved that her path, euthanasia, would also be theirs if they faced a similar medical crisis.

When I was studying death in the 1960s—and, without even realizing it, focusing primarily on men—I was struck by what seemed to be an almost universal fear of death in Western cultures and fascinated by the many ways people strove to live on through various symbols of immortality. Are mothers different? Does fulfillment of motherhood and the carrying forward of one's spirit by sons and daughters account for the many examples of courageous dying, the relatively few cases of apparent fear among the mothers in this book?

I am also using *spirit* in the sense of "life force" or "vital energy." During their lives, these women have an abundance of such élan. It is her life force which keeps Peter Najarian's mother, now in her nineties, still working in her garden, a peasant energy which her son both admires and envies. The life force of course falls away at the time of death, and some of our writers bear witness to this mysterious happening. I think especially of Allen Wheelis and his remarkable memoir of his mother's death at the age of one hundred.

My final notion of spirit is that of *essence,* the inner core of one's psychic being. Whether spirit, in this meaning of the word, lives on in some form or dies out like the life force is a question of belief beyond my competence and one that everyone must decide for herself or himself. But whatever our answer, spirit as essence can be very different from the outer persona, even from a mother's most striking life qualities. Gary Young is able to show, through fifteen brief poems, an essential beauty and hope underneath the turbulence of his mother's craziness. This connotation of spirit comes closest to what is usually meant by *spiritual,* or by the idea of soul. For a number of our writers—I think of Steve Masover especially—this spirit shows up unexpectedly when a mother is dying, shining through death itself. Despite a totally wasted body, a dying mother can evoke a striking beauty.

In a relatively spiritless world, spirited mothers have much to offer. If a man is receptive—and that is the big if—a mother can enspirit him. Peter Najarian knows this, so he hangs out at his mother's house as much as he is able to, even bringing her his laundry all the way from Berkeley to Fresno, and in the process subjecting himself to the taunts of his buddies. But Peter's male friends are probably defending themselves against their envy of him. For me, the richest and most moving essays in this book are accounts like Najarian's that show us how a man has been able, often after long resistance, to accept his mother's gifts, to recognize her great influence on him and acknowledge his many debts to her, as well as their common bond, their similarities as well as differences, and to finally accept the fact that she has been and continues to be a central person in his life.

Men, it is said, do not grieve easily. The comparison is with women. In *Iron John,* Robert Bly has made men's unspoken grief the center of his analysis, and getting men in touch with sadness and loss has been a big part of the practice of the men's movements. But Bly—as well as a host of others—sees only the father as the ghost whose loss has not been acknowledged, whose abandonment of his sons—in life even more than in death— haunts the male psyche. There is some truth in this. In over twenty years of teaching classes on men's lives, I have found the single most common lament, the most universally expressed feeling, among my female as well as my male students, to be a deep yearning for greater intimacy with a father who was simply not there. Emotionally, if not necessarily physically.

To grieve the death of one's father then is no easy matter. That death is also momentous, one that Freud, writing from the standpoint of his patriarchal era, called *the most important single event* in a man's entire lifetime. But men—and probably women too—have an advantage here: our father feelings are much closer to the surface, much more accessible to our conscious minds, than are our mother feelings. Mourning, after all, is simply becoming aware, pondering deeply, going through and getting past, all the varied feelings that we have toward a loved one, feelings that were there all along, but tend to be called forth dramatically by death. For our fathers we have learned to name those feelings, whether they are anger, loss, betrayal, admiration—the possibilities are endless. But with our mothers, the feelings have deeper roots. They originate in infancy, before the onset of language. They remain inchoate, often blurred and fuzzy, as well as ambivalent and suppressed. That's why it's not easy, even for an adult man, to look at his relationship with his mother with a clear eye, and that is why, with all the backlog of repressed emotion, the death of a mother can be a critical turning point, an opportunity for a man's growth and deepening, as well as an invitation to psychic disaster.

Psychological writings on men and their relationship to their mothers largely emphasize one theme: the need of the son, beginning in childhood, to *separate* emotionally from his mother so that he can then identify with male figures and grow up to be a man. Perhaps our mothers' spirits become so infused with our own in infancy and early childhood that some kind of "exorcism" is needed during our years of youth so that we can become independent actors in the world. But "separation theory" is a very one-sided view of male psychic development. We don't have to reject our mothers, even in that difficult process of growing up male. And even if we have rejected her—and I certainly did mine—it is possible, indeed I think essential, for a man's spiritual development that he "return" to her. The journey of return to the mother is a man's midlife task, and as we see in the narratives that make up *Our Mothers' Spirits,* it can take place either before or after her death.

According to Samuel Osherson, a most perceptive observer of male psychology, most men never even begin the journey of return to their mothers. Midlife men and aging mothers are often locked in relationships of alienation and distance, routinized obligation, often interlaced with anger, resentment, and disappointment on both sides. Which makes the writers in this book all the more remarkable. John Updike could be speaking for many other contributors when he writes in the opening selection that he has "forgiven" his mother for being his mother and has now begun to see her as a person in her own right. This too is not easy, because all of us are used to seeing our mothers as *just mothers.* We take her for granted, simply because she was, in so many cases, always there. And it is also hard because mothers are such archetypal figures, of mythic proportion to our psyches. There is the "Good Mother," the all-sacrificing satisfier of other people's needs, and there is the "Bad Mother," who is easy to blame for our problems in living. It is no wonder that our cultural discourses either sentimentalize or demonize mothers. The complex middle ground is hard to find.

With only a few exceptions, it is this middle ground that our writers occupy. They have found the clear eye that sometimes comes only from the writing itself. Writing about a loved one after death is also healing, an integral part of grieving. My essay "Mama's Boy" was simultaneously a way of keeping Esther Blauner alive and letting her go—getting some closure on her life and death. I suspect something similar was taking place for the other men in this book as they wrote about the lives and deaths of their mothers.

Our Mothers' Spirits

PART I

BEFORE DEATH: THE AGED MOTHER

When a mother is in her eighties and nineties, like the mothers of this chapter's three authors, death is a reality whose imminence cannot be denied.

In advanced old age, change can come rapidly, without much warning. At eighty, John Updike's mother was active and vigorous, but two years later, after a bad fall, the author senses a striking decline in her vital energy. Each time he's with her there's always that unspoken question: "Which visit will be my last?"

The mother of Russell Baker has already left this world, at least on the mental plane. But despite her senility, her son has learned how to be with her, to accompany her on her journeys to a distant past, and to enjoy her sometimes irascible company. Zaroohe Najarian, on the other hand, remains completely lucid at ninety, active and independent, the picture of happiness as she digs in her garden, a return, as her son Peter sees it, to her peasant roots. Knowing that their time together is limited, he spends as many weekends as possible with her, drawing strength from her simplicity and "groundedness."

W. D. Ehrhart's "Secrets," the poem that opens the chapter, suggests other realities in the life of an aged mother. Ehrhart is writing about his own mother, but her fate is a universal one: the aloneness of having outlived a husband, the silences of empty rooms in a house filled with memories. The poet-son regrets the still unknown spaces between them, her secrets, especially how she reckons the balance sheet of "hopes and disappointments" that "make a life."

SECRETS

W. D. Ehrhart

Each room except the room you're in
is empty. No need to check.
How many times in forty-five years
did you wish for such a silence,
just a moment to collect yourself
amid the chaos of a life too full
with other people's needs?

And now you've got more silence
than you'll ever need, more time
than anyone should ever have
alone, each memory another moment
in a world where time holds
nothing but the past
and someone else's future.

What do you dream of?
What do you fear each time

Reprinted from *Men of Our Time,* Fred Moramarco and Al Zolynas, eds. (University
of Georgia Press, 1992), by permission of the author.

you turn to hear Dad stirring
and you realize that what you hear
is just the silence of an empty house
an absence permanent as stone?

Surely such a silence turns
the heart back upon itself.
Do you find your husband there?
Four sons and four grandchildren?
Some little Brooklyn girl
in pigtails skipping rope
that once was you.

Mother, does it all come down
to empty rooms and half-imagined sounds
of someone familiar? So many hopes
and disappointments make a life.
What were yours? I'd like to know.

WHICH VISIT
WILL BE MY LAST?

John Updike

Men succeed, Freud tells us, because their mothers love them;
men become homosexuals, some lesser psychologists have the-
orized, because they cannot bear to betray their mothers with
another woman. Such a powerful personage must shoulder, like
God, a lot of blame. Prince Hamlet greatly resents that his
mother is anything *but* a mother, and feels entitled to scold her
and commit murder in her boudoir. The largeness of our
mother-myth has a paradoxically dwindling effect upon the
women concerned: they must be in all things motherly and
become therefore natural processes rather than people. Few
things are harder, in this era so preoccupied with the monitoring of human relations, than to get to know one's mother as a
person—to forgive her, in effect, for being one's mother.

My own is now eighty. She has just renewed her driver's
license and has upwards of twenty cats to feed—to feed and to
kill, for, motherly enough, her responsibilities toward her

The first part of this narrative is drawn from the essay "Mother" in *Odd Jobs,* copyright © 1991 by John Updike. Reprinted by permission of Alfred A. Knopf, Inc. The
second is from the author's book of memoirs *Self-Consciousness,* copyright © 1989
by John Updike. Reprinted by permission of Alfred A. Knopf, Inc.

adopted dependents are conflicted. She began feeding a stray cat to spare the birds around the place; more and more cats appeared at her back door; and now the perplexities of mercy ask that she keep their feline herd thinner. It is a bind, and not the first she has been in. She was, for the twenty-one years in which she and I shared the same address, not only a mother but a daughter. We lived, my mother and father, her parents and me, in a household with a strong undertow of Depression, a historical event that had happened to hit both my father and grandfather hard. One lost his job, the other his money. She helped out by working in a department store three miles away, in the fabrics department, for fourteen dollars a week. Later, in the war, she worked in parachute factories. But most of the time she was home writing, sitting in the front bedroom, with its view of horse-chestnut trees and telephone wires, tapping out pages to send to New York magazines in brown envelopes. The brown envelopes always came back. Ours was a big white brick house but much cramped by worry and need. At its center, squeezed from all sides, my mother held forth and held out, and pulled us through. Or maybe we pulled her through. In any case, she and I are now the only survivors of that five-sided family; and these last twelve years, in which she has been a widow, have been pleasant ones for me, of getting to know her, of tuning her in without the static of kindred broadcasting stations.

Her intelligence and humor, as she fends off the perils of old age, are startling. Though with a son's luck I have reaped most of the benefits, it was my mother who made the great leap of imagination up, out of the rural Pennsylvania countryside — German in accent and practical in emphasis — into the ethereal realm of art. I glimpse now how bright that little girl must have been to skip all those grades in her one-room schoolhouse and head off to normal school so painfully young. At college, she was four years younger than her classmates, of whom my father was one. This simple brightness comes in handy, as in solitude she calculates her taxes, administers her acres, operates her machinery, retypes her manuscripts, and entertains her grandchildren as they breeze in, not always unaccompanied, from their strange new world. She and I used to write letters; now, grown spendthrift and lazy, we talk on the telephone, and I hear how festive and limpid her wit is, and with what graceful, modest irony she illuminates every corner of her brave life. All this for decades was muffled for me behind the giant mask of motherhood.

When I try to pull "mother" from my childhood memories, I come up with two images, both of them, I fear, already embedded in some work of fiction or another. In one, my mother, young and rather formally dressed, is sitting opposite me on the floor, coloring at the same page of a coloring book. I marvel at how neatly she does it, even though from her vantage the page is upside down. She seems calm and comely and I am so proud it makes me shy. In the other, we are both somewhat older, and I see her, while standing at the ironing board, jump slightly and touch her jaw with her hand: a twinge of toothache, and my first unsolicited empathy into the pain of another human being. And this vision merges with the pathetic remedy our family used to apply to aches of all sorts, toothaches and earaches and eye-aches—a folded dishtowel, warmed by the iron. How many, in those pre-antibiotic years, sugar pills and dabs of ointment and spoonfuls of syrup went into the nurture of a sickly child, like those little pats of wind and rain that reassure a seedling and embolden it to lengthen its roots.

As I get older and older, my mother's genes keep sprouting in me. We eat alike, with a steady, enchanted absorption in the food. We laugh alike, and evade awkward questions with similar flurries of fancy. I hear her voice flirtatiously pop from my mouth. My hair, fine like my father's, went gray early like hers. Her old hobbies, which I thought eccentric—organic gardening, natural foods, conservation—now seem to me simple good sense. More deeply than any patriarchal religion, I believe what she instilled: the notions that we should live as close to nature as we can, and that in matters of diet and behavior alike we should look to the animals for guidance.

She can name all the trees and flowers and birds in her woods; I wish I could, and try to learn the names from her now,

since I paid scant attention when young. As we walk carefully
through these woods, with their treacherous footing of boul-
ders and mossy logs (both of us grown too brittle to relish a
tumble), the biological event that linked our two bodies seems
further and further away, the mere beginning of a precious
companionship. *(1984)*

My mother is old, she has not been well. This summer she fell
in the kitchen, and the fall hurt her back and abdomen and has
taken something out of her. She has taken to her bed, and says
it is too painful to get up and walk around.

I don't know quite what to do about her. *"She lives alone?"*
people ask me, with round eyes and an implication of filial
neglect. In this conservative region family members tend to
stick close to one another. Four generations of Mennonites live
all together on the neighboring farm. I am waiting for her to
tell me what to do about her. I find that the older she becomes,
the more my image of her is of someone young: the young
mother in the Shillington back yard with the fireflies and flowering cherry trees, the tall laughing college girl posing with my
father in his football sweater, and even the little girl raised on
this farm with a batch of complaining and ailing old people.
She taught herself from books to name the birds and flowers,
setting out a little wildflower garden under a black birch tree
that, grown thick and lopsided, is still there, though now only
weeds grow beneath it—weeds and wild raspberries and a few
scraggly Japanese lanterns brought from the Shillington yard
forty years ago. When she was very small, my mother once settled herself in a basket of clean wash in imitation of a nesting
robin, and was scolded by her mother for it. An only child like
me, she made her paradise, her escape hatch, out of the nature
around her, leaving no living thing on her father's farm
unnamed, much as I, once, could identify all the cartoonists in
Collier's upside down. Her diary, kept sporadically over the
years, takes note of the weather and the songs of the birds,
returning year after year, as they sound in the woods to the
west, through whose branches the red sun sets. During these

more than a dozen years since my father died, her voice over the telephone has always sounded young—quick and playful and interested in life, in the reality modulated by our "vocabulary," by our "gay-making" slant on the world. I am alarmed and depressed by what seems her withdrawal from the world—she stopped, after her fall, cooking, driving, watching television, writing, reading, and eating. All she manages to do is feed the dog and the cats and talk on the telephone to her well-wishers and to the numerous charity fund-raisers who call up relentlessly from Reading, asking an annual renewal of her little widow's mite of ten or fifteen dollars. There is no end of giving.

Her will to live, anciently involved with mine, has been slowly reviving this autumn. Tonight she let herself be driven out to dinner with some friends from Lancaster. Now we have returned, adjusted the dog and the thermostat, and gone to bed. Our bedrooms have between them a wall and door so thin we can hear each other breathe. My wife wonders how five of us once managed in this little house, all sleeping in this same upstairs, and all I can say is that at the time, to the child I was, it seemed big enough. My parents and grandparents each had a room and I slept in a bed in a space that served also as a kind of hall at the head of the stairs. There were voices, true—coughs and sighs and snoring, bedsprings creaking and the sound of my father patting my mother and making a humorous woo-woo sound that signified affection; but when one is young space curls up tight inside the blankets and it is not so hard to fall asleep through the hole that opens at the bottom of one's brain.

Now, it is harder. I am old, though not as old as my mother. It was not easy for me to drive her back from the restaurant, through an unseasonable sleet storm, early in this November. The wipers struggled against the freezing rain, the headlights coming at us were smeared and magnified, and she had been fearful that I was going to hit a deer, because deer did now and then cross this dark highway. Without saying so, I found her repeated concern rather sentimental and hysterical, especially since the deer would be slaughtered in hunting season less than a month away. Now the sleet patters on the windows and makes a crinkling sound in the fireplace, as the individual pellets tumble through, into the room. It would be cozy if the bed were not so cold, unwarmed by a woman. My wife stays away, as a gift, she says, to my mother. The room has two windows, a low ceiling, this never-used fireplace, and wallpaper, patterned with rosettes and little pink roses, that hasn't changed since I can remember. Even the decorative changes are slow: an uncompleted oil painting I did of my first wife was retired to a drawer around the time of our divorce, and more recently a felt piece of local kitsch I always disliked has been taken down. It showed an Amishman standing erect with a hammer and a carpenter's square, above the slogan WHAT A MAN DOES, THAT HE IS. I believe it but didn't like reading it. My suitcase is spread out open across two straight chairs, and a Harvard yearbook and an early Peter Arno cartoon anthology sit on a bedside table; these books never change, and in the table's drawer are pencils so old their erasers don't erase and even the graphite has gone waxy and refuses to write. Time moves slowly here but does move, and is overtaking my mother. Which visit will be my last? We do not know, or speculate. I can hear her breathe, with the loudness that signifies sleep. *(1988)*

Linda Grace Moyer Updike died in 1989 at the age of eighty-five.

WHERE'S RUSSELL?

Russell Baker

At the age of eighty my mother had her last bad fall, and after that her mind wandered free through time. Some days she went to weddings and funerals that had taken place half a century earlier. On others she presided over family dinners cooked on Sunday afternoons for children who were now gray with age. Through all this she lay in bed but moved across time, traveling among the dead decades with a speed and ease beyond the gift of physical science.

"Where's Russell?" she asked one day when I came to visit at the nursing home.

"I'm Russell," I said.

She gazed at this improbably overgrown figure out of an inconceivable future and promptly dismissed it.

"Russell's only this big," she said, holding her hand, palm down, two feet from the floor. That day she was a young country wife with chickens in the backyard and a view of hazy blue Virginia mountains behind the apple orchard, and I was a stranger old enough to be her father.

Reprinted from *Growing Up,* by Russell Baker, copyright © 1982. Used with permission of Contemporary Books, Inc., Chicago.

Early one morning she phoned me in New York. "Are you coming to my funeral today?" she asked.

It was an awkward question with which to be awakened. "What are you talking about, for God's sake?" was the best reply I could manage.

"I'm being buried today," she declared briskly, as though announcing an important social event.

"I'll phone you back," I said and hung up, and when I did phone back she was all right, although she wasn't all right, of course, and we all knew she wasn't.

She had always been a small woman—short, light-boned, delicately structured—but now, under the white hospital sheet, she was becoming tiny. I thought of a doll with huge, fierce eyes. There had always been a fierceness in her. It showed in that angry, challenging thrust of the chin when she issued an opinion, and a great one she had always been for issuing opinions.

"It's not always good policy to tell people exactly what's on your mind," I used to caution her.

"If they don't like it, that's too bad," was her customary reply, "because that's the way I am."

And so she was. A formidable woman. Determined to speak her mind, determined to have her way, determined to bend those who opposed her. In that time when I had known her best, my mother had hurled herself at life with chin thrust forward, eyes blazing, and an energy that made her seem always on the run.

She ran after squawking chickens, an axe in her hand, determined on a beheading that would put dinner in the pot. She ran when she made the beds, ran when she set the table. One Thanksgiving she burned herself badly when, running up from the cellar oven with the ceremonial turkey, she tripped on the stairs and tumbled back down, ending at the bottom in the debris of giblets, hot gravy, and battered turkey. Life was combat, and victory was not to the lazy, the timid, the slugabed, the drugstore cowboy, the libertine, the mushmouth afraid to tell people exactly what was on his mind whether people liked it or not. She ran.

But now the running was over. For a time I could not accept the inevitable. As I sat by her bed, my impulse was to argue her back to reality. On my first visit to the hospital in Baltimore, she asked who I was.

"Russell," I said.

"Russell's way out west," she advised me.

"No, I'm right here."

"Guess where I came from today?" was her response.

"Where?"

"All the way from New Jersey."

"When?"

"Tonight."

"No. You've been in the hospital for three days," I insisted.

"I suggest the thing to do is calm down a little bit," she replied. "Go over to the house and shut the door."

Now she was years deep into the past, living in the neighborhood where she had settled forty years earlier, and she had just been talking with Mrs. Hoffman, a neighbor across the street.

"It's like Mrs. Hoffman said today: The children always wander back to where they come from," she remarked.

"Mrs. Hoffman has been dead for fifteen years."

"Russ got married today," she replied.

"I got married in 1950," I said, which was the fact.

"The house is unlocked," she said.

So it went until a doctor came by to give one of those oral quizzes that medical men apply in such cases. She failed catastrophically, giving wrong answers or none at all to "What day is this?" "Do you know where you are?" "How old are you?" and so on. Then, a surprise.

"When is your birthday?" he asked.

"November 5, 1897," she said. Correct. Absolutely correct.

"How do you remember that?" the doctor asked.

"Because I was born on Guy Fawkes Day," she said.

"Guy Fawkes?" asked the doctor. "Who is Guy Fawkes?"

She replied with a rhyme I had heard her recite time and time again over the years when the subject of her birth date arose:

"Please to remember the Fifth of
   November,
Gunpowder treason and plot,
I see no reason why gunpowder treason
Should ever be forgot."

Then she glared at this young doctor so ill informed about
Guy Fawkes' failed scheme to blow King James off his throne
with barrels of gunpowder in 1605. She had been a schoolteacher, after all, and knew how to glare at a dolt. "You may
know a lot about medicine, but you obviously don't know any
history," she said. Having told him exactly what was on her
mind, she left us again.

The doctors diagnosed a hopeless senility. Not unusual,
they said. "Hardening of the arteries" was the explanation for
laymen. I thought it was more complicated than that. For ten
years or more the ferocity with which she had once attacked
life had been turning into a rage against the weakness, the
boredom, and the absence of love that too much age had
brought her. Now, after the last bad fall, she seemed to have
broken chains that imprisoned her in a life she had come to
hate and to return to a time inhabited by people who loved her,
a time in which she was needed. Gradually I understood. It was
the first time in years I had seen her happy.

She had written a letter three years earlier which
explained more than "hardening of the arteries." I had gone
down from New York to Baltimore, where she lived, for one of
my infrequent visits and afterwards, had written her with some
banal advice to count her blessings instead of burdening others with her miseries. I suppose what it really amounted to
was a threat that if she was not more cheerful during my visits
I would not come to see her very often. Sons are capable of
such letters. This one was written out of a childish faith in the
eternal strength of parents, a naive belief that age and wear
could be overcome by an effort of will, that all she needed
was a good pep talk to recharge a flagging spirit. It was such a
foolish, innocent idea, but one thinks of parents differently

from other people. Other people can become frail and break, but not parents.

She wrote back in an unusually cheery vein intended to demonstrate, I suppose, that she was mending her ways. She was never a woman to apologize, but for one moment with the pen in her hand she came very close. Referring to my visit, she wrote: "If I seemed unhappy to you at times—" Here she drew back, reconsidered, and said something quite different:

"If I seemed unhappy to you at times, I am, but there's really nothing anyone can do about it, because I'm just so very tired and lonely that I'll just go to sleep and forget it." She was then seventy-eight.

Now, three years later, after the last bad fall, she had managed to forget the fatigue and the loneliness and, in these free-wheeling excursions back through time, to recapture happiness. I soon stopped trying to wrest her back to what I considered the real world and tried to travel along with her on those fantastic swoops into the past. One day when I arrived at her bedside, she was radiant.

"Feeling good today," I said.

"Why shouldn't I feel good?" she asked. "Papa's going to take me up to Baltimore on the boat today."

At that moment she was a young girl standing on a wharf at Merry Point, Virginia, waiting for the Chesapeake Bay steamer with her father, who had been dead sixty-one years. William Howard Taft was in the White House. Europe still drowsed in the dusk of the great century of peace, America was a young country, and the future stretched before it in beams of crystal sunlight. "The greatest country on God's green earth," her father might have said, if I had been able to step into my mother's time machine and join him on the wharf with the satchels packed for Baltimore.

I could imagine her there quite clearly. She was wearing a blue dress with big puffy sleeves and long black stockings. There was a ribbon in her hair and a big bow tied on the side of her head. There had been a childhood photograph in her bedroom which showed all this, although the colors of course had been added years later by a restorer who tinted the picture.

About her father, my grandfather, I could only guess, and indeed, about the girl on the wharf with the bow in her hair, I was merely sentimentalizing. Of my mother's childhood and her people, of their time and place, I knew very little. A world had lived and died, and though it was part of my blood and bone I knew little more about it than I knew of the world of the pharaohs. It was useless now to ask help from my mother. The orbits of her mind rarely touched present interrogators for more than a moment.

Sitting at her bedside, forever out of touch with her, I wondered about my own children, and their children, and children in general, and about the disconnections between children and parents that prevent them from knowing each other. Children rarely want to know who their parents were before they were parents, and when age finally stirs their curiosity there is no parent left to tell them. If a parent does lift the curtain a bit, it is often only to stun the young with some exemplary tale of how much harder life was in the old days.

I had been guilty of this when my children were small in the early 1960s and living the affluent life. It galled me that their childhoods should be, as I thought, so easy when my own had been, as I thought, so hard. I had developed the habit, when they complained about the steak being overcooked or the television being cut off, of lecturing them on the harshness of life in my day.

"In my day all we got for dinner was macaroni and cheese, and we were glad to get it."

"In my day we didn't have any television."

"In my day . . . "

"In my day . . . "

At dinner one evening a son had offended me with an inadequate report card, and as I leaned back and cleared my throat to lecture, he gazed at me with an expression of unutterable resignation and said, "Tell me how it was in your days, Dad."

I was angry with him for that, but angrier with myself for having become one of those ancient bores whose highly selective memories of the past become transparently dishonest even to small children. I tried to break the habit, but must have failed. A few years later my son was referring to me when I was out of earshot as "the old-timer." Between us there was a dispute about time. He looked upon the time that had been my future in a disturbing way. My future was his past, and being young, he was indifferent to the past.

As I hovered over my mother's bed listening for muffled signals from her childhood, I realized that this same dispute had existed between her and me. When she was young with life ahead of her, I had been her future and resented it. Instinctively, I wanted to break free, cease being a creature defined by her time, consign her future to the past, and create my own. Well, I had finally done that, and then with my own children I had seen my exciting future become their boring past.

These hopeless end-of-the-line visits with my mother made me wish I had not thrown off my own past so carelessly. We all come from the past, and children ought to know what it was that went into their making, to know that life is a braided cord of humanity stretching up from time long gone, and that it cannot be defined by the span of a single journey from diaper to shroud.

I thought that someday my own children would understand that. I thought that, when I am beyond explaining, they would want to know what the world was like when my mother was young and I was younger, and we two relics passed together through strange times. I thought I should try to tell them [about] my mother and her passion for improving the male of the species, which in my case took the form of forcing me to "make something of myself."

She would spend her middle years turning me into the man who would redeem her failed youth. I would make something of myself and if *I* lacked the grit to do it, well then *she* would make me make something of myself. I would become the living proof of the strength of her womanhood. She would live for me, and, in turn, I would become her future.

THE ARTIST'S MOTHER

Peter Najarian

I've longed for someone since I can remember and not a night goes by when I don't reach for her. It's been hell having something between my legs instead of nothing, but as my mother would say, we must make the best of what we have and not complain of what we don't.

She's back in the valley and I just returned from the long drive. It used to be every four weeks but I made it three since she'll be ninety this year and I go as often as I can before one of us disappears. I once said it was for her sake, but now I admit it's for my own. She's a kick in the ass and I always look forward to it, my car packed with laundry as if I were going home again.

"You still take your laundry to your mother's?" Joe said the other night as we warmed up for basketball. "That's disgusting."

"Why?" I said. "It's better than the Laundromat, and anyway she wants it, it gives her something to do, she says my laundry is her happiness."

"That's disgusting," Joe said, "a man your age taking laundry to his ninety-year-old mother."

It's a pleasant drive after the windmills on Altamount and except for when I was away I've been going and coming for twenty years. When she lived back east I'd share a ride across country and when I lived in England I'd take a charter in the summer and write once a week the rest of the time. She's illiterate but I'd write my English simple enough for a mailman to read. I was eighteen when I moved out and since she was from the Old World she didn't understand why I didn't stay until I married like my brother, yet she was always better than I at living alone. She never asked anything but that I keep in touch.

Here I am, Ma, I would say, don't worry, I'm okay. I wasn't really, I was miserable as hell, but I would hate her worrying. Now when I want to tell her how miserable I am she tells me to shut up. "What do you got to be miserable about?" she says. "Be satisfied with what you have. Look at me, I'm satisfied. Whenever you're miserable, think of me and you'll be happy."

No, those letters weren't because I didn't want her to worry. Despite my need to cut the knot, they were to the only one who seemed to tie me to this planet. I was nineteen when I told her I was going to live in Mexico and write a book. "Don't worry," I said, "I'm taking a bus." Then I hit the road with my thumb out and lo and behold who was the first ride but old Po-Po from the neighborhood who spilled the beans while I was sending postcards from Memphis and Houston: "I just got off the bus, Ma, and I'm in the Greyhound station." Since then she's learned never to believe anything I write.

Sometimes I would love her so much I'd cry. In fact whenever I thought of her with love I'd cry as if she were gone and I'd never see her again. Yet I used to have dreams where I yelled at her with such anger I would wake in a sweat. My dream mother was not her of course, but they were related somehow. Leave me alone, I would yell, go away! I've always loved her, but we've had our epic yelling battles. She's from the Mediterranean and could yell like Anna Magnani. Even her Italian pals in the factory would say she was like Anna Magnani because of her strong nose and flashing eyebrows.

I used to hate her yelling and am still attracted to women with soft voices, my femmes fatales not at all like her in looks or type except in their vibrancy. I love vibrant women. I also hate them. There's no one I hate more than a woman I love who doesn't love me back.

Where am I? Oh, yes, I was just passing the windmills on my way to old Z in the valley, which is what I sometimes call her in my journal, Z for her name Zaroohe, which comes I think from Persia.

When I arrive at her home there's a piece of plywood in the driveway so the oil from my car won't drip on the cement. If it does she's out there with her wire brush as quick as Greenpeace in Alaska. She's one of those obsessive types, and though I always appreciated her clean sheets and cozy home, her extreme tidiness could make me scream.

"I was always this way," she once said when she admitted it does resemble a sickness. Even as a girl in the internment camp, she always made her bed after waking every morning. Never once, however, did she ever ask my brother or me to make our own, and we both scattered our mess wherever we wanted. When I was a child she even let me pencil my cowboys and horses on the wall by my bed as if it were a blackboard and when the weekend came she would scrub them away with Babbo and let me make more. Some people are like that in this life of ours, they just love to clean. I had my first wet dream when I was eleven and when she saw the gluey spot in the morning she laid a square cloth under the new sheet so the mattress wouldn't stain the next time. She'd wash that cloth too, of course, but the stains would linger like mementos from all my dreamgirls.

After I pull in the driveway, I dump my laundry by the washing machine in the garage and she sorts the colors from the whites. She really does love to do it and not only because she loves to work: It's not just any laundry, it's her son's laundry.

"Of course," she says in her matter-of-fact way, "if you had a wife I wouldn't do this for you." But I don't take this matter-of-factly, and with Joe's voice in the background my bachelorhood sinks into shame and failure. When I first left her I didn't want her washing machine or her food, I wanted to become a man and build my own home. Now I bring my sheets and take her jars not only because I don't like Laundromats and enjoy her cooking but because it makes her feel good. I wish I had a child whom I could feed and clean. It must be wonderful to be a parent. Remaining a bachelor son, however, can be so painful I want to die.

I used to think my death would be unbearable to her, but the older she grows the more enlightened she appears, and nothing seems to bother her except the ants in her kitchen. She might grieve like a Greek chorus should I die before her, but as she herself approaches death she accepts life in all its forms and wishes nothing but to go in peace without torture by a hospital machine. We sometimes hear how the approach of death can intensify life and bring a happiness to every last minute, and I see such a happiness in her when she hangs the laundry in the backyard by her fruit trees and vegetable garden. To be alive and stretch her arms to her son's underwear by the blossoming apricot is everything, and she has no wish for anything more. Renoir once said of his own peasant mother, "Her laundry was as important as the German Empire." I imagine infants feel this way when they smile like Meher Baba, who tells us to not worry and be happy. She often seems like a child now and like a Baba as well, an Old Z who tells her old son not to worry, there's really nothing to worry about anymore.

She was not always this way, of course. The vitality, the brightness, the Jimmy Durante twinkle, and the strength of an elephant were always in her, yes, but it was a hard road and I never tired of her turning it into a saga.

"Why do you tell people I never talked to you as a child?" she once said in Armenian. "Before your father got sick I used to talk to you all the time. In fact one day Baidzar came up the stairs and heard me talking in our kitchen when you were not even a year old. 'Zaroohe,' she said, 'who were you talking to, I thought your husband went to work?' 'I'm talking to my baby,' I said, 'I always talk to him.'"

"I didn't say you never talked to me," I said, "I said you never listened."

"Well," she said, "you're probably right, I needed to talk. But why do you complain about it? You can't have everything. Be thankful I at least talked to you."

Nevertheless she feels a little guilty now and tries to correct herself.

"So tell me," she will say, "how are things with you?"

"Well," I start to say, "I . . . "

But before I can finish my sentence she starts another of her own: "I had a wonderful week," she says like a child, "did you see my fava beans, how they sprouted so well?"

I let her continue. She's alone even more than I am and has so much she wants to tell me. As I've done since I was a baby, I sit like an audience for her tales that go back as far as she can remember.

Alas, it is not far enough and she can't remember her own mother's face, for she was only about nine or ten when they were marched into the desert to starve to death. She can remember details of her mother working hard like herself, but the face remains a blur and it is this blur that feels like the word *mother* itself.

Mother: What does it really mean? How revolted I would feel when women used it with pride and selfhood. As an old and crippled male who lost the rut to win a mate and so must wander alone for the rest of his life, I recoiled at so many females carrying their bellies like an insect queen who would squirt into this fallen realm more I's for an endless longing. Nor was my own mother pardoned from this horror where she was just another uterus for misery and death.

Yet the more my love deepens, the less she is *mother* than simply Z, though with her I might learn what the word really means. She, however, knows herself only as a mother. As I became an artist, so too she must have become a mother when she was just a barefoot orphan on her own path through life, as if in needing a mother she had to become one herself. It was her way of joining life, and it seemed to have worked well regarding my brother who had a family of his own, but with me it feels different.

I used to think how much better off I was than the poor girl who lost her family in the desert and almost starved to death, who at sixteen had to marry an older man she had never seen before and who as soon as she had stepped from Ellis Island had to sew in a factory twelve hours a day until it became eight when the union started, who when her first son was just an infant had to return to the factory and whose brief happiness was shattered when her second husband was crippled by a stroke, who when her second son was old enough for school had to return to the factory and care for a cripple and keep the refrigerator full and the sheets clean and the walls clean and everywhere clean because that's what being a mother meant, to feed and to clean and not complain about petty things. What a story, the story her boy kept wanting to hear as if the hardship were beautiful. What a hard life my mother had, he would think, how much better off I've been than she.

But I don't feel this way anymore, especially when I visit her wonderful home. She bought it when my brother moved his family to Fresno in '71. Before then her retirement plan was to buy a little house in Belmar on the Jersey coast about an hour from where he lived in Ridgewood. Unlike me, he always lived near her, and because of this I could feel free to wander without the guilt of leaving her alone. Once my father's death freed her from doctor bills she started saving her pay, and by the time she retired she had eighteen thousand dollars, which was just enough in those days. She chose Belmar because that's where the tribe would go in the summer and some, like her best friend Manooshag, had already retired there. Then my brother went through a change of life and decided to move to Fresno. I had come to Berkeley a few years before, so with her two sons in California she also came and bought a little house near my brother's in one of the developments that decimate orchards and fill them with monotony. I used to think it shameful, but for my mother the cul-de-sac couldn't be better. For the first time since she lost her parents she had her own home, with no worries about the heat or hot water. Ants, yes, but she could handle them, and the shopping center was a short walk and she would learn the bus system like a survivor in a jungle.

"I don't move anywhere I can't take a bus," she would say. "I'm not asking anyone to drive me around." She still takes them, and just the other day rode downtown for her checkup at the clinic which told her she's "okay." It is her good health that makes me feel how fortunate she is, and of course I mean her mental health as well. How did she get so healthy? I often wonder when I think of my lungs now black from all my cigarettes of despair.

One day, while working in her garden, she didn't see me looking when she lifted her skirt like a child to squat and piss by her grapefruit tree. It was then I fully realized who she was and where she had come from. She was a peasant child who had been exiled to a factory for fifty years and now she was home again with the sky and the earth. She herself once said casually as if it were just another fact:

"They took away my father's vineyard but God gave it back to me."

By *God* she meant that which she has always trusted, which has nothing to do with Jesus or DNA. If you ask her she'll tell you she's a Christian, because to her being an Armenian is being Christian and how could she not feel Armenian when her family was slaughtered as such? But churches mean nothing to her other than a place for funerals and her God is simply that which she never doubted. "You have to believe in something," she once said to someone who claimed to be an atheist. "It doesn't matter what, the sun, the sky, this little rock, but to believe in nothing is impossible." Once when someone talked about suicide in regard to a friend in a nursing home, she said: "It's easy to talk about it, but how could you kill yourself when your soul is so sweet?"

She's often wise when it comes to matters of faith and courage, but though she would be angry at my making it public, her ignorance is just as illuminating. She's as alert and inquisitive as ever, but I still can't convince her the earth is round or that there is north, south, east, and west. Calendars, maps, or anything Copernican is beyond her, and yet she managed to raise two sons and provide a home for them until they were ready to build their own, her memory and sense of direction sharpened by her illiterate and archaic psyche.

She is, in short, as natural and organic as they come, or "grounded" as we used to say. When I asked her one day what she thought of cremation, she said no, it didn't appeal to her, she wanted to be buried in the earth, as if to say her body, which she respects so deeply, should return to what she loves. Anyway, she had just bought a cemetery plot because it was on sale. She's one of those types that will walk a mile to save a nickel, and her eighteen thousand dollars didn't come easily.

It might give her mortal anguish to spend a nickel on herself, but her generosity is like one of her fig trees, which give such pleasure to her neighbors. She can't endure seeing food go to waste, especially in remembering the desert. She can be as frugal as a French farmer, but the five hundred dollars a month from Social Security plus the hundred from the union is more than she needs, so she always has some left over for her unemployed son. "I don't want it," I say, but she insists it's for the gas to come and see her. "What am I going to do with it?" she says, as if it were the figs she has to avoid because of their sugar.

One day she told me she could remember the mulberry blossoms falling on her face when she was a child waking in the morning. She and her parents and her two brothers all slept in the open from spring to autumn when there was no rain and she grew up playing among the trees and the vines. During the winter they all lived in one room in the city, but when the spring came they would return to their vineyard and live like peasants have since civilization first began. This was in Adana, by the Mediterranean, where Turkey curves into Lebanon and the sun is as friendly as in California or Provence. Their faces remain a blur, but she can remember her father tying the vines and her mother boiling fruit into syrup, the donkey sleeping under them and the mulberries as long as her finger.

In my darkness now I love to hear about them and search for new questions so she can tell me more. "Why are you asking me so many questions?" she says. "Are you writing a book?" "No," I say, "it's not for a book, it's because I like hearing about the *aki.*" *Aki* is her Armenian word for the vineyard, and the sound of it evokes a lost Eden to me now, that home of my mother's childhood, which gave her roots she could transplant after she was exiled. The genocide and the wars would come and go and she would endure because her roots would stay healthy and her arms would welcome life whatever it might bring.

No, I no longer think how much more fortunate I am to have been born in America and to have had what we call an education. I know how to read and I know the earth is round and I know north, south, east, and west, but I don't know what she knows and I don't even know how to sew. I have strived for success since I was a boy, and yet what have I done compared to her? With nothing but faith and courage and the grace of her God, she raised a family and built a home, and what have I done but wander in loneliness while longing to go home again?

During the old days all that psychology stuff tried to tell me it was because of my mother I was neurotic, it was because she abandoned me when she returned to the factory or held on to me in her loneliness, but it's all baloney now and even if it were true it wouldn't matter anymore. Nothing really matters but here and now and letting go of whatever holds us down. And I don't, I don't let go, especially of her, I still hold on to her, I still bring her my laundry, I don't want to lose her. She's all I've got, I feel sometimes; when she goes there's no one, and I will be like a kite let loose in the wind and never come down again. Often in my flying dreams I am rising in an overwhelming thrill and then in panic at never coming down I reach in desperation for a roof or pole to keep me grounded and maybe I once reached for a mother like that, for without her I might have never come back. Or maybe to stay I would have married one of the women who would have said yes instead of rejecting them because none was the true love of my longing. I would have married like my brother and I would have had a home and family like him and Joe and all the others I have envied, but no, I did not have to let go of my longing, I could go on longing and longing and whenever I flew too far to return I could write "Dear Ma" on a postcard or bring my underwear to her washing machine and she would always be there with her roots in the earth and her smile like a Baba. Without her, I think, I would not have become an artist.

Or perhaps I would have become a very different kind of artist. I used to think my becoming an artist had to do with my father, who sat like a crippled Hephaestus after Aphrodite had gone away, indeed he had been before his stroke a jeweler of delicate chains. Since I was a male I could not become like my mother, though she was the dominant parent after he was paralyzed, so instead I would be a cripple like my father and turn my pain into art. Yet who knows how anyone becomes an artist or anything else? I had genes for drawing and maybe even writing too, but my brother had even more and took a different road by wanting to work an ordinary job and live a simple life. I on the other hand ever since puberty thought only of how I could avoid work to have all the time I needed to become an artist.

There was no question of becoming anything else, it was the only way to survive. Already at five with no one home but a dumb cripple and a mother always gone, I was on my own in the wilderness of the city and the only way to survive was by longing for the sky as if someone were there. So off I went down the cliffs to the barges on the river like a little Wordsworth encountering the deep as if it were alive, always self-indulgent and fearless because come dinnertime I could always go home and the food would be warm on the table and the sheets would always be clean. I could go anywhere I wanted and do whatever I wanted because I had a strong mother who never said no and who let me draw on the wall despite her obsessive cleanliness. And I stayed that way for the rest of my life, always wandering and searching and longing. Yet what was I longing for but the very warmth back there by her side? So why did I leave in the first place? Why didn't I just stay?

I couldn't, of course, or I would have really become like my father. No, I am not a cripple, a healthy Zaroohe is in me somewhere, but I get lost, I get lost quite often and am like that little boy one day after kindergarten when he hadn't quite learned the long route through the perilous city and stood on the corner crying until Donald Negrini, the butcher's son, came and led him through the strange streets.

I've been getting lost like that a lot lately, especially in the waves of homelessness that engulf our venal and profane America. If I can't find a job and pay the rent, what am I going to do, where am I to go? No one's going to buy anything I paint and Donald Negrini is nowhere to be found. Could I live with my mother again?

"No," she said in her matter-of-fact way, "I don't want you to live here."

I was a little shocked until I realized what she meant. She's been losing her balance and has fallen several times while working in the garden. Fortunately she was able to cushion herself with her huge thighs, but she's afraid that if I came to live with her she wouldn't be able to clean my mess anymore. It's all she can do to care for herself now and not burden anyone.

Yet whenever I visit her she is still the same Zaroohe, with her washing machine and her dolmah that gets better and better, her sheets as clean as always. I sleep in the room near hers and once when I woke first I looked at her in bed with her legs sprawled and her arm out and I loved her so much I started to cry.

Why was I crying when she was lying there so alive? Why does love make us cry, as if like little children we are at the mercy of forces beyond our beseeching? I was crying as if I were a child who has lost his mother, but she was no longer the woman who woke and peed and washed her face and then joined me in the kitchen.

"Did you sleep well, my son?" she asked.

"I . . ." I say, and then she finished my sentence for me.

"I slept good myself," she said. "I had a good dream."

My own dreams are stormy and dark, but hers are often peaceful and filled with light. Sometimes she sees my father and they kiss and love each other. Most of the characters are dead, since she's the last of the old gang, but they come and go

like visitors. Then one morning she said as if she had an illumi-
nation, "I saw my brother, my son! I saw his face! I could see
his face so clearly! 'Boghos,' I said, 'is it really you?' 'Yes,' he
said, 'it's really me.'"

It was the first time since he disappeared into the desert
eighty years ago. For eighty years his face had been a blur and
now suddenly it was clear again. He was her older brother and
she had often told me how she remembered him always drawing.

"What did he look like, Ma?" I asked.

"How can I tell you that?" she said. "I know what he looks
like but how can I describe him to you?"

And as she said this he became a boy by the river near the
cliffs too far for me to see him clearly, he and his mother and
father and little sister all so far away; the more I tried to reach
them, the more they receded. "Ma!" I cried as a little girl once
cried in a desert, "Ma!" Ma, as in the *mah* that means death in
Armenian and Ma as in the last Pietà where a crippled Christ
was returning to stone, Ma that was beyond any breasts or
vulva and made absurd a feminist selfhood about nature and
the earth, Ma that had no gender or form but was the void that
would be plenitude by letting go. Let go, let go, it says, don't
be afraid, there will be light at the end of the darkness like a
warm dinner for a boy back from adventuring.

So I returned to an old Z sitting at the table peeling apples
who was not my mother anymore, yet through her I might
know the meaning of the word though she could just as well
have been a male. In fact she could pass for a male now, her
great nose and wrinkles like an old Black Elk invoking a grandfather.

In her bedroom there is on the wall facing her bed a picture of her second husband's father, one of my own grandfa-
thers. She enjoys all kinds of pictures on her walls, and though
she usually leaves the hanging to me she wanted on the wall
facing her bed the one of the old pop with the Wyatt Earp mustache who has remained there since she first moved in twenty-
two years ago, his handlebars looking down at her as she sleeps
every night. The picture is a tinted ten-by-fourteen blowup my

father had made of a little photo taken before the massacre. Unlike my mother, my father had several photos of his family, and since he lived with them until he was seventeen he remembered his father well, so my mother knew more about him than about her own father. She loved her own father very deeply and I imagine she had substituted for his face the one of her old father-in-law with the gray mustache, though he was only in his thirties when he was slaughtered. She doesn't think like this, of course; I doubt she looks at the picture except when she's cleaning the glass, but she has a father inside her and more than once while working in her garden she has turned to me and said, "I feel I have become my father now, I remember him shoveling like this."

So too as I sit here making lines have I become like my mother with her sewing machine. "My sewing machine is my *yo-yo,*" she says. "You have your *yo-yo* and I have mine." *Yo-yo* is her way of saying yoga, which she calls my sitting on the zafu she had sewn and stuffed for me.

Yes, Ma, I do my *yo-yo,* and you do yours.

Ninety-three now, Zaroohe Najarian still lives in Fresno in her own home.

PART 2

WHEN A MOTHER DIES YOUNG

For a very young child, every momentary abandonment by his mother evokes the fear of losing her permanently. Thus the very young too live in the shadow of mother loss, as Hank Heifetz's poem dramatizes. But for the five writers in this chapter, the possibility of orphanhood in childhood became a reality.

Losing one's mother produces "a hole in the world," to quote the apt title of Richard Rhodes's memoir of childhood. The loss, whether through death or abandonment, reverberates through the son's lifetime. In some cases, like that of Gus Lee, the author of the first selection, the mother's very memory is considered subversive by the reconstituted family and thus suppressed. And almost always the work of grieving such an enormous loss is beyond a child's capacities.

Such unresolved grief takes its toll: a well-known example is William Styron, who in *Darkness Visible* attributes his depressive tendencies to the "incomplete mourning" of his mother's death. His mother, like the mother of contributor Tim Beneke, died when her son was thirteen years old. Like Styron, Beneke also connects his depression to his mother's death.

Only when he grows older will a man who loses his mother in childhood be able to mourn her—if at all. A heart attack in his mid-sixties made Norman Sasowsky realize that he had never grieved for his mother. Sasowsky was taken at birth from a mother he never knew and his family "conspired" to prevent any knowledge of her. For Gus Lee it was a stepmother's jealousy; for Sasowsky, the stigma of a mentally ill relative.

Nick Davis was nine when his mother was killed in an automobile accident. In the form of a letter explaining why he *can't* contribute anything to this book, he reflects on the impact of that early loss.

Haki Madhubuti was sixteen when his mother died. Losing a mother in young manhood may be less traumatic than when one is small and dependent, but it is still harder to deal with than losing her in the middle years. And yet, though the death of a mother can sometimes be a liberation—Madhubuti, for example, gained some badly needed peace when his mother died—on the deepest level we are never truly ready to let her go. Every mother dies too young.

JOURNAL PAGE

Hank Heifetz

A quiet day. Do casual
small errands around Calcutta.
On one block see a beggar child
in the street, maybe
two, three years old
with his only clothes
shorts fallen to his ankles, crying
because his mother has left him.
She has gone down to the corner to beg
   there
but he doesn't know that
though I see her walking back
toward him as I pass.
Crying and crying,
head back and eyes closed
with the fear that he may be
abandoned forever,
he cuts through my heart.

MAH-MEE

Gus Lee

Her face was lovely, oval with large, deep-fired brilliant eyes, cheekbones chiseled softly from pale soapstone to hold haunting shadow and a mouth that seemed perfect in its fine linearity, its connectedness to the dimples that had been the common pride of her divided parents. A wonderful, joyous mouth that could laugh and grin and smile in a hundred expressions of precious, life-giving mirth.

She said the things that protect children from their fear of night, their anxieties about change, the terror of abandonment. I was so happy to be her son, her strength and beauty a shield against the glare of complicated and misunderstood days. She used to rub my ears with her fingertips, my cheek with the backs of her slender fingers.

"I love you so much, My Only Son," she whispered, clutching me to her as if she feared I would run away.

"I love you, Mah-mee," I managed, breathlessly.

I was five when my *mah-mee* died of cancer, never to hear her voice again. I experienced the loss so traumatically that it

Parts of this essay are reprinted from *China Boy* (Penguin Dutton, 1991), copyright © 1991 by Augustus Lee.

erased my memory, stunted my appetite, stopped my physical growth, deepened my myopia, and blunted my interest in the exterior world.

I never said good-bye to her. I was ignorant of her condition. When she went to the hospital I was told she was visiting friends. When she returned looking weak and unhealthily pale, I asked, "You sick, *Mah-mee?*"

"No," she whispered, her face saying, "Don't ask me." I paid her words no heed, looking for the message that said: "I will never leave you again."

I was then sent to stay with another family for a month. When I returned, I ran into the kitchen, darting from sister Betty's legs to sister Lily's legs. Back to Betty's. "Where's *Mah-mee?*" I asked.

"So, did you enjoy your visit to the country?" replied Betty Ying.

At the age of five I was clearly within the age of nondisclosure of my mother's passing. Mary Mei-Mei was in fact old enough to know, but Lily and Betty could not agree on whether to tell her, and there were no elder women to advise them. But Mary deduced *Mah-mee's* death quickly. With fierce willpower, she maintained the custom and did not tell me.

"Where *Mah-mee* staying—I do wrong?" I asked, my speech compressed, anxious. Our mother's absence had caught me between languages. My Songhai was pitiful, my Mandarin worse. My English was fractured. My Cantonese was nonexistent.

"What shall I read you?" Mary Mei-Mei asked in a tight voice, while Betty rustled the hair on my head. I thought someone was hiding my mother from me.

My sisters crafted letters to me, full of details of the busy harbor esplanade, the Bund of Tsingtao, the fat yellow fish from the Gulf of Po Hai, the austere greetings of my maternal grandfather, and the exotic foods of the White Russian restaurants of Shanghai and Harbin. They read them to me, tearfully.

They were signed, "I love you My Only Son, Mother."

I wondered why Father received no mail from her, and why

Mother had not taken me to accompany her to meet Grandfather and his tickling fish, to let me run in the compound's upper gallery and pluck mandarin oranges from the long branches of its treasured shade trees. I wondered if she had found Yip Syensheng, and Dog.

"When we go China, see Mother, Father?" I asked.

This no doubt made my father feel that he needed to find a mother for me, one who was older than my thirteen-year-old sister to cleanse the house of the complications of family consideration.

When I was seven, my father remarried, giving me a *chimu*, a stepmother. A fiery, emotive, literate woman who was born in the deep green, rolling-hilled farming country of the Pennsylvania Dutch, she was Caucasian in face, Germanic in child raising and fascist in opinion. She was as threatened by the memory of my dead *mah-mee* as I was encouraged by it. She treated my mother as if she were a vengeful divorcée, coveting her family and living vulturishly next door, liable to stop by for a free cup of sugar. My stepmother combated this threat by telling me, over the course of the next decade, that my mother had been corrupt, evil, illiterate, superstitious, and satanic, and that her greatest gift to me was dying.

I was required to regard my *chimu* as my *mah-mee*, and during a period in which everything I had been (Chinese) was transformed into a new personality (American), I forgot my mother, using that English word to describe the woman who now so powerfully dominated my life.

My true *mah-mee* remained interred in forgotten memory for nearly four decades. In a time of good fortune, I married and became a father to a daughter and a son.

When our daughter was seven, she asked me about her missing grandmother. I proceeded to tell her about my *chimu*. My wife pointed out to me that I was describing the wrong mother. It was in that moment that the gravity of my mother's fate first became clear. She had not only died, but been forgotten—not perhaps by neighbors, who remember her in any event, but by her only son.

I had cut the bond of *gang* with my mother. Chinese sons are pledged to their parents by a powerful tie called *gang* which involves filial piety and lifelong obedience. I had been undutiful and unforgivably dishonorable. Master K'ung Fu-tze—Confucius—would be very unhappy with me.

Now, propelled by my daughter's curiosity, I was willing to brave the strictures of the past and perform an archeological dig. The effort was launched in the name of my daughter, but I had waited unwittingly all my life for this chance to know my mother and to hear her voice, once again.

By that time I had been a criminal defense lawyer and a deputy district attorney. I interviewed my three older sisters as if preparing for a homicide trial, in which the prosecutor must strive to know the deceased through the stories of others. I asked endlessly about our mother, trying to make her life real not to a jury, but to her only son, the child with whom she had experienced a love made perfect by its shortness and irreplaceable by its purity.

So I asked: what time did she get up in the morning? What did she do first? What were her favorite foods, books, songs, clothes, and times of day? Was she a morning person? Who were her friends and enemies, and why? How corrupt, evil, superstitious and satanic was she? Show me how she walked. Imitate her voice. Did she have a sense of humor? Was she given to joy or depression? Was she intellectual? Describe her relationships to her mother, father, husband, children, mother-in-law. Was she political? What did she expect of me?

I compiled the often conflicting descriptions of *Mah-mee* (and the mother who replaced her) into a journal for my daughter. The journal became the novel *China Boy*. Thus the recovery of my long-dead mother's life led improbably to a change in profession, a reform of my parenting attitudes, and a sense of Providence in all we do—what once was a spiritual hole now covered with a warm feeling.

"Your name is Lee Jian-sun," said Mah-mee, looking deeply into my young eyes. She was beautiful and her voice was

like a soft caress. "Lee is your proud family name. Jian-sun'
means 'strong grandson.' You were named by your Gung-
gung, your father's father. You were born here, in Mei-gwo,
America, but he is so proud of you, anyway. You will be a
brilliant musician, a brilliant scholar." She closed her eyes
in pleasure.

When I was a child, my mother spoke to me in Chinese.
Only a few years ago, for the first time, I saw her English handwriting. It was on the back of an old, curled photograph, taken
of my youngest sister in wartime Chungking and mailed, with
great hope, in an airplane that flew over the Himalayas, toward
my father: "Honey, this is a snap of Mei-mei in her new holiday
dress. Do you like it? She misses you so much, and sends
kisses."

Through the browning of age, the fine, blue, fountain-
penned cursive words flow like beautifully harmonious and
uniform waves before a strong but kind wind, curving to the
same disciplined heights, but round and expressive between. It
is the handwriting of an English schoolteacher who has known
love.

My mother has been described by my father as "passion-
ate." My eldest sister describes her as "intuitive." Other women
sought her advice for any manner of problems. She could read
people's moods, measure truth within a *ts'un* – an inch – and
know what to say to drive men mad or cause them to concede
something they normally would not provide to a woman, even
in peacetime.

Chinese women were supposed to bear sons, and there is a
rumor afoot that even today, little has changed. *Mah-mee* bore
four daughters and in an effort to make her fifth child a son, she
scrutinized naked male Rodin statues while thinking reproduc-
tive thoughts. In opposition to her embarrassed husband, she
pinned pages from art books on the walls of their bedroom. The
selected art was representative of the European masters, but the
variations shared one trait: they all displayed the male organ. My
sisters would enter the bedroom and cover their eyes.

Mother would hum her favorite Christian hymns while looking at the pictures, praying in her wonderfully eclectic way to God Almighty, Michelangelo, and the Yin, the Goddess of Fertility. She lit joss sticks and closed her eyes, visualizing male babies. She attended Episcopalian churches and overdonated, murmuring, "For my Son, whom You will give me, thank You."

My mother believed in spirits, in brokering with capricious ghosts, in burning joss sticks to them in moments of reflection, in conversing coherently, and aloud, with her beloved father in Tsingtao while she was in a bathtub in San Francisco.

"The tub is perfect," she said. "I have come across the sea like the Ming admiral, Cheng Ho, to find this perfect tub. It is because of excellent deals I have made with the spirits of water and wind. The tub allows my feet to point to the west, toward Father, where the *feng shui*, geomantic forces, inspire calm and peace and allow the sun to sleep."

She was proud of her rigorous classical literary education, but paradoxically cursed by a mind that could not grasp the simplest fundamentals of the Newtonian world. She would look in mirrors, bewildered by the image. She could never understand why the gardenia in her hair appeared on the left in the mirror and on the right in photographs. "Magic," she whispered.

When something confused her, which happened regularly as the ticking of the magic clock, she giggled brightly, delighting in the mysteries of the world. She used to say that there was a small god inside the doorbell and she called him the Chime God. "Mr. Westinghouse and Mr. General Electric are *great* men! They have absolutely superior *shigong*!"

She loved electricity—ghost spirits in positive action. Reading one night under a lamp, Mother shrieked in abject horror when the lightbulb exploded, showering her with small glass shards. "Angry ghost!" she cried, throwing her book high in the air. When Lily unscrewed the hot bulb with a towel and inserted a new one, Mother looked at her as if she had turned ox dung into diamonds. "Lily Ah-wah! Promise me that you will be an engineer!"

Men who made passes at her were not rude ruffians but agents of evil river spirits. She would shop at Old Petrini Market on Divisadero Street and wonder why men stared at her. In China, men of my parents' social grouping developed peripheral vision and would not gaze openly at women.

"River-Spirit-Men!" she cried. "Why do they stare at me so? Why do they lick their lips like Gobi nomads at a well?" Even at the age of five I knew why. She was beautiful and wore tight, side-slit, high-collared, short-sleeved Mandarin dresses. She carried a parasol to keep the sun from her face.

"Spirits," my mother said, "are perfect because they never die and leave you. Women, My Only Son, have the great spirits. It is our gift."

In traditional China women were expendable birthing organisms for the glory of the family. Mother resisted this status. She did things most Chinese women would not imagine attempting in a state of final extremis. She refused obsequiousness, rejected submission, and exchanged restraint for spontaneity, stating the contents of her mind at the moment of the thought, however transient. She acted as if she were an enfranchised male.

My mother was born in Soochow (more a poetic "Sue-Joe" than a harsh "Sue-chow"), a city renowned throughout China for its beautiful and decorous women, its inspiring poets and quiet, soothing Venetian canals. She was the only daughter born to the Tzus, an influential and admired scholar-gentry clan that had achieved success in the age-old Chinese system of social ranking, where scholarship established status.

Her given name, Da-tsien, was diaphonous and opaque, attractive in sound and unclear in meaning. This was intentional; common family daughters were named Pear Blossom, Sweet Plum, or Beautiful Moon, pretty names with little mystery, all of the poetry on the surface, relating to the senses.

Aristocratic girls were given enigmatic names, shrouding them from the gods and hiding them from questing interlopers who would know them too easily. The poetry of their names remained hidden, relating secretly to the heart and the inner organs. Such names relied upon the horrific weakness of the

Chinese tongues: a rank overabundance of homonyms, where one sound could possess five hundred meanings. Chinese writers and name-givers exploit the differences in meaning to create endless, complex quadruple entendres and shifting interpretations. Thus, there is no poetry the equal of the Chinese, which offers so many tastes, nuances, and changing seasons with so few words. Like shifting clouds in a summer sky, one sees a mountain, a bird, a hint of a dream poorly recalled, or a face vividly replicated.

My mother's very name described relationships—between light and shadow, between scents and hints, between opposites, and between equals. The Chinese have made personal relations the essence of life. They do not look at the differences or similarities, for example between siblings, but instead to the relationship they form, the border where they meet.

Chinese focus energies not upon "achievement" or "ambition" but upon "success." And success is defined relationally. Good grades are not acquired for their own sake, or for recognition or later benefit alone. They are produced consistent with our *gang* to our parents.

A person who maintains good relations with others in China could never be a failure, regardless of his or her lack of economic success. The same does not necessarily hold in America.

In a society that honored firstborn sons and sneered at all daughters, Da-tsien held her tiny piece of ground and made it grow. "I don't care how Chinese girls should act!" she cried at her scandalized mother, my *Na-Bu*. "I think it's wonderful to tell *BaBa*, Father, that I admire how much he reads!" Thus in a culture that educated only firstborn sons of prosperous aristocrats, she learned to read and write, achieving a level many firstborn sons envied.

My mother's father, *Na-gung*, Outside Grandfather, was a wealthy heir and dedicated bookworm who disliked work. He moved the family to Shanghai, perhaps for the libraries. It was a wild, hedonistic, and diverse city, but traditions were still robust.

All marriages were arranged by canny *chih huo ch'ai che*, matchmakers. My mother was to wait submissively for her *yeh*, her karma, to take its course, presenting her with the husband who would pick her. *Yeh* and the matchmaker would bring her the man who would rule the rest of her life with either iron fist or firm hand, and usually both.

Mah-mee's spirit was too strong. At a very early age, she began to influence not only the behavior of others, but the very nature of the family's practices.

When she became a toddler, her mother and the servant women of the Tzu family gathered in the upper-level nursery to begin the traditional binding of her feet. The women, I imagine, felt the duty of the moment and the necessity of the sacrifice. No self-respecting gentry man would marry a girl with large, unbound feet. The only way to create a woman who would follow five steps behind her husband, walking with great vulnerability, was to break the toes in childhood and force them under the foot. The pain to be imparted was Chinese pain, structured along lines of status, given now to provide later gains.

As my mother told the story to my sisters, her father heard her crying that day while he was reading. He read everything, including books about the Western barbarian world and its curious religion whose leader was a *laoshr*, a teacher named Jesu, who treated children with the respect that Chinese gentlemen only provided to those above them.

The first wraps were already on his baby daughter when he used his well-educated but usually silent voice in action, something rare for him, a man of knowledge, manners, and quiet rectitude.

"Stop, please. You may not do this. It hurts her too much."

"*Aieyaa!* Husband! Are you crazy? If we do not bind her feet, they will grow like carp and she will not be able to walk gracefully and no *chih huo ch'ai che* will ever find her a husband and she will die lonely, without sons!"

"I don't care. I don't want her hurt anymore!"

"Husband! You hurt her worse, this way!"

"I don't agree. Times are changing in China."

Thus was born a bond with her father that would grow more dear as she grew older, as well as a tacit authorization for the little girl to believe in the decency of her own wishes.

My mother loved books and hungered for learning. Her father permitted her the outrageous luxury of a tutor to learn the minimum eighteen hundred characters possessed by all firstborn gentry sons. She also shared her father's sense of intellectual adventure.

Shanghai was one of the most cosmopolitan centers in all the world. The new tony tongue was English. *Mah-mee* asked American Presbyterian missionaries for English lessons. She did not care that the lessons described the Christian Lord, a Jewish rabbi named Jesu; she would have studied auto mechanics to acquire this troublesome, exciting literary form. She was by now high-minded, independent, and a curse to her mother. But still a teenager, carrying her favorite stuffed tiger as she walked with long strides followed by her short, obese, and very unhappy maid who kicked pebbles in anger and fear as they approached the church of the white devils.

Jesu offered her a personal relationship based on grace. He would forgive anything—her sentimentality about her father, her high-mindedness and failed *gang* with her mother, her quick use of her intuitions and loud use of her woman's voice in public. He might even encourage her learning English to acquire faith. Jesu, she learned, respected women equally to men and was a relational man who had died for her, who would remain faithful, regardless of her behavior, her faults, her passions. What Chinese man would do the same?

She converted formally to Christianity, accepting forever the companionship of the Jewish *laoshr*, Jesu.

By the time she was twenty, she had driven the matchmaker and her overtaxed mother to fits of delirious anger. She was tall and lovely, her face smoothly ovaled, her lips small and precise, her eyes large and commanding, her age too great to be single. In a high-necked *cheongsam* and her long black hair high above her head, she looked like a Chinese princess.

The matchmaker had come up with a new *beau ideal,* an elder merchant from a strong family, whose mother—read "tyrant-over-the-daughter-in-law"—had died. He would demand little of her, and his ample wealth was headlined by a kind heart. But she wanted someone whom she could relate with and not merely avoid. She wanted love and not security, friction along the yin-yang line, and not merely a recitation of differences, limitations, and man-made privileges.

There was a wretched but handsome boy who lived next door to their home. He was a Nationalist Army fighter pilot, which was about as terrible in those days as an upper-class family in Southampton having a son join the Mafia. He was the bane of the neighborhood as he drove up and down silent, elegantly forested Burkhill Road in the French section of Shanghai on a massive, ear-splitting BMW motorcycle. He was my *Na-bu's* worst nightmare—a handsome thug in boots and goggles, one of China's first bikers.

This was Dad. I can hear him snapping his fingers and saying in Wu, the tongue of Shanghai, "Hey, like hipsville, man. *(Snap, snap.)* Ya gotta go to where it's, like, happening. Crazy."

When she saw my father, she took a breath, exhaled her *yeh*, and nudged her unhappy mother. Her mother nodded in familiar defeat and set up a meeting of the families. The marriage was arranged. Perhaps the matchmaker changed jobs or left town.

My mother had selected her own spouse because she knew what she wanted, she knew that her wants were relevant despite the bindings of tradition, and that she was not doing this bold thing alone. She had a personal relationship with a long-dead but very gutsy Jewish rabbi, who must have reminded her of herself.

The Chinese civilian population, unlike the American, bore the brunt of World War II, as well as their civil wars and revolutions. The enemies of my father and his Nationalist Army presented my mother and sisters with the choice of flee or die. Three warring armies made this no time to attempt movement, much less emigration. Hordes of desperate refugees faced brigades of Chinese bandits and a host of warlord forces, while a million Japanese soldiers of the Kwangtung Army held China in brutal occupation. The Japanese Army summarily executed refugees, and men of all stripes routinely savaged women and girls.

Our mother, her feet unbound by an unconventional father, walked, pulled, led, and was pulled and led by Lily on a journey across the face of China, from Shanghai to Chungking, from Chungking to India, and from India to America. *Mah-mee* and the firstborn daughter used stratagem, patience, drama, and guts to manage the deceptions, the pantomimes, the speech, and the attitudes to permit survival in each new crisis.

Her beloved father had quoted the master K'ung: "Knowledge is easy, action is difficult." His daughter had mastered both knowledge and action.

I loved bedtime, when my mother sat by my pillow, held me in her lap to read the stories of Lu Hsun and told me about the twenty-five-thousand-man expeditions of Admiral Cheng Ho in the early fifteenth century, about good boys who were good pupils.

My mother revered scholars and musicians; I liked soldiers.

"Jian-sun, recite for me the story of the good student Tzu-han-ren while Elinor brushes my hair."

"Mah-mee, how do you want your hair brushed—back or up?" asked Elinor.

"Dear. Please. Brush my hair so it will look windswept, as if I were standing on the beach barefoot on a warm day, singing to my father, facing China, with typhoons coming to me from the Yellow Sea!"

My mother loved Ocean Beach because it was the closest she could get to her father across the horizon. Throwing Janie Mei-Mei and me into the old Ford, she drove like a suicide candidate to the Pacific Ocean, jerking to a wild halt on the Great Highway, bouncing us off the dashboard. Removing her shoes and dashing across the busy street, she sighed as her feet found the wet sand. I ran with her, consumed as small children are in the passions of their mothers.

Putting her bare, graceful feet in the frigid seas, she expended two books of matches before wild fortune caused a match to accidentally ignite the joss stick.

"I hope it is hot on the Tsingtao Bund today!" she cried into the crashing surf, the joss stick hissing.

"Then the water that touches my feet is the same that touches yours, and you can know how I miss you, and revere you, and respect your learning!" Mother had to speak aloud to her father across the sea, because he could not read her facial expressions from afar.

"Do you think of me? Do you forgive me for leaving you? I am so sorry, Father!" she cried into the cloaking roar of the waves, the mist of the sea kissing the tears welling from her eyes.

"Mother abandoned you! I promised I would never do the same! And I am now in another world! Oh, my Christian Lord.

"Do you know?" she asked the wind as it carried her words to China. "The Americans made the black people their slaves. They took them from their homes in Africa. I think the war has done the same to me."

Her death had begun when she left China in a cheerless lonesome dawn, without a kiss from her parents or forgiveness from her father. She was never to see them, or China, again. In her last days I think she regretted the separation from her father in Tsingtao and the greater extended family in Shanghai more than the deprivation of a long life in America or the permanent separation from us.

"Yes, Son, put these fingers here and press. Ah, it's beautiful. Play more! No no no, son, fingers on here, the kang ch'in keys. There! Oh, Jian-sun, you're incredibly perfect!" She clapped her hands, but more quietly than had been her practice. She was not as strong as she used to be. She touched my cheek and I leaned my whole face into her cool hand. "Jian-sun, you will be the most wonderful kang chi'in chia! You make me so happy, I cry."

Mah-mee wanted a son and got one in me. Five years later she was dead, her influence upon me presumed to be gone with her. She wanted me to be a prodigy in music, and there are few fields in which I show less promise or ability. She hated war and disliked the profession of arms, as only a woman can who has seen her culture destroyed by the work of soldiers. I became a soldier, and came within a *ts'un* of choosing the military as a noble career. She wanted me to be a Christian man, but my father and stepmother were atheists, and I was lucky to be agnostic.

Her ardent desire for me to become a quiet pianist playing before an adoring world was a pure extension of her own wishes. This is of course natural. What is unusual is that because I was once her flesh, I was always her flesh. I did not have independent dominion over my future, because I was using her body. So many Chinese mothers have coddled their sons from a hard physical world, knowing that if they raise warriors, their flesh will die. The mothers were born in a cruel world, and sought continuing life for their clan. Thus I think the impulse for pianists, engineers, doctors, and scientists.

My *mah-mee* wanted many grandsons and I have given her but one, a wonderful and remarkable boy. He was born in America and owns his own flesh. He loves sports but can play the piano.

I also have given *Mah-mee* a granddaughter who is the match of anyone and should remind my mother of someone she herself once was. For this girl believes in the decency of her own wishes.

Attending to them, through her heart, is my mother. I hear her voice now. I feel as if a long looping arc, wandering lost for forty years, has closed the circle it was meant to form. I understand to some degree who she was, what she valued, what she wanted.

My father filled me with a will to succeed and the encouragement to develop physical and professional strengths. But it is my mother whom I need in my biggest jobs of parenting and husbanding. This is not because she was my mother—but because of who my mother was. She was the one who died young, but had found faith in life. She was the one who felt relationships should be inspired by the divine and not by rules of female subjugation. She was the one who urged upon me a life of relational good faith, to make both K'ung Fu-tze and Jesu, the Chinese and Jewish teachers, proud of me.

I often wonder how I found my wife. She is unlike any woman I have ever known, with her fiery belief in family, undying loyalty to her children, the ability to take long strides in the interests of the clan. She is highly relational, widely read, and the recipient of difficult advisory questions from many women. She was raised Christian.

I can look at my wife, at our daughter, and at our son, and see them through the eyes of *Mah-mee*. I cry with the happiness taught me by a woman who was fiery in her beliefs, who understood *gang*, who took long strides for her family in the company of a Jewish rabbi, and who taught me love when she was my mother.

REMEMBER

Norman Sasowsky

It took fifty years and the treatment for a severely blocked coronary artery for me to realize that I had not grieved for the death of my mother. Had I closed part of my heart?

The unexpected discovery of my arterial disease and the following angioplasty made me very sensitive to what was going on in my upper chest. One evening during a joint baking event with my wife, I began feeling tired and not up to finishing my part of the project. My experience was that I was not performing as well as I should—that I was somehow deficient, not living up to some abstract expectation. Not pleasing my mother? I felt constriction and a choking feeling in my throat, as if there was something I "had to bring up." Then it exploded. I began uncontrollable sobbing. Why was I crying? It seemed to have emerged out of nowhere. I had no idea why this was happening. Then I realized that I was crying for the loss of my mother fifty years ago. I felt how much I missed her love (a love that I never experienced) and how much I missed her (a mother I never had). When she died I was thirteen and had not been given the opportunity to grieve for her. I had never allowed myself to do so.

Someone at the corner candy store came to our Brooklyn apartment two-thirds of the way down the street and said we had a phone call. I was sent to get the message. Looking back, I have no idea how this system was set up, but I assume few of us in the neighborhood had phones. I have very little memory from that part of my life. My uncle Ben was on the phone. He was my mother's oldest brother. He said: "Tell Harry [my father] that Fannie died." Dutifully I took the message and went back to the apartment to report it. I have no other memory of the event. I remember—I think—going to the funeral, but little else.

It was as if it never happened: my mother's life or her death. Her life was a mystery shrouded in family silence. I knew that she was "mentally ill" and confined to an institution. I vaguely remember that I might have been taken to see her once. I'm not sure if I imagined this, or it really happened, or I wished it.

Over the years I was able to piece together bits of information about her life. She had given birth to twins before I was born. They had not survived. She and my father had married because "they had been found together." I was a difficult child. I was colicky. She suffered from a common postpartum syndrome ("blues"). This was why she was confined. Perhaps she had tried to harm me or herself? No one said anything. In later years when I would try to open the subject my family told me there was no use in revisiting the past.

My maternal grandparents took care of me in my first years. I think my father considered giving me up for adoption or to a foster home, but couldn't go through with it. After a while—I don't know how long, but I know it was when I started elementary school—I went to live with my paternal grandparents. This grandfather always resented me and was jealous of the attention my grandmother gave me; he was very insecure in their relationship.

My mother's father continued to visit my mother and attempted without success to bring her home. He always came to visit and took me out for the day. I was his first grandchild and I knew that he cared for me. His face was always filled with love. I believe he saved my life and made it possible for me to find love in the world.

We were never sure that there would be enough funds for the family. Both my father and his father were gamblers and lost much of the money they earned. The other members of our family, aunts and uncles on both sides, were kind to me in various degrees. However, there were times that I was unsure about my place in the world. I sensed that I was extra baggage on a difficult family journey. My grandmother had raised four children and had an unreliable partner. However, she was there for me, even if she did not provide me with a feeling of unconditional love that one hopes a mother would provide.

My father was absent most of the time. I saw him as a weak person who had great difficulty coping with the world. My memories of him are of his weaknesses, and I think my presence in the world made him feel his failure. He considered me, to my surprise, a "failure" until I gave him a grandchild on whom he could bestow his love. He lived only three months after my son's birth to enjoy this.

To this day I am not able to find out much about my mother. I realize that it never occurred to me to ask my father about her. Probably I thought it was dangerous territory. I feel I did her a great injustice. For many years I harbored an anger toward her for having "abandoned" me. Ultimately, I forgave her, realizing as I got older that it was not in her power to be there for me. Nevertheless, she deserved to have a conscious place in my memory.

I have only a few family pictures which I keep on my studio wall. One is the entire maternal family with my mother, at the far right, as a very young woman. Another is my mother and father standing outdoors.

When the explosion occurred I could recognize what unfinished business I had left. I had never allowed myself to feel my loss, and the family, thinking this was best for me, unconsciously conspired to not let my mother live in my memory. She must have had a terrible life. I don't know how she died. Had she died of natural causes or taken her own life? I suppose, since my own life was so difficult, I was reluctant to probe deeper. I worried that I might have "mental illness." I sensed that my family shared this concern, although in reality I never got the sense they spent too much time thinking about me. They were busy with their own children. I never got a sense of my own value. Later, it was mostly teachers and others outside the family who helped me value myself, at least what I could do.

I am lucky to have married a woman who has some of the same qualities my mother had; she was very generous. My mother was also gifted musically. I chose to be an artist, maybe unconsciously trying to fulfill my mother's talents in another form. I know that she bestowed many gifts on me and inadvertently helped me to develop certain strengths. And I also realize the great hurt that occurs when one has lost so valuable a resource. One continues to seek the approval of others and a secure place in the world. I was too busy surviving to take the time to realize what had happened to me, what had helped form my behavior, my fears, my way of dealing with the world. It is only now that I am a grandparent that I realize how important it is for children to have the love of their parents, how valuable that love is, and how hurtful and long lasting that loss is. The world is filled with terrible abuse and neglect of children. We can only estimate the ongoing damage this does to children and the people in their lives.

Because of the explosion, I can now talk about my mother. It has been painful. Though I am active in a very effective men's group, I found that I had to approach talking about her slowly, for fear of how I would react. First, I hinted at the subject. Two weeks later, after having shared some of the experience with my sons and a few friends, I felt secure enough to talk about it with the group. Each time it has helped me to acknowledge her life, to let her live again, and to forgive myself for having allowed her to be "put away."

Lastly, I thank my mother and father for the life they gave me. Though they could not nurture it, it was nurtured. How can you remember a mother you did not know? How can you not remember?

MAKING MY
MOTHER REAL

Timothy Beneke

A woman friend who had followed my work as an anti-rape activist once pressed me to explain why I became a pro-feminist man. There are many reasons, reasons I have explored elsewhere. But one reason I could identify with women's fear of male violence was my own fear, as a child, of my father's violence. And in my twenties, as my pro-feminist consciousness coalesced, I wanted to please the women I knew—who were all feminists. And behind that was a deep-seated desire to please my mother.

Mother:
Since your death thirty years ago your presence is a film covering my experience, darkening it and making the world, the world of my life, seem farther away. If I could pop you open, a thousand memories would appear and move me, breaking and healing my heart,

Originally written for this volume; an expanded version of the author's mother story appears in his *Proving Manhood: Reflections on Men and Sexism* (University of California Press, 1997).

and making the world real again. Your unreality places the world so far away. Your unreality makes my life unreal. But I can't, don't know how to pop you open, and as I move deeper into middle age, wonder whether the attention I give you is worth the effort. But still, I sense, until you are real, I will not be real.

Or so it seems when I think of my mother. She died when I was thirteen, quickly, in agony, of cancer. She was told it was a slipped disc. I think I was in love with her. By the time she died I had lived in twelve houses in nine cities. I barely knew anyone outside my nuclear family and was, with good reason, terrified of my father. She was it.

I remember the day she died. My father put his arms around me and my brother and said:

"The doctors don't think your mother is going to make it through the day."

(I sob as I write this, but my sob feels as much like a physical convulsion as an emotion, as much like a cough as a cry; maybe a third of the meaning is in it. My body sobs at the thought of her death—my psyche denies most of the meaning. Sobbing with much of the passion missing: This is the ongoing story of my grief; my body wants to grieve but something in me resists the meaning of it . . . as if over time my soul is trying to reenter my body. Over the years my tears for her have never felt quite real. I—my body—can cry over her, but I can't quite feel the sorrow.)

The three of us wept. That night at the hospital, she lay howling in pain, making gurgling noises. My brother and I sat on either side of the bed crying. She was mostly bones by then. In four months she must have gone from 140 pounds to 60. I doubt that it is possible for a person to be any bonier. She howled. When we left we kissed her on the cheek and for the first time she gave no recognition. Her mind had been going for a couple of weeks.

My father told us we would remember Mommy as she was with a clear head.

I remember going to sleep that night. My father came and woke me up:

"Mommy's in heaven. She's gone."

I felt a sense of relief that it was over. I remember crying. I remember some faint image of heaven. And I remember something else. I went into the bathroom and stared into the mirror and, smiling angrily through my tears, thought to myself, "I'm not going to let this get to me."

I think I had been playing with my emotions for years.

When I was ten my father beat up my mother, ran everyone out of the house, and broke most of the furniture. It is by far the most powerful memory of my childhood. For the next couple of years he was often on the edge of violence. I never again felt safe around him, and lived with the unthinkable fear that he would kill us all. With my father ranting outside my door, I spent many nights with a pillow over my head and butterflies in my stomach, praying I would fall asleep and wake up the next morning with him gone to work. (He was a colonel in the army.) I organized my time to avoid him. When I was around him, I constantly assessed his mood. At times he was better, at times worse; there was much about him that was good and that I loved, but I was never again unafraid of him.

I saw the bruises on her the next day, and remember her lying with ice packs against her discolored jaw. But in the strange way such things are possible, I never actually admitted to myself that he had beaten her up.

At the funeral I stared and stared and stared at her as if I were staring her down. I liked it. I was in some altered, trancelike state. I stared a long time and then was led away by the funeral director as if I needed looking after. I resented this. I was fine and wanted to stare some more. Maybe I was trying to cultivate some cold-bloodedness; maybe this was an expression of rage. Maybe I was trying to protect myself from overwhelming grief. No doubt. I imagine the funeral director thought I was showing signs of shock. Maybe I was becoming an embarrassment.

Afterwards I was angry at God and decided he must not exist if he could allow this. The problem of reconciling evil with God bothered me.

After she died my father, my brother (Richard, who was sixteen), and I did not talk about her. *Did not talk about her.* Or almost never. Our grief was private, for the most part.

We were three men living on an army post in the Deep South, in 1964, with tanks stored four hundred yards away. We did not know how to comfort each other or how to grieve or how to vivify her memory. She had been the emotional center of our lives. None of us had enduring sources of emotional support apart from her.

Once my father came to me in tears.

"Why did this have to happen to us? You and Rich have your school, but you are all I have."

I remember his face when they closed the coffin for the last time; I remember how he fought with his tears walking back to sit down with us.

Another time he came to me:

"You know your mother was one of the smartest people who ever lived. You could come to her with a problem, and she would help you talk about it and work it through."

My father hated his own mother; he addressed my mother as Mommy, a letter he wrote her in 1953 begins "Dearest Mommy," and ends with him saying what a great mommy she is. Despite the cold, terrifying anger he was capable of, he could be wonderfully tender. I still cherish the way he would tuck me in as a child and tell me that he loved me with the dearest sweet talk.

When someone close to us dies, we are left with a hole in our lives. Ideally, as we grieve, we slowly acknowledge what we have lost, and the hole is filled with memories of the person, with warm feelings of love; with a recognition of how the person lives on in ourselves and the world. The void becomes rich and fertile as the deceased becomes a source of energy and strength. Nothing like that happened when my mother died.

I cried, a lot, for some time. And because of that, I assumed that I had properly grieved my mother. But as I got much older, in my thirties, I slowly came to recognize that I had not.

It is sometimes said that unresolved grief is at the core of depression. I have, in varying degrees, been depressed much, maybe most of my life, in ways recognizable to those close to me. What is the connection?

My mother is a presence who comes and goes. I have intuitions, intimations of her presence, her meaning in my life, but for the most part she is mystified. I am forty-three. I begin to feel that by the time I die I may understand her effect on me. It is very slow going. In writing this I want to speed her up.

She manifests herself in so many ways . . .

A running joke for several years: When someone does something I mildly disapprove of, I say, "If you *think* you are hurting *anyone* but yourself, you are *very sadly* mistaken." This usually gets a laugh.

When I say this I am saying something my mother said to me many times. I am simultaneously assuming her identity and power and mocking it. And I am using her to get a laugh.

Sometimes I reflect upon the women I have been involved with and I think: "It is all *one* woman; all one woman underneath. At my deepest center I do not discriminate, do not notice who is there at my side. . . . At my deepest center is one woman I am responding to, tailoring my personality to, entertaining, impressing, charming—my mother."

We were very affectionate, my mother and I. We kissed a lot; she hugged me a lot. I was physically precocious, five foot seven and shaving at twelve, the first in gym class to have pubic hair. And lust-ridden at an early age and unable somehow to masturbate to orgasm. In our own way my mother and I possessed some physical, even sexual, connection I do not understand. I have said this since I was about twenty. I am not entirely sure what I mean.

Exactly a month before she died, she came home for a night. I remember ministering to her. She could not walk by then. I remember getting her a pitcher of some sort to enable her to urinate as she lay in bed. When I placed it near her genitals I was jolted by a vivid glimpse of her vagina. I felt a powerful, confused thrill. I had not looked head-on at a woman's vagina in this way before. I felt like I was seeing something I was not supposed to see.

At my father's funeral I was surrounded by relatives I had mostly not seen since my mother's funeral some twenty years before. A first cousin of my father's said he was struck by how much my and my brother's facial expressions resembled our mother's. I have no idea what he was talking about and probably never will. The thought that I wear her on my face, in my facial expressions and manner, is both terrifying and comforting.

She was buried some seventy miles south of us, in Nashville, Tennessee. I remember on cold rainy nights wondering what it must be like out there, in a box in the rain. When I was twenty-three, I wrote a fragmentary poem about it. I called it "Your Mother Wears Combat Boots!" and it went something like this:

> YOUR MOTHER WEARS COMBAT BOOTS!
> my mother wears no shoes
> she's in a box
> outside
> in the rain
> in the rain
> in a box
> she wears no shoes, hears no views, sings
>   no blues
> in the rain
> in the box
> underground
> not a sound
> does reach her
> not a sound
> goes round
> in her head

or her toes
no one knows what it's like in a box in the
    rain
with no shoes
it's insane what that box could contain
just insane

For a long time I would cry at evocations of goodness. I remember seeing a segment of *60 Minutes* about a couple who had adopted some fifteen "problem children" and, apparently, through giving them love, had enabled them to adjust to life in a family. I cried when I saw this without knowing why. Once when I was twenty-three I played the last five minutes of *The Wizard of Oz* over and over and cried at Dorothy's line, "There's no place like home!" Watching Clinton's inauguration cere-monies, I sobbed when Marilyn Horne sang the Shaker song "'Tis a Gift to Be Simple, 'Tis a Gift to Be True," and a song about children of different colors, "Make a Rainbow, Make a Rainbow." I taped this and would return to it and cry again and again. For a long time I had little idea why I was crying. Then slowly over the years, I came to believe that it had something to do with my mother. But what is the connection?

I came across these words in a book on romantic love by Stephen Goldbart and David Wallin: "becoming aware of the goodness of love in the present can, unexpectedly, trigger grief. . . . We may grieve for what we have had and lost. Or we may grieve for what the past has never given us" (*Mapping the Terrain of the Heart*, p. 203).

This told me what I knew but hadn't quite thought. My mother's goodness, her affection and kindness and goodwill, which gave me joy and safety—however romanticized—is gone and will not come back. But I carry it inside somewhere, and the presence of human kindness awakens my simultaneous longing for it and grief at its absence.

UNSPOKEN LESSONS
FROM AN EARLY DEATH

Haki R. Madhubuti

My mother was ill-equipped to nagivate the economic, social, and political pressures of her world. All of this drove her to alcohol, drugs, and death at the age of 36.

I was born in 1942. Then in 1943, my mother migrated from Little Rock, Arkansas, moving, as John O. Killens would say, "up-South" to Michigan. She came with me, an infant child on her knees, and with my father, who stayed long enough to father my younger sister.

Those years, the 1940s and 1950s, were not kind to us, and my father wandered in and out of our lives from the day we hit Detroit. My mother, alone with two children and no skills, ended up working as a janitor in an apartment building owned by a Negro preacher/undertaker. My earliest memory is of her cleaning that three-story, sixteen-unit building each day, carrying garbage cans on her back to the alley once a week. Seldom did I see her without a broom, mop, or washcloth in her hands. By this time, I was eight years old, and my sister was seven, we

---

became self-elected helpers and assisted as much as possible because we knew that staying in our basement apartment depended upon our mother's sexual involvement with the Negro building owner. These encounters took place when we were at school or while we were asleep. My mother began to trade her body quite early in order for us to live. In the 1940s, there were few safety nets for single women with children. Consequently, my mother became a victim in a white supremacist, monied system, which allowed some Black men to become surrogate oppressors.

With no family in Detroit and left to her own limited resources, my mother sought to survive with her children in a way that would have the least possible negative impact on us. However, due to the violent nature of her relationship with the landlord, we stayed in our Lower East Side apartment only until she was able to find work less threatening and taxing on her physically and psychologically. At least that is what my sister and I thought. What I've failed to tell you about my mother is that she was probably one of the most beautiful women in the world. I've seen her beauty not only stop traffic but compel men to literally get out of their cars to introduce themselves to her. Her beauty, which was both physical and internal, was something that few women she associated with could handle. Women would stare at her with dropped mouths. Her beauty would ultimately place her in an environment that would destroy her.

My mother's next job was that of a barmaid. She started serving drinks at one of the newest and classiest locations in Detroit, Sonny Wilson's. Along with this job came the slow but destructive habit of alcohol consumption. Also, she began to run in very fast company. She was named Miss Barmaid of 1951, carrying with that title all of the superficiality and glitter of the Negro entertainment world at that time. To cut to the bone of all of this is to note rather emphatically that my family's condition of poverty drove my mother into a culture that dictated both her destruction and great misery for my sister and me. By the time I was thirteen, my mother was a confirmed alcoholic and was fast losing her health. When I turned fifteen, she had moved to hard drugs and was not functional most of the time.

My sister, who had just turned fourteen, announced to us that she was pregnant. This was in the late 1950s and pregnancy out of wedlock was not a common or acceptable occurrence. I went looking for the man who had impregnated her. He was a local gang leader, twenty-one years old, who had as much potential as a husband or father as I did at fifteen. After briefly talking to him about my sister's condition and getting virtually nowhere, I did what most "men" did in similar situations at that time: I hit him. And he, in a rather surgical fashion, responded by literally "kicking my ass." After reporting this to my mother, she, in a drunken stupor, gave me another whipping for getting whipped.

Shortly after that incident, my mother's need for alcohol and drugs increased. She prostituted herself to feed her habit. Many nights I searched Detroit's transient hotels looking for her. Needless to say, I had grown up rather quickly and felt that there was no hope for me or my sister. Just before I turned sixteen, my mother overdosed on drugs and died. She had been physically and sexually abused by someone so badly that we were not able to view her body at her funeral. My sister was pregnant again. By the time she was twenty, she had three children. Before she was thirty, she had six children and had never been married. She has endured a life of pain and difficulty that often has been the exact duplicate of our mother's. To this day she lives in great pain.

I could not cry at my mother's funeral. My heart was cold and my mind was psychologically tired. I felt a quiet feeling of relief and release at her death, but also an underlying tone of guilt. At sixteen, I felt that I had not done enough to save my mother. However, it was clear to me that her final days had been filled with long hours of tragic suffering over which she had no control. All I could do was watch in confused pain, hostility, anger, resentment, and rage.

At first, I could not understand my anger. Why did she have to die so young and so viciously? Why were my sister, her baby, and I alone without help or hope? Why were we so poor? It seemed that my life was one big fight. There was no escape from problems and very little peace. And I guess my mother's death brought a moment of peace. The fight to survive remained uppermost in my mind. Yet it seemed I was being torn apart from the inside. A part of my own fear was connected to how my sister and I were going to survive. I had seen and been a part of too much destruction and death in my young life. I knew that the only person who really cared about our future was me, and that was not enough.

A part of the problem that my mother, sister, and I faced in America was that our skin color was neither Black nor white, but yellow! The unusual beauty that centered in my mother was not only due to the distinctive bone structure of her face and her small, well-connected body. It also had to do with the fact that all of her physical beauty was wrapped in yellow. Yes, we were "Arkansas Blacks," but my mother could easily have passed for Puerto Rican or dark Italian if she did not have to open her mouth. Her language was Southern Black English, and it carried in it the rural slowness that urban America does not have pity on.

However, it was her beauty, illuminated by very light skin color that attracted the darkest of Black men and, of those I remember, the most abusive of Black men. They seemed to be steaming in anger, hatred, and internal rage. It seems as though by being with her, they were as close to white women as was allowed at that time. And their often intense love/hate relationship with her was only a mirror of the fight they were having daily with themselves and the white world. They could not touch or physically retaliate against white people, but my mother was there for many of them to play out their deepest hurt in the "loving" and abusive treatment of her. I was not to understand, until much later, the deep color-rage that plagued them and that lay at the surface of my own reality.

That understanding would come first from reading and then from life, especially from my involvement in the Black struggles of the 1960s. After my mother died I knew that I didn't want a life like hers, but I didn't know yet what I did want. I knew that I had to leave, to get out of the area before it consumed me too.

My mother, not a deep reader herself, had encouraged me to read. She had sent me to the library when I was thirteen to get books by Richard Wright and Chester Himes. But at thirteen my self-hatred kept me from asking a white librarian for *Black Boy,* a book by a Black author with "Black" in the title. Later I went back, found the book on the shelf, and couldn't let it go. When I finished *Black Boy,* I was somehow different, more concerned about the shape of things around me. My questions about everything changed.

It was through reading Black women writers that I first learned to have empathy for women, to understand women. In the military which I joined after high school and especially in the 1960s when I worked with CORE, SNCC and SCLC and later the Black Arts movement, I met strong independent Black women. I had to learn how to negotiate working with them. I began then to realize that men and women were essentially the same. Aside from biology, superficial appearances and cultural roles assigned to us by society and its institutions, not very much separated us from each other.

Sometimes this understanding, this ability to empathize with women, would hurt me, especially with other Black men, given the climate of the movement in those years. Sexism covered the Black community like polluted water and was consumed by all, almost without question.

But out of this I came to understand my mother. As I grew into adulthood it became very clear that my mother had done the very best that she could have under the racial, political and economic realities of Apartheid in America and the cultural reality of Black life at that time. And as I gained this understanding, my feelings of anger and alienation rolled away, and finally by the time I was thirty, I was at peace with her and myself.

Out of this peace and understanding, I was able to view my mother in a different light. While other eyes would be fixed only on her beauty, which in the eyes of most men and many women defined her, I could see that my mother was not just beautiful, she was also very intelligent. She was verbal in her soft-spoken Southern manner and she gave me her way with words, the ability to use words to get what I wanted. But she was not able to find a place where she could use her intelligence, to have it valued.

My mother had a generous and giving heart. In fact my mother's heart was almost too big. But from her I got my sense of goodness and kindness, the assurance that one should love quietly and unconditionally. She gave me the understanding that it was not my lot to join what Ayi Kwei Armah has called "ostentatious cripples," those who live out America's creed of materialism and consumerism without consideration or care for the less fortunate of this earth.

Above all I got from her my independence, a fiery streak of self-reliance, and an understanding of the absolute need for an enriching and enlightened culture and for deep personal love in one's life. I've never wanted to work for anyone but myself, to depend on other people outside of my race and culture. But at the same time her example taught me that one person— alone—can't break through the alienation of racist institutions or America's Apartheid. Her life made it abundantly clear that I needed family commitments and a positive information bank. I also needed an intimate knowledge of what it meant to live a good and healthy life which incorporates productive work, spiritual insights and practice, holistic education and political and economic activism.

My mother didn't have a family or a community to fall back on. Her legacy to me was the idea that you can do whatever you want to do. Ideas and the creators of ideas run the world. The questions for me were: Where were the African/Black ideas? How do we move to ownership of ideas, ownership of the space that we occupy? I've tried to answer these questions by building Black institutions in my community and by helping to maintain a strong family with my wife and our children.

My mother's early death in such an inhuman manner forced me, a teenager, to confront life—in all of its mystery, creativity and wonder—on my own terms. I've learned much from her errors and the mistakes I've made. But unlike her, I did not allow them to defeat me. My mother's absence has taught me about the power of love. I realized that blind love is a weakness and the need for "too much" love can be a sickness. That whole people grow into love and that enlightened people do not abuse the love of others. And, if the human race is to develop and progress we must understand that all love is precious, yet there is something unspoken and special about the love between a mother and her son.

SINCERELY

Nick Davis

Dear Bob,

Thank you so much for inviting me to be a part of your book about men and their mothers. Though I'd love to participate, I'm afraid I'm going to have to decline. I wish I knew why.

I'm writing you from a place called The Writers Room, a large office space in lower Manhattan where writers come and rent desks. The only rule in the room is silence: except for the occasional nod on your way to the pay phones or bathroom, you have very little contact with other humans, and most of us here seem to like it that way. The day before yesterday, though, I rode up in the elevator with two women who chattered on like Monty Python housewives. One wore a gray overcoat, the other a red ski parka, and though I didn't recognize either of them, as their conversation meandered through a variety of subjects—the Hudson River, Russian pianists, Nelson Mandela—I realized that the one in the red parka was actually quite smart. She had a sly wit and used the phrase "second-thoughted," and when, after we reached our floor and Gray Coat had trundled past me with her keys, the other gave me a quiet smile that reminded me, quite impossibly, of my mother.

My mother died when I was nine, so I've had over two decades of things impossibly reminding me of her—tunes on the radio ("Those Lazy-Hazy-Crazy Days of Summer," "Seasons in the Sun," anything by Charlie Pride) or the sight of a Greenwich Village stoop, or the way Italian dressing can seep into a hamburger bun—and I've become used to the feeling. She died suddenly, in a freak car accident, so I didn't have a chance to say good-bye, or catalogue things about her to remember. Maybe that's why the reminders still sneak up on me: Here's something else—the way iceberg lettuce snaps apart—I don't know why, but put it on the list.

So my mom was very much on my mind as we all entered the outer room of The Writers Room to sign in for the day. (Signing in is an odd ritual here—in addition to your name, you note the time, so at the end of the day you can say to yourself, Well, seven hours and twenty-five minutes, there must be some good work in there *somewhere*.) Gray Coat signed first, and then her friend, but as I took up the pen, I recognized something and gave a nearly unselfconscious gasp.

"Um," I said declaratively to Red Parka. "You were friends with my mother."

She looked me in the eye. "Well, who are you?"

I said who I was, Johanna's son, and her face softened. "My God," she said. "I was just talking about her yesterday." Then she looked at me again and she said, "Let me give you a hug," and she did.

I am not a particularly impulsive person, Bob. I don't usually gasp, and I certainly don't hug people, but I haven't enjoyed a hug like that in years, probably since my first girlfriend headed off to France the summer we fell in love. It was nice, this hug. We broke it, shook off any embarrassment, and stood back from each other and talked. We didn't have much to say, said it quietly and politely, and before we entered the room, we made a tentative date for coffee in the afternoon. Then she paused and looked at me and said, "Of course, I can see her face."

I got to my desk, plugged in my laptop, opened up the screenplay I've been working on, and started to cry. I had never hugged a woman of that age before. My stepmother is about ten years younger than my mom would have been, and the various hugs I've gotten from aunts or friends, or friends' mothers, they haven't felt the way this hug felt. This hug, I said to myself, rather stupidly, felt good for one simple reason: It felt the way a hug from Mom would have felt.

But the problem is this:

When I was six, my family rented a house in Long Beach, an hour away from the city. My mother was working on a novel she would publish the year before she died, and my father was commuting to the city every day. And the dominant memory I have from that summer is of my mother, crying and laughing, pounding on my father's chest after he'd come home far later than he'd promised one night. It probably wasn't that late: It was twilight behind my parents as they stood on the curb, her fists hammering away at him, and his joyful yelps of pain as she whomped away. I never saw them truly violent with each other, but the memory is triggered by the word "hug" and the idea of a hug from my mother, because what I really want to tell you, of course, is that my mother was the best hugger in the world, you'd have loved to get hugged by my mother, oh, Bob, there was nothing like a hug from Mom. But any such sentiment, even when dimly articulated as it was the other morning at my Writers Room desk, is always checked by its exact opposite, which in this case is the scene of her walloping my father's chest.

And that's why I can't contribute to your book, Bob, try as I might. Because all that's left of her for me now are just loose scraps, stuffed randomly into my brain, and the contradictions don't end up teaching me anything; they're just contradictory—Mom lived. Mom died. Mom hugged. Mom punched Dad in the chest. I went through a difficult period about six years ago of hating her for dying, and realizing that she wasn't the perfect loving goddess I always remembered, but lately the feelings are so incredibly jumbled, and the memories are such a scattered mess, I've pretty much sworn off trying to make sense of them.

So I had that coffee with my mother's friend.

It was like a blind date, where you can only talk about the third person, the one who set the two of you up.

"Your mother," Red Parka said, as if the phrase were her invention, "lit up a room." And more: "God was she smart," "God was she funny." (And this, I said to myself, from a writer.) "She had a way . . ." and she let her eyes fill with tears.

And when she'd finished with my mom, I listened to her own "funny" stories—this editor screwed her, that magazine slashed her piece on South Africa without understanding the structure of it—and all the while a strange but incredible rage was building in me: Why was I here? What gave her the impression that I cared? Wasn't there some place better for me to be than listening to a middle-aged woman complain that the *Times* had ruined her piece on Irvine Welsh? And then of course came the awful doubts: Would my mom be like this? Would she be boring? Do I only find this boring because it's so close to home? Or would I have built up a resistance to being bored had Mom lived?

Summer 1974. My family drove across the country, west to east, after a year in California. One afternoon, my mother was driving along a highway in Wisconsin, the sun was beating down on our Volvo, the bugs were killing themselves on the windshield, and my father was quizzing my older brother and me on trivia.

"For ten points," Dad would say, "who were the three—"

"Mazzini, Cavour, and Garibaldi!" we'd interrupt with glee, remembering his standard question about the Italian revolution.

"Excellent," he would say. "Now, boys, for fifteen points: Saturn is not the only planet with rings . . . "

When we heard the siren, I darted a glance at the speedometer, silently cursing myself for not having paid more attention to Mom's driving. The speedometer was at 63, and coming down.

"Shit," my mother said. "Shit, shit, shit."

"Calm down," my father said. "Josie, calm down," and now she was pulling over.

"Calm down yourself, I know how to handle midwestern cops."

So when the midwestern cop approached the car, my mom was all innocence. There was no way she was doing over 55, simply no way, officer.

"I'm sorry, Ma'am, but I had you on radar."

"No, I'm sorry, officer, because your radar must be faulty."

"I had you at 67, Ma'am."

"I wasn't doing 67."

"Yes, you were."

"No, I wasn't."

"Yes, you were, Ma'am."

"No, officer, I wasn't."

It was time for me to speak.

"Yes, you were, Mom."

What I remember after that was a long ride into a town called Sparta to pay a huge fine, my brother taunting me, telling me that I had betrayed the family, my mother chiming in with a reference to Benedict Arnold, my father telling me that although he understood my position, there was a time for prudent silence as well as dogged lawfulness. And then the jail in Sparta, where we paid the fine, my shame deepening so that by the time we got back on the highway, I was pouty and miserable. Everybody was angry at me, but all I'd done was speak the truth; I wasn't the one who had broken the law.

My mother finally had to pull the car over by the side of the highway, and I took my pillow out with me as she dragged me out of the car and held me by the arm and said that what I'd done had been stupid, but it was over, and let's forget about it and be friends and love each other again. And though I didn't agree with her (it hadn't been stupid; it had been law-abiding), I felt better that she loved me again, and we got back in the car and ten days later she was dead, her head smashed against a mailbox in Greenwich Village after two taxis had collided and one had spun around and thrown her high into the air.

And is it something I can make sense of, ever, my feeling that all I'd wanted in Wisconsin was to be safe, and that I'd been mocked for it, by her and everyone else, and then she'd died? Or my feeling that my betrayal had led to her death? Is it something I could really put in an "essay" for you, Bob? Something I could whip up in The Writers Room, polish, and fax off to you like one of the countless others here, the whirring and clacking of the keys audible to me even now, as I contribute to it?

My mother's friend and I parted quickly after coffee. There was no hug. I was headed back to The Writers Room and she had to go pick up a repaired handbag, so we just waved and I scooted across Astor Place, back to the Room, hoping I could finish up my work on the screenplay for the evening and sneak out without being seen. . . .

Good luck with your book.

Sincerely,
Nick Davis

PART 3

GOOD DEATHS, BAD DEATHS

Is it possible, in the shadow of the twenty-first century, in an age dominated by technology and bureaucracy, to die a "good death," one that flows organically from the life we have led? A death with dignity, a death of completion, a dying that is not managed and directed by others: hospitals, doctors, family? This question of dying well has been a leading concern of philosophers and religious thinkers throughout history.

In this chapter the death of T. S. Matthews's mother comes closest to the medieval ideal of the "good death," the *bona mors*. Like the patriarch of the Middle Ages described by the French social historian Philippe Aries, Mother Matthews died at home, spending her last days sitting on a chaise longue by the window, looking out at her favorite tree. There she said good-bye in turn to each of her eighteen grandchildren; then, in long "exit interviews," to her husband and her children. In contrast, a sudden death—for example, by an automobile accident, as in the case of Nick Davis's mother in the last chapter—allows no opportunity for good-byes or other avenues of closure.

Unlike the mother of T. S. Matthews, most of us will probably lose control over the conditions of our dying. Although there is a movement for home deaths just like home births, most people still die in institutions—old age or nursing homes, above all hospitals. In her last days, Martin Duberman's mother was tied down to a hospital bed, screaming to go home. And we live so long that in many cases we have lost our mental faculties and other powers. Allen Wheelis's mother died at the age of one hundred, but the story of her last decades was the story of her physical and mental deterioration.

What stands out in Kirk Douglas's description of his mother's dying is her dignity, an inner peace, a sense of completion. Though the circumstances were very different, I think my own mother was pleased with her death: a final heart attack gave her just enough time to call both her children and the ambulance. Dying on the way to the hospital, she did not have to inconvenience anyone!

I call this chapter "Good Deaths, Bad Deaths," but the very words oversimplify. Like life itself, most deaths are mixed bags. Even in the case of a death which appears to be completely arbitrary and without meaning, it is sometimes possible to take something positive from it, to learn from such a loss a larger lesson about life.

And "the best deaths" are still fraught with pain, regrets, sadness, something missing. Poet Donald Hall's mother died well, but she slipped away at a moment when her son was not present. To the questions I posed earlier—Is a good death possible, and what would it look like?—there are no easy answers.

TWO UNTITLED POEMS

Donald Hall

1

At ninety, bed-bound
in the facility, my mother gasped
as she sucked oxygen
through cannulae. Shyly she confessed
her tormenting obsession
to eat a piece of apple pie.
We watched her chew
the slice from Letha's Family Restaurant,
smiling as she paused
to breathe, her face gorgeous with
    happiness.

2

I sat at her bedside
every afternoon for half an hour,
dwelling in the luminous

air of her pride and affection.
She died quietly
and quickly on a morning in late March
before I could reach her,
while a tender woman held her hand.
I sat with her white body
half an hour and kissed her forehead,
and at night the telephone
rang although no one was calling.

DYING IS HARD LABOR

T. S. Matthews

One of Mother's most often-repeated threats—she didn't make many—was that when she got to be a grandmother she was going to wear a lace cap and smoke a pipe. I didn't much like the sound of this, when I first heard her say it; the prospect of Mother getting old was disagreeable in itself, and this professed desire to take to a pipe was a disquieting indication of the unknown amount of repressed Irishness in her. But when she did become a grandmother, and the lace cap, vastly becoming, duly appeared, I was almost disappointed that the pipe didn't follow suit.

She was to be an old lady for years and years; that was the idea. Our idea, anyhow. Whatever Mother really thought or guessed about her future, I can't think that it was a great surprise to her when she learned that she was going to die.

We were all used to her arthritis, but that turned out to be a side issue after all. It had been a useful cover-up for what she must have suspected was something worse. When we learned that she "had to have an operation," and the dreadful word "cancer" was breathed, I think for the first time in our lives

Reprinted from *Name and Address* (Simon and Schuster, 1960), copyright © 1960 T. S. Matthews.

Mother came into focus as a person in her own right. I know that it was then I first noticed how really brave she was. I couldn't help contrasting her behavior, on the eve of her operation, with the way my father had acted a few years before under similar circumstances. I had been very much moved at the time by his display of bravery; he obviously considered that he was facing death, and indeed mentioned the prospect in prayers that he himself conducted in his hospital room, the night before the operation. But Mother was cheerful and deprecated any display of emotion; she didn't want a fuss.

The operation was a success, we were told. For some reason I was delegated by my father to have a further conversation with the surgeon, just to make sure. This surgeon was a fine-looking man whose quiet certainty inspired the same trust you would feel in a veteran sea captain; you knew he had weathered all the storms, and that when he was on the bridge everything was being done that could be done. Nevertheless, as we talked, as I kept trying to get him to answer my persistent question ("Will there be a recurrence? Could there be?") and his not-quite-satisfactory replies grew more impatient and finally angry, I realized that I had encountered for the first time the doctor who lies from principle—out of pity, perhaps, for the layman who can't bear the whole truth or be trusted with it. I had forced him further than he wanted to go; in his determination not to tell me everything, he refused to admit that there was anything more to tell, and this answered my question. Though he did his best to deny it, I knew that Mother was still in danger, perhaps doomed. Then, as she made an apparently complete recovery, I found it easier to put the surgeon's ambiguous answers out of my mind; perhaps we all did.

Nevertheless, not many months later, when my father's noncommittal telegram arrived, saying that they were going to Johns Hopkins hospital for an examination, I knew it was a summons and what the summons meant, though I didn't want to believe it. We all got to Baltimore as soon as we could. The hospital Mother was in was a famous one, but I was no longer awed by a hospital's reputation, having had enough experience of them to be more angrily skeptical of their red tape and superinefficiency than Mother ever was about doctors.

In a few days the X-rays had rejected the final appeal and confirmed the verdict: death, in a few weeks. As usual, my father rose to the occasion; as usual, my mother didn't have to.

She hadn't looked well, we now realized, for some time; but for the next week or so she was like her old self. It was as if there was a great load off her mind, and she no longer had to pretend. She was quite unaffectedly cheerful and calm; there was nothing whatever, now, she had to worry about. It was late summer and the trees and flowers were looking their best. For most of the days, at first, Mother lay on her chaise longue by the window, in her prettiest dress and her grandmother's lace cap, and looked at her favorite tree. This tree (was it an elm? I can't even remember that) had one great branch with a V-like dip in it that Mother thought particularly beautiful. In a picture she wouldn't have liked it or seen its relevance, but she loved it where it was.

In these first days, when she was able to be out of bed and on her chaise longue, her eighteen grandchildren all came to say goodbye to her in turn. If she was in pain she never admitted it, but she grew obviously weaker, and after a few days had to take to her bed. It was only a matter of four weeks from the time she came back from the hospital till she died, and since then I have watched a longer struggle, but Mother's dying seemed the lengthiest and most difficult ordeal I had ever witnessed or could imagine. As it drew toward its end we took turns sitting in her room through the night, to relieve the nurses. As I watched her gaunt profile, the mask of Tragedy, with silently shouting mouth, against the night light, and listened to her hoarse breathing and her spells of sharp, dry coughing (so different from the well-known self-conscious clearing of her throat) I saw that dying is hard labor.

A fantasy that still haunts me formed in my mind. We—my father, my sisters and I, all of us except Mother—were in a transcontinental train, air-conditioned and luxuriously comfortable. As we met in the dining-car for breakfast, after our good night's sleep, we looked through the closed windows at the desert landscape, baking, dusty, waterless; and there, plodding along beside the track, as she had been all night and as she must through all the days and nights to come, was Mother, with no food, no drink, no arm to help her. She was too exhausted even to look at us, but she was condemned to stagger on, night and day, with no rest, until she died. On board the train our life went on, under a strain that we knew was increasing but that we also knew was temporary. Every day for us was a new exercise in patience—with Mother, for taking so long to die; with one another, for forcing us all to such mutual forbearance. And, as in all confined situations, the patience and forbearance were in daily danger of cracking. Every day brought us the renewal of a mental and moral struggle to behave at least decently, if we could not act always in love. We could only ease our pent-up irritations in a low key and in oblique directions; in bitter skepticism about the art of medicine, in indignation against the hard professionalism of certain nurses. But mostly we had to swallow our feelings, and they stayed inside us like a lump of ugly pain. I had read, with no conviction, about the political maneuvering and conniving that used to surround the deathbed of a monarch; now, in our own house, I saw and joined in those politics.

Outside in the desert Mother was undergoing a simple, more continuous and infinitely harder experience: dying.

Up until the last few days of flickering consciousness she was able to keep in touch with us, though her touch grew daily feebler. I still have some notes from those days:

"Aug. 8—She said how blessed she was in 'this kind of an ending'—without having lived so long that her mind failed her, and with her children all about her. She said she was sure she would know about us after she died; that (with a twinkle in her eye) 'she would keep an eye on us.' She looked forward not only to seeing much greater distances through space and time, but she was curious to know whether a theory of hers would prove to be right (and she thought it would): that she would be able to see *into* things—see how a tree's life goes on inside it, for instance.

"Aug. 15—They put her in an oxygen tent today, and she said from inside: 'This is a queer arrangement.' My father leaned towards her and said, 'I see you through a glass darkly, darling.' Hours later she woke from a nap and said to him: 'I see you quite clearly now.'"

(The oxygen tent brought out all her old distrust of doctors. She suspected, in spite of solemn assurances to the contrary, that its purpose was to prolong her life—which she considered unfair, and she was not going to be made a party to it. The doctor and my father finally persuaded her to try it, but the trial lasted only a day: she made them take it away again, saying that she felt too cut off from us.)

"Aug. 16—She opened her eyes and said drowsily to me: 'I dreamed you were Secretary of State.' The way she said it made it sound like a criticism.

"Aug. 19—Early this morning (about 6:30) Mother woke and said with surprising loudness and clearness: 'Can't talk. Can't breathe. Can't move.' She said it twice. The nurse asked her if she'd like a hypodermic. Mother muttered something, and then said, 'Try anything.'"

It must have been a day or so after that when she wrote her last note to me: "Tom darling—Please make Daddy go to bed at once—he is *dead* tired—has had a long hard day without one bit of rest. It will be lovely to see you—your loving Mother."

By "seeing me" she meant our final private meeting, which was to take place the next day: the last "little talk" we ever had. Like her grandchildren, all her children came in turn to say their farewells.

My last interview with Mother was a failure; at least, I thought so at the time. Now I am not so sure. To make certain that I said what I meant to, I had written it down. I sat by Mother's bed and read it to her. I was so moved by my own words that as I read them my voice choked, and I wept. Mother listened dry-eyed, with a smile. I think she patted my hand. If I had not known her so well (could I say, now, that I knew her at all?) I would have said that she was a little bored.

A few days later she died; and then suddenly all the things

she had not said, all her life long, filled the emptiness and
silence like a fanfare. Then that died away too, in the hushed
bustle of preparations for the funeral, whose details, she hadn't
wanted to bother about, but which was efficiently arranged and
managed by my father.

During her long dying we had watched her, every day and
part of every night, seeing with anxious and helpless anguish
how difficult it is to die even when you are willing, even when
you are being a "good patient" about dying; that although you
may have resigned yourself to death, your body will not resign
and goes on refusing, every inch and every moment of the way,
with a silent implacable will of its own, yielding only little by
little and more slowly than you would think humanly possible;
that it is the hardest physical labor you will ever be called on to
perform, and that you have to do it with no rest or let-up to the
very end, alone, against an increasingly deathly weakness which
you must somehow fight until the weakness grows so overpow-
ering that at last it can be fought no longer and at the end
helps you to get there, where you have been struggling all this
time to go.

We had also seen that when you are dying you become so
preoccupied with what you are doing that you have no more
strength or caring left to spend on anything else, including the
people whom you used to love but whom you are now forget-
ting; that it does not matter to you now that they are watching
you or that they feel a terrible anxiety about you in this suffering labor. They see your deathly weakness, and they cannot distinguish it from suffering; perhaps there is no distinction. You
are the one who knows, and you cannot tell them. Their anxiety
about you is not only that you may be suffering—in spite of the
doctor's reassurance that you are "feeling no pain"; how can the
doctor or anyone else but the dying person know what dying
feels like?—they are anxious that you should die well.

Bona mors, a good death: meaning one that the onlookers
can applaud. If you behave well, to the very end, it will be less
painful for them. They want you to reassure them, by dying
well that even dying is not out of character. They see, though

they shudder and reject the evidence, that you are giving them a preview of their own end, and they want you to set them a good example, one they can understand and admire and hope to imitate. But how can we tell how "badly" or how "well" a dying person is really acting? Why should we believe that they control their vanishing, their increasingly invisible, behavior? And which of us is in the position to judge?

My mother made a good death. If it were possible to impute motives to the dying, I would say that she did it on our account, so as not to give us more anxiety than she could help.

MELANOMA

Martin Duberman

My mother had been operated on in 1976 for a rectal tumor that was thought benign; immediately following the operation the surgeon had told me he was "certain" cancer could be ruled out. Then came the first pathology report, shocking us all with the diagnosis of "malignant melanoma." Her doctor scheduled a series of tests to see if the melanoma was anywhere else in her body; he was "hopeful" (not "certain" this time) that it was not.

The next month was a roller coaster of contradictory findings, raised hopes, sudden deflations. On October 28—my mother's seventy-fourth birthday—her doctors decided to reoperate: a "tiny recurrence," the surgeon said, adding that he "had to go pretty deep" and was "keeping his fingers crossed" that she wouldn't lose control of her sphincter muscle. She didn't, and was soon out of the hospital and back working every day in her tiny resale shop, Treasures and Trifles.

A woman of bedrock courage (belied by a surface habit of petty complaint), she refused to let me—or anyone else—accompany her to the chemotherapy treatments that had been prescribed. She carefully worked out the logistics, timing her return leg of the car/bus trip (she had impatiently dismissed the suggestion that she take a cab: "Why throw money out?")

from the doctor's office in Manhattan to her apartment in Mount Vernon, so that the vomiting that always followed a treatment would only begin after she was safely home.

Before the treatments were even completed, she decided to cook one of her legendary family dinners; "my welcome back to life" was how she billed it. We were a small family, but almost everyone showed up. And Ma outdid herself, doubling the usual feast. She prepared *two* sets of hors d'oeuvres; turkey, pot roast, *and* tongue; strawberry *and* banana shortcakes. My sister proposed the right toast: "To a gallant lady." As evening came on and people struggled homeward, I saw the deep melancholy settle into Ma's eyes, heard her unspoken thought: "the last time ... almost certainly the last ..." I saw her firmly shake her melancholy off, determinedly rejoin the conversation. Who expects nobility in one's own mother? Having harbored for so long my youthful set of grievances against her, using up what compassion I had on myself, I got a belated glimpse into the stunning brave woman who was so much more than Marty's "difficult" mother.

It did prove to be her last family dinner. By the summer of 1977, she had developed swollen lymph nodes and (a woman who had had insomnia all of her adult life) began to spend an unnerving amount of time asleep. Her doctor told me on the phone (my mother allowed me to call, if not appear) that "melanoma is fickle." He imperiously ticked off his contradictory findings: yes, we're "virtually certain" the nodes are affected; no, chemotherapy is not "entirely useless" in combating the spread; yes, her endless sleeping does suggest neurological complications; yes, one could just as logically ascribe the sleeping to effects of the chemotherapy.... He warned me against telling her the truth about her condition, which, as we moved into late summer, he spoke of as "hopeless; nothing more can be done medically, and she would not be able to handle that news."

I had always thought of her as a person who could handle anything. She had been the rock in my life, the superconcerned, omnipotent guardian angel who could make everything come

out right; her shamanistic power remained with me even after
my teen years, when I had stopped telling her anything important about myself because I didn't want to risk getting near the
subject of central importance—my homosexuality.

Yet I decided to go along with her doctor's advice. I had
never been convinced of the dictum that "a patient has the
right to know." *I* wouldn't want to know; I would want some
hope to hang on to. My mother was more of a stoic than I, but I
wasn't sure how much more. And as for the touted right to face
death directly, with Dignity, I doubted there could be much
dignity in dying other than that conjured up by fake serenity or
religiosity—neither of which were part of the family heritage.

I knew her minimal financial affairs were in order, and I
couldn't bear to think about the disarray of her emotional ones,
the long-repressed feelings she might now want to let out. Ours
had been a deeply entangled relationship, the emotional bond
powerful, the ability to express it minimal. Her unquestionable
love for me had been so embedded in invasive, suffocating control that as a teenager I had retreated into monosyllabic silence
when around her; it had long since become habitual: perpetual
anger at her relentless intrusion when I was growing up, perpetual guilt over the fortified behavior it had protectively induced
in me. I couldn't bear that she was going to die with so much—
and especially so much love—left unexpressed, that she was
going to leave me bereft of what felt like my one true ally.

I decided I would take my cue from her; if she pressed for
more clarity about her condition, I would *try* to provide it. But
that decision wasn't easy to implement. I kept changing my
mind about how much she already knew, and what more she
wanted to know. More than once (but not often), she would
whisper that she was dying, even threatening now and then to
kill herself. A day later, she would insist that she felt much better than last week, that her sleepiness must be due to the
chemotherapy treatments and that she didn't need me "hover-
ing" over her all the time.

Some of the family had planned to gather in early August,
in celebration of my birthday, at my cousin Ron's house in

Saratoga. My mother insisted we proceed with the outing, and once we were there, insisted on going along with us to the racetrack. Her gallantry got her through five hours of muggy heat and engulfing crowds. But the following day she was noticeably more feeble—"all broken up," as she put it.

She propped herself up on the living room sofa, emaciated and weak, trying to keep awake, trying to maintain through sheer force of will some semblance of her usual place in the family tableau. The piercing high spirits of Ron's two young children, as they dashed gleefully back and forth through the room, provided some relief, though anguishingly highlighting her own debilitated state. She smiled sadly at the exuberant two-year-old at one point, then across the room at me, remembering (so I imagined) the antics of her own adored cherub forty-five years before.

In our few minutes alone, she listlessly went over and over the advisability of continuing this or that medication, believing this or that diagnosis. She acted as if real decisions were at stake, but her tone confirmed a gut-level awareness that the debated options were nonexistent. Toward the end of the day, she became nearly comatose. As I carried her to the car for the trip back home, she seemed angry at my touch, brushing away my arm with what little strength she had. ("So now, when it's too late," said her furious, unspoken words in my head, "you are willing to embrace me.")

That night I wrote in my diary, "I broke down at one point, but turned away before she could see. For all I know she wants to see, wants confirmation that someone cares, wants permission to mourn together. We don't trust ourselves. We can't comfort others. The family talks of the need to make her last days 'peaceful'—meaning easy on *us*. Our automatic response is evasion. So we bicker over tactics, scapegoat each other, or offer false support. All in the name of sparing *her*. What shit! *We* don't want pain. Bury it! Bury her! Quick, quick! Before anyone discovers anything. About being human."

After the Saratoga trip, my sister and I took turns staying with her during the days while her unmarried sister, Theresa, with whom she had long lived (my father had died some fifteen years earlier) was at work. Mostly we just sat in her apartment while she slept. Looking in at her asleep on the bed, her slight, thin body appeared almost girlish, and it would set me to thinking sorrowfully of how little happiness she had ever found. Beautiful, smart, dynamic, she—like most women of her generation—had never had much of a chance. She had gone to work straight out of high school, had made a mostly prudential marriage, had poured her prodigious energy into housewifely routines and, when her marriage turned loveless and sexless, had poured it into contentious altercations with friends and driven devotions to grandchildren—leavened, happily, by a resilient, good-natured ability to make fun of herself.

When she was awake, it was even harder. I could barely choke back tears watching her hand tremble as she tried to raise a glass to her lips. Listlessly, she would go over and over the "mistake" she had made in letting them do the original operation; or, angrily, would adamantly reject as a "waste of money" my suggestion that she let a housekeeper come in for at least one or two days a week. Sometimes she would seem so perky and rational that I would start to wonder all over again— using *her* words—whether the original diagnosis had been right, whether her current weakness wasn't (as we had kept assuring her) merely the by-product of the accumulated chemotherapy treatments, whether she hadn't entered a stage of remission.

The family felt she should be hospitalized, but I fought that decision, arguing that she should have the comfort of her own home, that there was nothing left to do medically that hadn't been done, that at this terminal point in her illness, the hospital doctors would only torture her, probe and test solely for *their* information. But by mid-August, she was sleeping almost continuously, refusing food and, when awake, growing increasingly disoriented.

The day finally came when we had to take her by ambulance to Mt. Sinai Hospital. Everything I feared would happen, did. She became instantly alert, terrified, angry; convinced that they would operate again and that she was dying, she began to tremble with anxiety, even as she furiously denounced the "needless expense" of a private room. The hospital staff, in turn, seemed infuriatingly indifferent; her doctor never showed up that day, she was refused sedation ("we have to have her clear for the brain scan") and I couldn't even get a nurse to bring her a blanket. Choking with rage, I had simultaneously to invent rationales for calming her down: "Only a few days for tests," "You need care and intravenous feeding to build your strength back," and so on.

When I finally got back to my apartment that night, I felt, as I wrote brokenly in my diary, "helpless, defeated ... *they've* got her now ... couldn't spare her this final horror ... I think of her alone in that dark room, the needle in her arm, eyes glazed with fear ... she would have managed to prevent that from happening to me ... I'm okay when with her in the hospital, can't stop crying back here in the apartment ... feel so fucking alone ... the family keeps saying 'she's in better hands now.' Yeah, sure. We're better off, Ma's not."

When I arrived the next morning she seemed less frightened—or too weak to express it; her voice was so low I had to put my ear next to her lips to hear. She was mostly rational, except that she kept asking me whether "everyone has had lunch," and warning me to watch her pocketbook: the condensation of two lifetime obsessions. Her doctor finally appeared, said he'd begun "tests," thought the melanoma had reached her brain and that "the ballpark figure" was, "best guess," only a few weeks. But, he warned, "she could last five, six months; your family had better start thinking of putting her in a nursing home."

They moved her that day into a two-bed room with another woman dying of cancer who kept screaming "Marion! Marion! ... Help, oh help! Get me out of here! ... They've burnt my legs off! ... We're stranded!" She went on screaming all that night. Next day, I learned Ma had tried to get out of bed and had had a bad fall; they had then tied her down. When I arrived that morning, she was rattling the metal guards on the sides of her bed, moaning and tossing. As soon as she saw me, she begged, "Take me home! Take me home!" Over and over she repeated the words, her glazed eyes forlornly appealing to me. Then, in a conspiratorial whisper, she told me to go to the closet and get her clothes: "Shush . . . not a word or they'll hear . . . get me dressed . . . we'll slip out . . . they'll never notice . . . into the car . . ." She looked feverishly around the room for her "dress," as her roommate took up the keening chorus, "Get us out! Get us out!"

In my shock, I tried to placate her: "Okay, Ma, yeah . . . I'll get your stockings . . . just be patient . . . one minute." I dashed out to get a floor nurse. "I'm the only person on duty," the nurse at the desk responded coldly. "Your mother will just have to wait. She has private duty nurses. Let them take care of her." I tried to explain that the private nurse hadn't shown up for her shift and that my mother needed attention *now.* I got a blank, hostile stare. She returned to her charts.

Racing back into the room, I discovered my mother had slid halfway down the bed, feverishly determined to escape. This time I tried admonition: "You *can't* go home now . . . two more tests . . . you must get the tests while you're here . . . you *must* be patient a little longer . . . I'll take you home *soon* . . ."

"Not true," she responded to each phony phrase. "Not true! . . . Not true!"—her voice strangely firm and adamant. I didn't know if she'd suddenly become rational again or whether, in some bitter, final defiance, she was bent on unmasking all the false blueprints that had been handed her for a "happy, meaningful" life. Two hours later the private duty nurse finally arrived, and Ma subsided into mumbled agitation. I could hardly bear to look at her—my dynamo mother turned into a tiny, yellowing bag of bones, her voice gone, her eyes glazed. But I couldn't stand not being in the hospital either.

Her doctor reported that the brain scan was "negative," but quickly added that it "only picks up gross infiltration." He thought she would become increasingly and rapidly comatose, yet doubted she was approaching death. He urged me to proceed with my long arranged plan to fly to Los Angeles for a few days, where my play *Visions of Kerouac* was in rehearsal. He said he could always call me back if her condition unexpectedly changed. The family urged the same course, as did, more insistently still, the play's producer, Lee Sankowich.

Lee had been phoning daily from Los Angeles, begging me not to delay any longer. He had already postponed opening night once, and could not do so a second time. Lee was a soft-edged, decent man, but his latest call had been agitated: the *Los Angeles Times* was offering to do a big spread on *Kerouac*, but it was contingent on my availability for a personal interview within the next several days. Lee insisted the article was "essential" to the play's success, and begged me to leave for Los Angeles at once.

Everyone insisted that I go, that there was nothing more to do for Ma, that she was unable any longer to recognize anyone, that it was now essentially a vigil. Torn apart, I finally decided to risk the trip. The night before I was due to leave, Ma's face lit up when I walked into the hospital room: She did momentarily recognize me, her beatific boy, her adored baby—then lapsed quickly back into vacancy, patting her hair distractedly, her blank eyes frantically searching the room for some unnameable, supremely precious object just out of reach. I broke down in tears. . . .

The hospital called at 4:30 that morning. She had died a few minutes before. Typical, I thought, between the tears: she didn't want to inconvenience me.

"Don't Be Scared, Issur!"

Kirk Douglas

Issur walked slowly toward his mother's hospital room, down the long linoleum-carpeted corridor. He pushed open the door to the hushed, dark room. Ma was in bed under an oxygen tent—a transparent plastic dome, the kind of thing his son Peter would like to play under. She lay there breathing heavily, suffering from pneumonia on top of a heart condition and diabetes.

"Hello, Ma. It's me," he whispered.

She gave a feeble smile. "My big-shot son."

Issur was glad that Ma was alert. "Oh, I'm not so very big, Ma."

"Yes, you are." Her head turned a little toward the nurse. "This is my son. The whole world trembles when they say his name."

Rustling, whispers, giggles from the hallway. Issur looked up. People peeking through the door, pointing. "Look! There he is! That's him!" They didn't see Issur with his dying mother; all

---

they saw was somebody from the movies. Issur's problems were not theirs.

Issur remembered as a child thinking that if his mother died, he would die too. He had seen his mother lose control only once. They were seven starving children, squalling for food. Ma had started screaming, too. "There is nothing! I have nothing! What do you want from me?" twisting her flesh as if she would pull off chunks to feed them, as she ran from the house. Issur and his sisters stared at each other, suddenly silent. If Ma was gone, they would die.

Issur and his sisters stayed with Ma for days as she got weaker and weaker, drifted in and out of consciousness. At dusk one day, she roused herself. "What day is it?"

"Friday."

"Don't forget to light the candles for Sabbath."

They didn't want to leave Ma, but she insisted. So they all went to Betty's house and lit candles. Issur said the evening prayer. They all returned to Ma and told her they had done as she asked. She beamed at them, her daughters and son at her bedside. *"Gut Shabbas,"* she said.

Issur's sisters returned to their families that night. Issur stayed. He sat with Ma, held her hand tightly. He was over-whelmed by his mother's composure and dignity, remembering the look in his father's dying eyes: fear.

That same look must have been in Issur's eyes. Ma looked up at him, a clear, serene smile on her face, the smile that was there every Sabbath as she sat on the porch in her rocking chair, Bible open on her lap.

"Don't be scared, Issur. It happens to all of us."

Issur choked. Holding his own breath, he watched his mother breathe so slowly, in, then out, each breath causing her pain. Until a long, deflating exhale followed by ... nothing. Issur reached a finger out, touched Ma's forehead. It felt strange. When you're dead, you're really dead, he thought. Issur's mother was like the chair, the table, the bedpan: an inanimate object. Issur cried.

The private nurse came in and handed him a bill. She

wanted to be paid immediately. Numb, Issur reached into his
pocket, pulled out some money. He handed it to the woman
without looking at her.

Both Issur's mother and father were dead. He had only his
sisters now, and his mixed feelings about them. They buried Ma
apart from Pa. Ma wanted it that way. Issur resented it. Why,
even in death, could the two of them not be united? After the
funeral, Issur never went to visit his mother's grave; he didn't
like that cemetery. But he found great solace at the grave of his
father in the Jewish cemetery, in Amsterdam, New York. It was
a peaceful little place.

A parent's death makes you grow up, and growing up is
hard. You think that when you do grow up, something wonderful will happen. No more problems, like magic. Then, you grow
up. You become a "big man." Your voice is lower. But inside
you're still a child. But you look like an adult, and other people
think you're one, so you pretend to be one; you return the
favor by pretending that they're one. You all buy into the same
fiction.

The truth was that Issur was a forty-two-year-old orphan
pretending to be Kirk Douglas, a grown-up, flying back to the
heart of the world of make-believe so he could pretend to be a
man who lived two thousand years ago—a slave called Spartacus.

THE LIFE AND
DEATH OF MY MOTHER

Allen Wheelis

The numbers at the end of each section indicate the pages from which the passage has been taken.

"Son ... come closer. There's something we must talk about." I sit on the edge of the bed. She takes my hand, holds it between both her own, strokes it, looks away into the distance. She is thinking, wants me to be prepared for a weighty matter. The bones of her hands are covered with a yellowish film with dark brown blotches. No flesh remains; the papery skin with its tangle of black veins sinks in between the bones. "Son ..." She focuses on me, lowers her voice. "Son ... we've been associated together a long time. And so ... it's only natural ... that we have become very *fond* of each other. It's been a long ... and a very close ... association. And so ... after all that time it's only natural ... we might want to get married." She pauses. "We

From Allen Wheelis, *The Life and Death of My Mother* (Norton, 1992). By permission of the author.

don't have to do it right away, though. No need to rush into anything. But it's only natural . . . "

"I'm already married, Mother."

"You're already married?"

"Yes."

"Who is your wife? What is her *name*, son?"

"Ilse . . . Do you remember Ilse?"

"Well . . . would she . . . be jealous?"

"Yes."

"Well . . . we certainly don't want to upset her. We don't want that. We just won't rush into anything."

"Mother, listen. We *can't* get married. You're my *mother*, I'm your *son*!"

"Yes . . . well . . . that's true, that's certainly true, and we've been very close, very close together . . . for a very long time. That's true, isn't it?"

"Yes."

"But we don't want to upset anyone. We mustn't cause a stir. But I want to tell you something, son." She strokes my hand tenderly. "We have plenty of time. No need to rush into anything. So . . . if you want to look around first, try out some of the younger girls . . . see how you like it . . . if you want to do that . . . I want you to know, I won't mind. You look around all you like. I'll wait for you." *(118–119)*

When I was fourteen my sister went away to college. My mother and I were now alone with each other. In the mornings she would get up first and prepare breakfast, which we would then eat together. She would leave for work the same time I left for school. She taught third grade, and I was a junior in high school. When we arrived back home in the afternoons she would often walk the mile or so to the grocery store. Returning, she would make beds, sweep, clean, wash, and prepare dinner. Afterward she would wash the dishes while I studied. When all the chores were done she would sit at the kitchen table with checkbook, budget, bills all spread out before her and "do the accounts," as she put it, which meant trying to figure out whether we could make it to the end of the month, and if not what expense could be cut, or postponed. She had "no head for figures," as she said, so this was a tedious and inconclusive task, always to be continued the next night. Sitting at the table under the dim hanging light, she pondered, she moved her lips, repeatedly moistened the pencil on her tongue as if a hyperreadiness to write might make the bleak figures come out better, a deeply troubled expression on her face. If I showed concern she reassured me. "Oh, don't worry, son. We will find a way." Or, "It will all turn out for the best. God will look after us." But she didn't act as if she counted on help, from any source, but as if it were all up to her and she were failing.

About this time I gained a different image of her, came to see her life, not simply as she lived it day to day, but in extension. For six years she had enslaved herself to my father, a twenty-four-hour nursing duty, day after day. And the outcome of all those years of toil and devotion—he died, he was gone, and that wild piercing cry she flung after him, and no response, nothing. Where he had been was but a void.

She pulled herself together then, but only to begin a different kind of servitude: to her children. She had no special training or ability or experience, and no confidence in herself. She offered piano lessons, sold encyclopedias, finally got a job as study-hall teacher, went to night school and summer school, finally obtained a temporary teacher's certificate that had to be renewed each year by more courses. She was never sure we could make it. She knew we would not starve, for, at worst, we could move back to Louisiana and live with her parents and brothers; but it seemed important to her, for her children, that we have a home of our own. This was what she was struggling to achieve and to maintain. And was succeeding—but just barely.

It was about this time I came to see where her life was heading, and that she herself could neither see what lay ahead nor do anything about it. She enslaved herself to those who would leave her. June had already gone, and in two years I would be leaving—I could hardly wait. Then she would be alone. I worried about what would happen after I left. *(52–54)*

Increasingly it seemed to me that I was the architect of my mother's life, and as the years passed—straining and adventurous for me, gray and impoverished for her, years of waiting, always waiting for my rare and brief visits—it seemed that I unintentionally had designed for her a barren life, and that she was obediently following my blueprint, unable to break away from my spell, and I powerless to free her.

So perhaps my dying father was right to fear that she would fall for the first man to lay a hand on her flank, but he could hardly have known that that man would be I, that therefore the promise not to remarry which he extracted from her could not protect her. *(86)*

During her eighties my mother's upper spine slowly collapsed, diminishing her height by about six inches. Her esophagus, now much too long for the shortened distance from her throat to her stomach, formed kinks, and the swallowing of solid food became difficult. Several times a morsel of something like steak would fail to pass, would lodge there, halfway down, creating in her a helpless choked discomfort. Sometimes it would take days to pass. I was constantly urging her to take small bites, to chew thoroughly, to drink water as she ate.

A huge lump formed on her back. At ninety she was deeply stooped over, walked with a cane in small, slow, shuffling steps, and what presented forward as she came toward me was not her face but the crown of her head. Her face stared at the ground; she had begun her final plunge into the earth. When she heard my voice and saw my feet before her she would reach out and climb my arms with her hands, thereby managing to lift her face enough to see me.

When she was eighty-three it became evident that she could not continue to live alone. She was doddering and indecisive in street intersections, got lost on the way to the grocery store. She would put something on the stove and forget it until the house filled with smoke. She could no longer walk to church or to prayer meetings, could not visit friends, was increasingly isolated. I urged her to enter Trinity Towers, a nearby retirement home where several of her friends now lived. "Meals will be prepared for you," I told her, "and it will be easy for you to find companionship." She was reluctant. "I will keep your house intact," I promised her, "just as it is. You can move back anytime you like. Only if *you* decide to stay there permanently, only then will we sell this house."

At ninety she became incontinent of urine and had to be diapered, needed assistance in dressing and undressing and in bathing; so I moved her from Trinity Towers to Spring Park, a nursing home. She was no longer steady enough to walk with a cane; she got about the hallways slowly in a walker. In the short distance from her room to the dining room she would lose her way. *(95–96)*

Always I delay calling my mother—because it is so hard to get off the phone. One thing reminds her of another; the chain of reminiscence is endless, ranges not only over her own long life, but gathers in friends and relatives, extends back into what her grandmother told her about her great-great-grandmother. After five or ten minutes I begin trying to say good-bye: "It's time for me to stop. I must help with dinner now." Whereupon she tells me what she had for dinner, and the wonderful dinners her mother used to prepare, the vegetable garden when she was a child, and Mamie the black cook, and the time when her sister, Mit, left the arsenic in the pantry and everybody got sick and they all thought it was Lit the handyman who had done it. "Now I really have to stop, Mother," I say. "There are things I have to do before ... " "Yes, I know," she says, "and I mustn't keep you, before we say good-bye I want to tell you that..." and off into another story.

That's the way it was until her ninety-seventh year when, one day, I realized with surprise that I had called her during my ten-minute break between patients, that I had fallen into the habit of calling at such times, and that it was easy to get off the phone. The stickiness was gone. Her densely peopled past had, like old film, faded to uniform gray. *(96–97)*

As she lost the past, she also lost the present. Vision blurred and dimmed; she could not read or write, could not make out what was happening on the television screen. Books and newspapers fell away. She no longer hears the telephone: I must call the nurses' station, ask that someone go to her room and pick it up for her. No more does she shuffle down the hallway in a walker; she lives in a wheelchair. *(98)*

A telephone call from the nursing home. "Your mother is crawling around on the floor. We can't think what's got into her. Never been like this before. We pick her up, tie her in her chair, but first chance she gets she'll slip right out, sorta slide down, and then there she'll be, crawling around again." I ask the nurse to put her on the phone. After a while I hear the struggle, the labored breathing. "Hello, Mother. How are you?" Pause, then the thin, infinitely tired voice. "I guess I'm all right, son." I ask about the crawling. She begins to cry. "I've lost my rings."

The world is lost to her. Those rings were its vanishing point. When next I see her she still slides down out of her chair, gropes about on the floor, but no longer knows what she seeks. Everything is slipping away. She still has a grasp of me, though at times she stares blankly as if I too were fading. *(105)*

My sister develops Alzheimer's disease. Gradually her memory slips away. After a few years she knows nothing, can no longer feed herself or wipe her behind. Francis [her husband] puts her in the nursing home alongside my mother. Neither recognizes the other. My sister wanders the hallways, smiles benignly, but does not speak. Francis dies of cancer; she knows nothing. She comes upon her mother down on the floor, stops and stares down at her with a fixed and uncomprehending smile. My mother stops groping for her rings, glares up. "What is that woman doing here?" she cries angrily. "What does she want? Why is she staring at me? I don't like that! Something ought to be done about a situation like this! Where is the management? I'm going to report her!" *(111)*

•   •   •

"There's something wrong down here, son." She pushes at the bedclothes.

"Do you have pain?"

"No . . . a kind of itch, a burning."

"I'll ask the nurse to get you something."

"They don't know about such things. I've already told them. They don't know."

"Well, I'll ask your doctor."

"You're my doctor, son. Remember? You saved my life. Twice. If it weren't for you I wouldn't be here today." She has pushed down the covers, is pulling up her nightgown. "Have a look, son. See what you think."

"No, Mother, it's better that . . . "

"It's all right for you to look, son. You're a doctor."

She opens her legs, raises her knees. Her belly has disappeared, is draped against her spine; the aorta throbs visibly beneath the blotchy yellowish skin. Mons veneris has disappeared: no more that spongy rounded mound, no more that thicket of dark hair. A few spare tufts of white sprout from the bare bone of pubis. No flesh anywhere to be seen. The buttocks have vanished; the skin which once covered those ample cheeks now falls from the iliac crests as a gray curtain, pools on the sheet like candle wax. The bony architecture of the pelvis looms up from the mattress like a ruined and haunted house—of which I am the appalled ghost. *(117–118)*

My mother is one hundred years old, has been dying for a long time. For years. Two months ago I was called by the nursing home; that was perhaps the beginning of the end.

She has stopped eating, the nurse tells me. She sits at the table in her wheelchair, pushes the food about with her spoon. If the nurses put it in her mouth she spits it out. If they persist she becomes cross. Occasionally she will swallow a few bites of ice cream. I speak to her on the telephone: "I am coming to see you soon, Mother. I *want* you to eat. Are you listening? Mother? You *must* eat—so you will be strong for my visit." A few days later a call from her doctor: She has lost a lot of weight, he wants to hospitalize her, to begin force-feeding. I refuse. She is confused, I tell him, could not possibly understand what was being done to her, would be terrified by the tube in her throat. I speak again to the nurses: "Offer her small amounts. Frequently. Encourage her to eat. But don't force her." I try to speak to her on the phone, hear the nurse say, "Hold it to your ear, Mrs. Wheelis. It's your son!" "Mother!" I yell into the phone. "Mother! Can you hear me?" She drops the phone in her lap, mumbles unintelligibly.

When I arrive she is not in her room. I glance in the open door. Her blue mohair shawl lies in a heap on the bed. I go looking for her—in the halls, in the TV room—return presently to discover that my mother herself lies beneath that crumpled shawl. A tangle of bones in a bag of skin. Her body makes no impression on the bed. I take her hand, call her name, shake her slightly. The smeared eyes open blankly. "Mother ... it's me. Your son. It's Allen." Suddenly the skeleton hand tightens on mine, a smile comes to her face. She struggles to lift herself, to turn toward me. She falls back, but presently, out of that waste, two stick arms rise up to embrace me.

I stay with her three days. From my hand, when I command it, she will eat. Constantly I am lifting something to her mouth, urging on her yet another sip of liquid protein. She gains some strength, is able to talk, can sit up for a few minutes. *(16–17)*

These are the last hours of my mother's life. And she knows nothing. Only I observe her blind, stumbling arrival at the end of a century-long journey. I hope it may be different as I lie dying. I hope that I will be able to take myself as the object of reflection, see my life in extension, the whole course—taking off like a ballistic missile, soaring, leveling off, falling—and, just before the end, achieve, like the computer in a warhead at impact, a view of the whole trajectory.

I doubt my mother has ever done this, or would want to. For years now, she has had no awareness of death. Death got lost as memory failed and reality slipped away. The last time she grappled with it was six years ago. She was ninety-four, frail and failing. She took my hand, solemnly, between both of her own, her voice dropped, her manner became portentous. "Son, I want you to know . . . *you* know . . . I don't want to live forever . . . you know that . . . son, some folks nowadays . . . they just hang on and on, no use to themselves or anybody else, taking up space and costing money. I don't want anything like that. I don't want you to take any special measures . . . you know what I mean?"

"Yes, Mama, I know."

"I've lived a long time, and when my time comes . . . when it's right for me to go . . . well . . . I'm ready. I leave that all to you. It's up to you."

"I understand."

"I don't want to just hang on when my mind is gone and I'm no use to people."

"You're still in good health, Mama. You have a lot of life before you. I want you to keep living as long as you can enjoy things."

We sit in silence. She strokes my hand absently, brooding, troubled. Her breathing becomes irregular, she wants to speak. Can't find the right words. She sighs. "Son," she says after a bit, "son . . . tell me . . . how long do you think I will live?"

I realize she is afraid. "You have a lot of vitality, Mother. You've always been very strong . . . "

"That's true."

"You've pulled through bad sicknesses that would've been too much for most people."

"That's true."

"So I think you might . . . live to . . ." I canvass her anxious face, extend my estimate. ". . . you'll probably live to be one hundred!" Wildly extravagant. But maybe she will buy it. Perhaps it will make her happy.

Her expression doesn't change. She fixes her eyes on mine, judiciously weighs, examines, my estimate: "That's not very long, you know." *(19–20)*

• • •

There is a fecal smell in this room. On the bed, unconscious, my mother is slowly bleeding to death from the bowel. Over the radio, faintly, Mahler's Fourth Symphony. I have switched off the light. Outside the window the shadowy gestures of poplars.

Daylight says life is knowable, night tells the truth, says we know not what lies hidden, neither in the darkness out there nor the darkness within. Day is pragmatic acceptance, night is infinite longing.

All of life is here: the smell of shit, the sound of music, the surrounding dark. *(15)*

Her breathing now is a labored rattle. The legs are blue to above the knees, the arms to above the elbows. I cannot feel a pulse. *(119)*

We look into the deaths of others, even much-loved others, as in a dark mirror. We seek a glimpse of our own. *(15)*

MAMA'S BOY

Bob Blauner

My mother was the custodian of my memory, particularly that of my childhood, which was much more vivid and detailed for her than I can ever recall it for myself. I am not talking only about the early years, when childhood amnesia, especially for boys, is almost total and to be expected, but of experiences well into my teens and beyond. Fortunately she kept every possible memento of her children's lives. She passed these souvenirs on to me during the period when she was cleaning out her closets, preparing for her death. In a box of assorted letters, clippings, photographs, copies of the high school paper with my sports columns, I found a note I had left her in the summer of 1945, shortly after my sixteenth birthday. She was working at the Chicago Public Library, and since I would not be home on her return, I wrote that I was off to play tennis with Spunky Zimberoff (Spunky and I would be vying for the last position on Sullivan's tennis team the coming year) and that when I got back home, I wanted her, my mother, to wash my hair.

That my mother was still washing my hair at age sixteen—because I didn't know how to do it myself, after all she had never taught me!—was less of an eye-opener (forty years later) than the whole tone of that note: affectionate, tender, and very intimate. Because during my twenties and thirties I put great effort into distancing myself from my mother, I had not only "repressed" the memory of the particular event, I had forgotten how long I had been a mama's boy, and more important, how much in those days I loved my mother.

Writing this so many years later I can still feel some of the shame I must have felt at being so closely tied to my mother, as well as the feeling of emptiness and yearning for the father who had retreated into the shadows of our family life. So if it has taken most of a lifetime to reclaim my mother, to place my love for her in the center of my consciousness, much of it undoubtedly stems from our peculiar family. Though my mother and father lived together for forty-two years, they were so at war with one another that my loyalties were inevitably divided. Growing closer to the distant father of my childhood, a task that consumed me during my twenties and thirties, meant not only holding my mother at arm's length, but actively learning to dislike her. For decades I was bewildered by her many and vibrant friendships, by the acclaim and respect with which so many people viewed her. Could this be the same person I had known all my life, a woman so anxious, insecure, and superficial in her tastes and values and approach to life? The same woman whose fears, rigidities, and coldness had left me with a lifetime of emotional problems to overcome?

The death of my father in 1966, instead of freeing me from this impasse, only intensified it. It was partly the tendency, after death, to identify with the dead. My wife of that time said I took on many of his worst qualities: depression, withdrawal, irritability. Freud wrote that it takes a son seven years to mourn the death of a father. With so much unfinished business to deal with, it was more like ten or twelve for me. And part of the grief work, a large part of the unfinished business, was becoming aware, on a gut level, of my old anger toward my mother.

There was also new anger at her reaction to his death, which in its circumstances was almost a metaphor for their relationship. He died alone, in his sleep, of a heart attack, evidently suddenly and without pain. My mother, though they shared a bedroom, but not a bed, was not there because she was visiting her grandchildren in Boston. My father never went along on these trips. He would have said that his wife, whom he characterized as "a monopolist," excluded him. Being introspective, honest, and relatively undefensive, he would also have admitted that he had excluded himself, through his withdrawal and strained relationships with wife and daughter.

So that when my mother returned to her small apartment two weeks later she was greeted with the unspeakable stench of a decomposing body and bedroom walls that were turning yellow from the evaporate from my father's bodily fluids. When I saw her six weeks later—an airline strike had prevented me from getting there earlier—she could focus only on this horror: You would have thought she had just emerged from Auschwitz. I wanted to talk about my dad and his life, but she would talk only of herself and her horrifying experience. Finally I got her to address my repeated question, "Didn't you have any feelings about him and his death?" Her answer: "Of course I was unhappy. I don't like to see anyone die."

I think that statement and the fact that she spoke with much more warmth and sense of loss about a former library boss who had also recently died sealed inside my heart an anger and hatred that would take another fifteen years to soften and forgive. But the death of Samuel Blauner did free his wife, Esther (better known as "Sunny"), in many important ways. (Having referred to my mother only as my mother up to now, as sons especially but perhaps all children are wont to do, it is time to give her a name and some personhood of her own.) Two years later, at the age of sixty-nine, she moved herself to Los Angeles, where she had a second and in many ways better life. The appeal of Los Angeles (besides the fact that she had several cousins and lifelong friends who had made the move to California as early as the 1930s) was the warm weather. Chicago's cold winters had been aggravating her heart condition. And Los Angeles was close enough to Berkeley so that she could expect to see me from time to time. She must have also known that we did not get along well enough to live in the same city, though she probably would not have admitted this to anyone.

Mark Twain's witticism about how parents improve in their old age is meant to imply that it's only our perceptions that change as we grow up and gain some distance from them. Perhaps so, but I'm convinced that my mother did grow and deepen in her old age—and I would like to think this is true of many elderly people. In my twenties what bothered me most about her was her conformism, an exaggerated concern about what other people thought. The contrast was my Bohemian, unconventional father. But in her seventies—perhaps it was the California influence—she became more open to new ideas, her tastes and feelings seemed to have more substance to them. My first divorce (I was thirty, she sixty) almost shattered her: She became very depressed, talked of suicide. It was the stigma of public opinion as well as the psychic meaning of a broken family that was so devastating for her. Twenty years later when I divorced again, mindful of her sensibilities, I flew to L.A. to tell her in person rather than by phone or letter. I was surprised by her calm acceptance, her philosophical attitude, her nonjudgmental support.

She loved her one-bedroom apartment in West L.A. and lived there the last eighteen years of her life. She had friends of all ages, would talk to six or eight of them on the phone daily. Never without a book, she would read at least one a day, if necessary rereading and rereading her favorites. The circulation problems she developed in her legs in her eighties made it impossible to take the bus to the local library. Though she had trouble asking for help, for books she made an exception and her friends filled the breach. One of my finest hours was my present on her eightieth birthday: eighty books, mostly used, which I had selected from the offerings of the book sale at my children's school. It gave me the chance to reciprocate for those childhood years when she would bring me books from her library. Sick in bed and home from school, I would surround myself with my favorite authors—Dumas, Alcott, Altschuler, and Ralph Henry Barbour—on the same table as her cure-all cup of hot lemonade.

She went to lectures at UCLA, took a Spanish class where

at seventy-five she still felt she had to be the best student. (She was only second best, the honor went to a woman named Judy Cole.) There she met people fifty and twenty-five years younger who would become her close friends for the rest of her life; to Judy, who would visit her often, sometimes twice a week, she became a second mother, and to each of Judy's children as they came along, she was Grandma Blauner who always provided their favorite cookies, sodas, and other sweets. But what impressed me most was the brailling class she took when she was eighty years old. She had always identified with the blind and wanted to do something for them. And she was bored just sitting in her old age, especially as more and more of her friends died. She wanted some real work. So every time I went to Los Angeles, one of the most important errands in my rental car would be our trip to the Blind Center for brailling paper. Sitting on a small card-table chair at the little brailling machine—she was small herself, only five feet in her prime, now in her eighties shrunk down to four feet nine at best—she would pound out the symbols, regularly berating herself for the mistakes she was making and would have to correct later ("The corrections are the worst part," she would always say), but still completing in perfect fashion two very long and important books, one a biography of Bernard Berenson that she especially liked, books that nonsighted people are reading to this day.

But even as my admiration for her grew, I did not find it easy to be with her. Though I was outwardly a dutiful son, I saw her only rarely, perhaps once every year or two. And this despite the relatively short distance between us and the cheapness of airfare, at least until Reagan's deregulations. On each of these visits, she would come to the door, usher me to the dining room table, set for lunch, the packaged coleslaw and potato salad from the Market Basket (later Ralph's) on Wilshire already on the table, the chicken breasts staying warm in the oven. I would tell her the news of my family and friends and ask about her health; she was most interested in my children. In the evening we went out to dinner at Bruno's or a Chinese restaurant in Westwood where she always paid the bill. Then, after we listened to music on her phonograph or watched television, she would retire to her bedroom with a book and I would throw some sheets on the living room couch, hoping to catch a good night's sleep, vaguely uncomfortable at our proximity, too aware of her breathing, coughing, snoring, and other old-lady noises in the next room.

Predictably, the second day I would begin to feel claustrophobic. Her talk now seemed like chatter—empty, anxious, jarring. In the car driving her here and there, tension and strain hung in the air between us; I suppose as I became quieter and more withdrawn, she reacted by talking more nervously. Never did we address the situation directly. We were still pretending that this was an ideal mother-son relationship. At least once, though, I shortened my stay because two days of her was all that I could endure.

A creature of habit and fixed routine, she would call me every other Sunday morning, promptly at ten minutes after ten. (On alternate Sundays she would phone my sister.) One Sunday when there was no call at the expected time—it was December 1982—I heard instead from Judy that she was in the hospital with a heart attack. It was her third, but much more severe than the others. She almost died, and it was weeks before it was clear that she was going to pull through.

This illness was a turning point for me and for our relationship. Up till then I knew, of course, that she would die, and that it could be any time. But the knowledge was intellectual, I did not truly feel it. I can recall precisely when the realization came, because I was in the bathtub and I take a bath maybe every two years. Lulled by the warm water, I started to shake with fright. Then I began to cry, sobbing that I didn't want her to die because I still needed her, I needed her to be my mother. For the first time in decades, perhaps in my entire lifetime, I felt how deeply I loved my mother, acknowledged it without reservation. I was still the mama's boy of childhood, and what is wrong with that, then or now?

Seeing her after that was different. I no longer had to

ration my visits. I saw her three times in five months, first in the hospital, then on her return home, then on a surprise trip to take her to the movie *Tootsie* on her birthday. I no longer felt as claustrophobic, no longer found her presence stressful, her talk as strained or nervous. Things about her that had particularly bugged me no longer seemed that important: the way, for example, she would begin a phone conversation with "Everything's all right, isn't it?"—not giving me the space to say how I was actually feeling. I could express better my affection, acknowledge my worries about her condition, and instead of waiting—in part with anticipation, in part foreboding—for that biweekly phone call, I would call myself during the interim. Though we never talked about all this, I assumed she sensed these changes in me, and welcomed them—except for my phone calls, which jolted and confused her a little, upsetting her need for order and routine.

During the height of the Great Depression, Libby Wolf, my mother's younger sister, was working as a social worker in Chicago's Loop. On a lunch hour she noticed a beggar, old and decrepit, dirty and altogether down and out. He looked vaguely familiar. It was her father, whom she hadn't seen in thirty years, since the time he abandoned his four children shortly after their mother died.

Aunt Libby took her father home to her tiny apartment, where he lived out the rest of his life. Esther Blauner was still too angry to see him, so we never visited my aunt and uncle until after he had died. My cousin Alan grew up with a grandfather; I never knew any of my grandparents. I thought all of them had died.

My mother was seven and a half when she lost her mother. With her younger brother Sam, she was placed in the Marx Nathan home, an orphanage on the West Side, financed by Orthodox East European Jews. Libby and David, the two youngest, were placed in the Chicago Home for the Friendless, which was supported by the Reform German Jewish community on the South Side. I never met my Uncle Sam either. His institutionalization for mental illness was another family secret.

Orphanhood and the orphanage must have been the crucial formative experiences of my mother's life. Though she would have denied it, I think "orphan" was her deepest identity, and it brought with it a profound sense of being unworthy and unloved. Alongside her competence and her cheeriness—it was in the Marx Nathan Home that Esther Shapiro earned her nickname "Sunny"—there was also a bereft quality about her and an ever-present anxiety that could only be assuaged by constant activity or by the company of people. Not until she graduated high school would she find a real home with her Aunt Rae and Uncle Jake and their five girls. She became a second mother to the smallest children, particularly Rosella, and remained connected to her cousins all her life. But so powerful was that feeling of shame and stigma, according to Rosella, that all the time she worked in the library she lived in fear that someone she had known in the orphanage would come in and give her secret away.

Otherwise library work was perfect for her. Had there been enough money, she would have preferred to go to college and become a teacher. But in the library she could share with others the books she loved, be with people, serve them. In an old journal I have recorded a childhood memory of her behind the desk: "I'm waiting for her to finish work. It feels cozy, comfortable, safe. I like my mother at work, she keeps her distance. I like her waiting on other people." Looking back at her life, just months before the end, she viewed her work as one of the great satisfactions of her life. The other was her children. Her marriage was a disappointment, but she would not dwell on failure or unhappiness or anything unpleasant. "The whole subject is too painful," she told me in refusing to record on tape her early memories.

She and my father were a mismatch from the outset. Even their family origins clashed. Her Russian Jewish family was from Minsk, an urban center; they were "superior" Litvaks, educated, *sheyn* (refined, literally "clean") people, some of them well-known poets and rabbis. His family was from a small Polish village (Dembitz); they were inferior Galiciani, *prost* (uncouth, "vulgar") people who lived in their bakery. My mother was born in this country, my father was an immigrant. To her, I think, his earthiness and sensuality must have seemed crude. He was also a Bohemian and an intellectual while she was much more conventional and status conscious. Even temperamentally they were opposites: he moody, she even-keeled; he an unworldly romantic, she practical to the bone.

But they both loved books, and this is what brought them together. Samuel Blauner was finishing the Kent School of Law when they met and was also an aspiring poet. (His idol was Edgar Lee Masters, another Chicago lawyer-poet.) Friends of the writer Lawrence Lipton, they had access to the Dill Pickle Club and other Bohemian and literary circles. So there was a period—from the 1920s through the early 1930s—when they had a "normal" family life, filled with friends, talk of books, and evenings of bridge.

But the Depression changed all that. My father lost much of his income and was reduced from a respectable and varied legal practice to the undignified work of collecting bad debts from clients like the Sam Cassell Cigar Company. The loss of money and status must have opened up old wounds. He too came from a family where his mother had died young, his father deserted, and one sibling had gone mad.

As my father told it—and I never got her side of the story— his wife would not stand by him in his time of troubles. Instead she became openly contemptuous, viewing him as a failure. I can also imagine that my mother was looking for a reason not to sleep with a man who was too unpolished for her. And with her status consciousness, she would have found it hard to be associated with someone who was not measuring up to her expectations and who could not provide the standard of living to which she aspired. Twenty years later, when I quit my graduate studies to spend five years working in factories as a political radical, she never told any of her relatives or friends what I was doing.

They were a reasonably happy couple until about 1933 or 1934, my dad told me in the early 1960s. Something of a Freudian, he wanted to feel that my early childhood had given me the foundation for a healthy adulthood. Having just read Harry Stack Sullivan in graduate school, I was convinced that she had been an "anxious mother" with a "bad nipple." No, she was relaxed and serene, he assured me. I did not believe him. Nor can I know how far back their alienation went. In 1974 my mom told me that, to her, only the first two years of their marriage were happy ones.

I have no memories of love or warmth or happy talk between them. I remember instead silence, tension, anger, contempt. On rare occasions some civilly uttered request to pick up a bottle of milk on the way home would punctuate the great silence—more often, cross words. It would not be much of an exaggeration to say that they lived together for thirty years of their marriage virtually without speaking.

As in such novels as *Sons and Lovers* and *Call It Sleep,* where husbands and wives are similarly alienated, the mother-son relation in my family too became eroticized, though not to my belief overtly sexual. But our classic oedipal triangle was complicated by my uncle David, who lived with my parents from the time he left his orphanage to the time he got married fifteen years later. She doted on her little brother. It must have confused and pained me to see how loving and affectionate she was with him, so cold to my own father.

There is a Jewish mother joke about a psychiatrist who has been trying over and over without much success to explain the intricacies of the Oedipus complex and its dire consequences to the mother of the mama's boy whose neurosis he is treating. "Oedipus, Shmedipus," she replies. "As long as he loves his mother." That's all that counts for her, and of course that is not all that should count, but as I get older I can see the underlying wisdom of her position. Psychoanalysis, despite its virtues, does have a way of making overcomplicated the simple truths of life, of undermining the innocence of our attitude toward the everyday and ordinary, subtly and not so subtly encouraging an overcritical, judgmental stance toward people, motivations, and worst of all, toward our own selves.

With my father out of the picture, my mother, my sister, Sonia, and I were effectively the family. Indeed, she was like a single parent of today, holding it all together and making possible that semblance of family life that accounts for the fact that most of my memories of her are happy ones of mundane family activities—unlike most of my memories of my father, which are sad and painful, tinged with deep longings. We sat around the big dining room table doing homework and listening to Fred Allen, cracking jokes and reciting poetry, talking about school and baseball, eating cookies hot from the oven. In the summer it would be the three of us walking to North Shore beach. Waiting for the light at Sheridan Road, we'd call out the out-of-state license plates on passing cars; one summer we took the train and visited relatives in Los Angeles, again without my father.

On birthdays and holidays it was she who would make sure there were baseball gloves, sleds, and stamps for my collection. Through most of elementary school she'd be waiting for me when I came home from school; she did not go back to work until I was eleven. I'd tell her, without waiting to be asked, what games we had played at recess, how I was the only one in my class to know the capital of so-and-so. She was interested in everything I did and thought, from each new playmate to the latest baseball card. Though I have one memory of getting into trouble at school and imploring the teacher not to tell her, otherwise I do not remember hiding anything from my mother.

If I was filled with an underlying sadness, if I ached for a happy family and a real father, I did not know it then. My mom kept her despair and disappointment to herself, protected us as best she could from the fallout from their relationship. Still, often in the middle of the night I would wake to the sounds of fighting, my pop yelling and screaming, my mom trying to quiet him down, "You'll wake up the children." The pall that all this cast on the atmosphere of my childhood did not seep into my conscious awareness until years later. For if she said I was happy, then I was happy, or at least believed I was.

Though I may have dodged her hugs and kisses, found her at times vaguely intrusive, even felt some of the mama's boy's shame, as a child I accepted our closeness. I wanted to please her. Living vicariously through her son's accomplishments, like so many women throughout history, she stayed with my father because she felt Sonia and I would be traumatized by "a broken family." That she had gone through once too often.

To view her critically I had to leave home. Encountering new ideas and interests at college, I began to see hers as shallow and superficial, her tastes and convictions too easily influenced by others, including, as I grew older, myself. Married now with children of my own, I cringed when she fawned over them, making too much of every word and gesture. Had she been so all-consuming with me? Had she really loved me for myself, *unconditionally* (I was reading psychology now) or for my accomplishments, which she could use for her own self-aggrandizement?

And I began to withdraw from her. My letters were more perfunctory, I toned down the expression of my affection. When she visited, I left her to Ginny (my first wife), later to Rena (my second). Of course such "kinship work" typically falls to women in our society. It was not just my growing disdain for her. Once married, mother love seemed to conflict with a commitment to a mate. Divided loyalties again. The year Rena and I lived in Chicago, we visited as infrequently as possible, and when we did I found particularly galling her continued pretense of normality. When my mother called my father "Dear," I would want to scream.

My view of my childhood changed most dramatically in my mid-forties. Through a version of primal therapy, I recovered whole chunks of my childhood, and especially those feelings that she must have deemed unacceptable, and which, according to the metaphor that then appealed to me, she had literally stolen—or kidnapped—from me. Reclaiming these "bad feelings," I discovered that my childhood had not been happy after all. My father's sadness, their lack of love, even my sister's anger and jealousy, had all made me a fearful child, afraid of the world, even of school, where I had so excelled. And pretending that everything was all right had been driving me crazy.

Lying on the floor in a darkened room of a restored Victorian house in West Berkeley during a three-week period away from home, I told my mother to stay away from me, expressed early rages, hurts, and shame, and re-created the way she had made me feel: wrong to my very core, dirty and smelly, because that's the way boys are. Her presence I experienced as scary, creepy, as Death itself. She became a monster, the witch who, in a flight of poetic fancy—we were allowed to record our feelings in a journal—"turned baby boys into girls, and whose front of sweet light and innocence rendered her invulnerable to attack . . . while the little boy was fighting to see, to feel, to call a self his own."

My therapist was a kind of exorcist, exhorting me to feel these long-repressed feelings more deeply, especially the presence of my mother and her influence inside me, then to expunge them through expressing my anger bodily, pounding at her image on the mats I lay on. I took to him in large measure because he saw my mother as the parent most responsible for my difficulties in living whereas my psychoanalyst had viewed my father as the main culprit.

After a period the pendulum began to shift. I began to yearn for a mother who was soft and gentle. I could feel how much I had needed my own, as well as the love for her that had been there along with the pain and conflict. I began to accept some of the positive things that we shared or I had gotten from her: my physical vitality, basic optimism, stability, and sense of responsibility. But the turnabout was not sufficient. When I returned home and could once again talk to her, I found that "the tone, the beat, the constant humming of her voice, the franticness, the anxiety, the terrible tension . . . made me want to gag." And I felt once again possessed by her when she said that "each day of the three weeks I was gone were the longest days of my life."

It got somewhat better. I found her useful as a check on my still spongy memory. She became an ally again, this time in the project of re-creating my personal history. She verified the details of my birth, the existence of Molly, a beloved nursemaid who had cared for me until I was two, and many other important events and feelings whose facticity I had only intuited from bodily and other nonverbal sensations. But there was much tension between us, feelings unspoken and unresolved, that made her visits to see her grandchildren quite difficult for me.

By the summer of 1983, my mother had regained her strength after that near-fatal heart attack, but it left her with a circulation problem in her legs. Her doctor felt that her heart was too fragile to risk an operation. Instead he gave her more medication, not only for her heart and legs but also for her arthritis, indigestion, and other complaints: Her medicine cabinet was a virtual armory. For the most part she kept her sunny spirit and brave front, but it must have been humiliating as well as damned inconvenient not to be able to get around on her own, to walk to the store for groceries, to take the bus to Santa Monica to shop for underwear or toilet water. By 1984 she was no longer saying, as she had been for the last fifteen years of her new life in California, that it felt like a miracle to wake up in the morning each day and be alive to enjoy it. With the pain and the restrictions on her movement, it was no longer worth it—she felt she had lived long enough. Indeed, she would say that with modern medicine most people live too long these days.

Her doctor, as well as Judy and other friends, began to worry about her living alone. What if she should fall and not be able to get up? What if she had another heart attack, too far from the phone to call for help? They persuaded her that it was time to move to a retirement home. Against her better instincts she went along with the plan.

It fell on me to make the arrangements. So on Christmas Day 1985 I flew down to L.A. to spend the next two days visiting prospective places with her. At dinner she was not her usual contained self. She was visibly upset at the prospect of leaving her apartment, doubtful that we could find a place that was right for her. It wasn't only giving up her independence, she hated the idea of being in a home with old people. Esther Blauner might be eighty-six, but she wasn't really old. Not her.

And I was having troubles of my own, besides being agitated by the sadness of my mission and apprehensive at the prospective loss of my "home away from home." For over a year I had been in the midst of the worst depression of my life. I would have liked to have covered up my mental state so as not to further upset her, but I could not. Driving to find various retirement homes, I kept taking wrong turns, retracing the route, and losing my way, I was in such a panic.

We saw three of them. The administrators were invariably nice, the conditions apparently humane. A few of the residents seemed active and alive, but perhaps half were sitting in their chairs like zombies, vegetating with catatonic looks about them. And these were not even nursing homes, but residences for "vital," healthy senior citizens. One facility seemed a little better than the others, and my mom seemed to be actively considering it. I had my doubts and was relieved that she had changed her mind when we got home. One of her friends suggested I call a senior center for more alternatives. The case worker, who came to the apartment within an hour, sized up the situation immediately and insisted that my mother stay put. They would provide support services.

Moving would have literally killed her. A "home" would have been the orphanage all over again, but with no prospect this time of getting out. Though she only lived five more months, it was on her own terms, in her own familiar terrain.

Another mother-note I've saved, this time written by my daughter Marya when I was out: "Grandmas @ Cedar Side [Sinai] Hospital, Room 5226." The cardiac intensive ward again. The doctors told me (now relying on my own hasty scribble on the same note): "Aortic stinosis. The last valve narrowed, blood backing up to heart. Results congestive ht trouble, causes difficulty . . ." Here I stopped writing, I had gotten the message. She didn't want the operation her doctor would recommend, the additional pain and the long uncertain recuperation. She had already lived long enough, she kept reiterating.

When I talked to her the next day, she seemed calm and in good spirits. Always the favorite of doctors and nurses who responded to her sunny disposition, she seemed to like being taken care of in hospitals, even though she hated calling on her friends for help. I would insist: "It's your turn now, you've helped other people all your life." I told her to hang in there, live another few years, I wanted her to see my book finished. I had been writing it for almost ten years, researching it twice as long. The next day, thinking better of it, I called her back. "Die when you're ready to die," I told her. "Don't hang around for me." I think she appreciated that. She had lived too much of her life for others, she could at least die for herself.

And she did. And in her home, or more accurately, in the ambulance which was taking her from the apartment to the hospital. Before, she had a peaceful month in her own place, except for agonizing as to whether or not to have that valve operation. Ironically she had finally come around, had decided to enter the hospital on Monday. By Friday and Saturday she was having acute chest pains. Misreading them as angina, she took more "nitros" and refused offers of her friends who wanted to stay overnight with her. Perhaps she just wanted to die without anyone in the way to stop her.

The day she died was my ex-wife's birthday. They had stayed on good terms, so remembering her social obligations to the last, she called her ex-daughter-in-law. Rena told me later that she could tell something was different, she was really saying good-bye. My call came a half hour later. Oddly, it was our usual ten after ten, a Sunday morning. By now she was really scared, could tell it was the end. So sensed I, but we didn't quite say it, didn't quite say good-bye. At least not directly. She sounded very alone. I told her to call 911. By the time I phoned St. John's Hospital she was already dead.

On the airplane. I'm feeling strangely good and very alive. Reading Bernikow's *Alone in America*, I'm very moved. What a fine book, won't Mom love it. I catch myself. It hasn't hit me yet.

At the hospital. First order of business is signing the death certificate. Then I've requested some moments alone with her. How long? they ask. Maybe half an hour. But there was not that much to say or do, just notice the look on her face. A smile of satisfaction? And try to give a final hug. We never hugged easily, both of us inhibited, self-conscious. But try it with a corpse. How quickly she had turned rigid and cold. There will be no burial, no funeral. She wanted no fuss over her. No send-offs. No belief in an afterlife either. "The end is the end," she had told me when, unsure of my own beliefs, I had pressed her for hers, only a little while earlier. Her body will be going to USC. I am already dreading next fall, anticipating the med students' sick jokes, poking fun at my mother, that tiny, wizened old lady. I used to make fun too, called her "the midget." But I sign the release papers.

The memorial at her apartment. The culmination of a difficult week. Sonia and I have been staying at her place, going through her things, deciding what to sell, what to give away, what to divide among us. Hard decisions, but we made them. But not without getting on each other's nerves, our styles of mourning clashing, ancient resentments and rivalries surfacing.

After the bagels and the cream cheese, after the wine and the soft drinks, after the hugs of commiseration and the wiping away of tears, I give my little speech, saying good-bye to my mother before thirty of her remaining friends. I say how it was a good death because she had a full life and was ready to die. But I wasn't ready for her to die, maybe I never would be. Something in the tone of my elegy, maybe it was my depressed state, bothered Judy's husband, Danny, who tried to reassure me that our loved ones remain with us in our memories and in our hearts.

But that was little comfort then because I wanted my mother to be with me to see my new house; meet my new friends, especially the women in my life; see my kids grow up; above all, see myself my self again, the book finished, dedicated to her and not to her memory. To be able to walk to the front door, pick up her *Los Angeles Times,* and one morning on the same page as the crossword puzzle with which she drank her first cup of coffee, find my first book review.

Having begun this memoir with a note, I shall end it with the last one I left her, as I walked out her door that final time she was in the hospital. The last written communication of mine she would read, which her friends later told me had been a source of comfort in the last month of her life.

> Dear Mom:
> Welcome Home!
>   It was so nice seeing you and I hope you recover miraculously and have a long time to enjoy your nice apartment, all your friends, and your memories of a wonderful life. And if you don't, that's all right too, as long as you don't have to suffer too much pain. You've had enough.
>   So now I'm off to get [her granddaughter] Susan's card and see you at the hospital, but I wanted you to find this note on coming home.
>   You're a wonderful mother and a wonderful person and I love you very much.

PART 4

TAKING HER OWN LIFE: SUICIDE AND EUTHANASIA

A suicide is the subject of each of the selections in this chapter, but otherwise the four stories couldn't be more different. As Gary Young describes his emotionally disturbed mother in a series of surreal poems, self-destruction was such a persistent theme in her life that her actual suicide comes almost as an anticlimax.

The mothers of Andrew Solomon and B. J. Nelson, on the other hand, made conscious decisions to end their lives. Suicides like that of Mrs. Solomon (and that of Charles Wertenbaker in the book *Death of a Man*) can be seen as an individual's assertion against "the system," a kind of revenge against all the machinery of modern medical technology that will keep us alive whether or not we want to be kept alive, whether or not the life that remains is worth living. Above all, it means taking charge of one's fate, rather than surrendering that control to authorities and institutions. By deciding that she would, when the time was right, swallow her plentiful supply of pills, Mrs. Solomon was able to die at home, surrounded by the love of husband and children, a family that participated in her death. The irony for me is that this death by suicide is not only a good death, but perhaps the best of all the leave-takings in the entire book.

The death of Marie Brett is much less satisfying, since she was not supported by a large and extended family but only by one son, the author B. J. Nelson. She died embittered, mother and son squabbling almost to the very end.

Thus every case of euthanasia does not a good death make.

The mother of Daniel Oberti jumped from the cliffs above the Pacific Ocean, but instead of ending her life as she had intended, she was rescued. Alice Oberti would live for many years afterwards, crippled physically and emotionally. "The accident," as her fall was euphemistically referred to, would irrevocably transform her son's life.

What is striking in all these accounts is the way these writers are able to convert the pain of their mothers' suicides into writings of power and beauty.

I WANT TO SING

Fifteen Poems About My Mother

Gary Young

> Zeng Shen said, "I once heard the Master say no man reveals his true self, except perhaps when he is mourning his parents."
>
> *The Analects*, Book XIX, no. 17

My mother was a beautiful woman. She had been a beautiful child. She danced for the soldiers, then, and sang for them, and everyone clapped and cheered. When her period came, she thought she was dying. Her face broke out, and her mother screamed, how could you do this? How will we live? Who will love you now? Years later, my mother turned to me. I was twelve. We'd stopped to rest in a little town. She put her hands

An original compilation first appearing in this volume. Ten of the fifteen poems have been published elsewhere: "I was home from the hospital," "My mother loved violets," and "The light from her room" in the *Denver Quarterly;* "My mother was a beautiful woman," "My mother had the flesh," "My mother entertained the troops," and "Terrified of another pregnancy," in the *Kenyon Review;* "My mother wouldn't ride" in *The Prose Poem: An International Journal;* "Tell me a story," in the *Santa Barbara Review;* and "I last saw my mother" in *Days,* by Gary Young (Silverfish Review Press, 1997).

on my cheeks. Let me get that, she said, and she dug her nails into me, picking until I bled. That's how it starts, she said, and it wasn't the shock of the pain, it was the look on her face that made me want to cry.

I was home from the hospital and not expected to survive. My mother had come to visit before I died. She needed my attention; she was still weak. She had tried to take her life again. I have trouble breathing, she said, and tapped a gold coin hanging from a choker at her throat. It's to hide the scar, she said. But the coin was too small. I gave her my hand to sit; I gave her my arm to rise. When friends arrived for dinner, she danced for an hour, beautifully. Everyone agreed she had a talent.

Tell me a story, she says, one I haven't heard. So I tell her, it was autumn. Mother took us to see George. I'd made him lunch, but he couldn't eat; he was dying then of cancer. No, she says, a happy one. I tell her, you were three. There was a party in the old house. They dressed you like a flapper, and everybody danced. It's strange, she says, I can't remember, and you can't forget. I stole money to buy you food, I tell her. I know, she says, you told me before. I hid the food under my bed, but I couldn't bring myself to eat it.

I waited for my mother in the greenhouse. It was warm, and I could feel the presence of the air. I practiced words in my breath on the windows. I thought I was alone, but an older boy in the corner called my name. I asked, how do you know me? And he said, I'm your brother. He said our parents had sent him away, but he knew me, and watched me every day. That night my mother said, someone is playing a joke on you, but I knew she was lying. I believed him, I still believe him, an orphan, a boy I could never be.

The burning house turned our night clothes yellow. Standing at the curb, my brother batted ashes with his hand. We had a puppy, and my mother shouted, where's the dog, and then, my God, where's Cathy? I remember the sound of breaking glass, and walls too hot to touch. I remember pulling my sister from her bed, and leading her out into the world again. I did not wonder, then, how I'd found her, or how my mother could have turned so easily to send me back into the smoke and flames. It was my house; I knew where I was. I could find my way even in the dark.

My mother cut her toenails and her cuticles every night until they bled. She'd take a little pick and peel away the skin; she'd cut the pale flesh away with shears. I couldn't stop her, and if I asked, are you finished, she always said, no.

   I sat on her bed and watched; my attention was all I had to give. It was all she ever wanted.

Terrified of another pregnancy, my mother asked the doctor to remove her uterus, and the doctor did. After the surgery, our dog made a nest of torn rags in a corner of the house. When we stroked her belly, our hands came away wet with milk. The vet said, she isn't having puppies, she's just a high-strung breed. She began to have seizures. Her body convulsed, and her small eyes jerked in her head. I'd pry the jaws apart, feed her raw eggs and whiskey, and she'd relax. She'd lick my face in gratitude. My mother used to say, that dog is almost human; she really is like one of the family.

The light from her room was penetrating, otherworldly, blue. I didn't recognize the smell, but I remember thinking, the air is burning. I was afraid to go in. I could see her lying on the bed. Her skin was blistered; she'd fallen asleep under the tanning lamp. That winter, she did it again. They covered her face with a salve, and she seemed to be melting. While she was away, I lifted the lamp over my head, and let it fall. When she discovered the lamp was broken, she screamed, nothing's safe, I can't keep anything for myself.

My mother entertained the troops in Vietnam. When she came back, she handed me the photograph of a soldier, and said, he was killed sneaking into the camp the night I sang. You may not believe this, she said, but I've never felt as safe as I did while I was there. The Vietnamese soldier in the photograph is hanging by his wrists. A curtain of blood fans out from his neck. His hands are swollen; he was still alive when they strung him up with wire. My mother said, those boys couldn't do enough for me; they treated me like a queen in Vietnam. I still have a picture of the one who gave her his life.

My mother wouldn't ride, but when the horses had been turned out to pasture, she'd pour salt on our cabin floor and dance all night for the cowboys. One summer she missed a turn driving into town, and rolled her car into a ditch. She was so happy to be hurt, to be an event. In the hospital she introduced me to a girl who'd spent two days pulling slivers of glass from her teased and bloody hair. My mother asked, did you miss me? But before I could answer, she turned to the girl and said, we have had such a time.

My mother had the flesh burned from her lips; she had the skin peeled from her face. She wanted to look young again. When the scabs fell away, and she couldn't bear the bright, new scars, she poisoned herself. I have so much to tell you, she said later. She said, I left my body. I knew I was dying, and I could see my body there. I floated away from it, down the hall, and through the door into the street. There were people everywhere, she said. It was beautiful. They wanted me to lead a parade. Mother, stop, I said, I was there.

My mother practiced Yoga. She leaned forward from her waist, pulled her legs behind her neck, and said, my vagina's collapsed; the doctors say there's nothing they can do. In the mental ward she met a young man from Texas. He had small, hard muscles, and his face twitched when he showed me his tattoos. He and my mother talked about home, and madness, about the future and electric shock. They fell in love. When they were released, he terrorized my mother, broke into her house and beat her again and again. I should have had him arrested and put away, but she was so happy, so excited, that I didn't have the heart.

My mother loved violets. When she spent whole days in bed for days on end, I bought her violets, and put them in a cup on the nightstand by her head. I skipped lunch all week for the money to buy them, and the florist would nod, and say, violets again. When I brought them home, my mother said, you precious thing. Then she'd look at the flowers and say, they're beautiful, but they never last.

My cousin had a dream last night about my mother. He said, I was sobbing, and she held me, and rocked me in her arms as I cried. She turned, and looked behind us, at a room full of people, and I asked, do they know you're here? And she said, no, no they don't. My cousin said, I'd never dreamed of her before, and I woke up happy; I was still crying, but I felt all right. Then he stopped, and I asked, how is she? And he said, great, great. She looked great.

I last saw my mother a week after her suicide, in a dream. She was so shy; she was only there a moment. I'd called her stupid. How could you be so stupid? Eight years later she's back. What do you want, I ask her, what do you really want? I want to sing, she says. And she sings.

A DEATH OF ONE'S OWN

Andrew Solomon

Since my mother's death, there has been a certain tendency toward denial in my family. My father doesn't care for sad movies or plays anymore, and in trying to look away from his own loss he tends to overlook a certain sadness in my brother and in me, as though he has forgotten that grief unites us. Unlike the uniting sorrow of other deaths, this one has in it the weird legacy of our once secret history. With time, I have come to understand that being active in euthanasia circles is both a means of working through agonizing feelings and a means of holding on to them.

My mother's ovarian cancer was diagnosed in August of 1989. During her first week in the hospital, she announced that she was going to kill herself. She was not at that time speaking of a considered agenda of terminating her own symptoms—she had scarcely any symptoms—but rather was expressing a sense of outrage at the indignity of what lay ahead and a profound fear of losing control of her own life. She then spoke of suicide as people disappointed in love may speak of it—as a swift and easy alternative to the painful, slow process of recovery. It was as though she wanted vengeance for the snub she had received from nature: if her life could not be as exquisite as it had been, she would have no more of it.

The subject lay low as she went through an excruciating, humiliating bout of chemotherapy. When, ten months later, she went in for exploratory surgery to assess the results, the regimen proved to have been less effective than we'd hoped, and a second round was prescribed. After the surgery, my mother lingered for a long time in a state of resistance to consciousness. When she finally began to speak again, a flood of anger came out of her, and this time when she said she was going to kill herself it was a threat. Our protests were thrown back in our faces. "I'm already dead," she said as she lay in her hospital bed. "What's here for you to love?" Or else, "If you loved me, you'd help me out of this misery." Whatever meagre faith she had had in chemotherapy was gone, and she laid down as a condition of her accepting further punishing treatments that someone get her "those pills," so that she could stop whenever she was ready.

You tend to accommodate the very, very sick. There was no answer to my mother's rage and despair after her surgery except to say yes to whatever she demanded. I was living in London at that time, but now came to New York every second week to see her. My brother was in law school in New Haven, and he drove down often. My father neglected his office to be at home. We were all clinging to my mother, who had been the center of our family, and we wavered between the lighter tone that had been our customary mien and a darker solemnity. Still, when my mother had relaxed into a facsimile of her usual self, the idea of her suicide, though it had gained resonance, once more receded. Her second round of chemotherapy seemed to be working, and my father had researched half a dozen more options. My mother made her remarks about suicide on occasion, and we continued to tell her that it would be a long time before such measures could be relevant.

At four o'clock on a blustery September afternoon in 1990, I called home to check on some test results. We would continue with this therapy while we explored other options, my father told me, trying to sound upbeat. I had no doubt what other options my mother would be exploring. So I should not have been surprised when she told me, in October, over lunch, that the technical details had been taken care of—she now had the pills. In the early stages of her illness, my mother, stripped of disguises, had suffered as a side effect of her treatments a loss of beauty so obvious that only my father could contrive to be blind to it.

She had found the physical damage of chemotherapy intensely painful—her hair was gone, her skin was allergic to any makeup, her body was emaciated, and her eyes were ringed with perpetual exhaustion. By the time of that October lunch, however, she had begun to take on a pale, illuminated, ethereal beauty, completely different in its quality from the all-American looks she had had during my childhood. The moment when she actually sought the pills was also the moment when she accepted (perhaps prematurely, perhaps not) the idea that she was dying, and this acceptance afforded her a radiance, both physical and profound, that seemed to me that day more powerful than her decay.

I protested, as we ate, that she might still have lots of time, and she said that she had always believed in planning carefully. Euthanasia is a deadline matter, and I asked what her cutoff would be. "As long as there is even a remote chance of my getting well, I'll go on with treatments," she said. "When they say that they are keeping me alive but without any chance of recovery, then I'll stop. When it's time I'll know. I won't do anything before then. Meanwhile, I plan to enjoy whatever time there is left."

Everything that had been intolerable to my mother was made tolerable when she got those pills, by the sure knowledge that when life became unlivable it would stop. I would have to say that the eight months that followed, though they led inexorably to her death, were the happiest months of her illness; and that in some obscure way—despite, or perhaps because of, the suffering in them—they were the happiest months of our lives. Once we had all settled the future, we could live fully in the present, something that we had never really done before.

Euthanasia offers a remarkable liberation, for the imminence of death, once it is fully acknowledged, can be the basis for a stripped and pure honesty that is not possible under ordinary circumstances. I should emphasize that the vomiting, the malaise, the hair loss, and the adhesions were all relentless; that my mother's mouth was one great sore that seemed never to heal; that she had to save strength for days to have one afternoon out; that she could eat almost nothing, was a mess of allergies, and shook so badly that she was often unable to use a fork and knife—yet the excruciating business of the continuing chemotherapy seemed suddenly unimportant, because these symptoms were permanent only until she decided she could take no more, and so the disease was no longer in control of her. In "A Short History of Decay" E. M. Cioran writes, "What greater wealth than the suicide each of us bears within himself?"

A few days after my mother told me that she had the pills, I had lunch with my grieving father. We talked through the logistics. My mother, in a euphemistic discussion with one of her many doctors, had complained of insomnia. The doctor suggested Halcion. My mother said she had taken Halcion. They had once talked in the abstract about euthanasia; it was not mentioned now, but it seems likely that the doctor knew why only Seconal would do. He wrote a standard prescription for twenty pills. Two months later, he would write another. Meanwhile, there was also discussion with a psychoanalyst my parents knew, whom I shall call Moses Grey. They had previously discussed the matter of euthanasia, and Dr. Grey had provided great emotional support. Now he obligingly prescribed Seconal in response to complaints of sleeplessness. The bottles took up residence in the back of my mother's medicine chest. In yet another euphemistic conversation, my mother asked a doctor how he would feel about signing a death certificate for someone who "died peacefully at home after a long illness," and he said, perhaps understanding her meaning, perhaps not, that he had done that before and would be willing to do it again. If a death certificate says suicide, or if an unprepared doctor suspects suicide, there is usually a police autopsy and anyone who was nearby when the suicide took place may be subject to questioning.

My parents had bought a book from the Hemlock Society, "Let Me Die Before I Wake," which was a less explicit precursor of the volume "Final Exit," and was written in a cautious vocabulary of ostensible fictions; "Alan and Ruth were planning a cruise of the Caribbean in a chartered yacht in April, but when Alan noticed traces of blood in his semen he went for a checkup with a urologist," one story went; it ended, "Dr. Browning gave Alan nearly two dozen injects each of a quarter of a grain of morphine solution." From the book my mother had worked out details, and my father, who is also given to careful planning, went over the whole thing with me, as though a dress rehearsal would exhaust in advance some of the pain of the event itself. We talked about how my brother and I would come to the house, how my mother would take the antiemetics, and what time of day would be best for this exercise; we agreed to hold the funeral two days after the death. We planned it together, much as we had on previous occasions planned parties, family vacations, Christmas.

My mother talked in that period about how much she loved us all, and unearthed the shape and structure of that love: she contrived in the course of a few months to resolve old family differences. She set aside a day with each of her friends—and she had many friends—to say goodbye; though very few of them knew her agenda, she made sure that each understood the large place he or she occupied in her affections. She recruited me one afternoon to help her buy my ninety-year-old great-aunt a handbag, and although the expedition left her exhausted to the point of collapse for three days, it also renewed us both. She set about having all our furniture reupholstered, so that she would leave the house in reasonable shape, and she selected a design for her tombstone. Perhaps you can talk about euthanasia in public after the fact, but you certainly cannot talk about it in advance, and so we fell into a sort of conspiracy that made us feel like a group of fifties Communists. In the context of my rather conservative and highly reputable family, this was a profoundly strange sensation: we were liberated by our newly clear emotions, but entombed in our collusion. No longer fully honest with friends, we became even sadder and more isolated and more dependent on one another than we had been.

After my lunch with my father and my lunch with my mother, we didn't discuss suicide very much. But, though we all wanted to believe in Chemotherapy No. 3 and Chemotherapy No. 4, we also understood that we were really playing for time. Bit by bit, the fact that my mother's suicide plans would become reality seemed to settle on us. Later, she said that she had considered doing the whole thing on her own but had thought that the shock would be worse than the memories of having been with her for this experience. As for us, we wanted to be there. My mother's life was in other people, and we all hated the idea of her dying alone. It was important that in my mother's last months on earth we all feel connected, that none of us be left with a sense of secrets kept and intentions hidden.

If you have never tried it or helped someone else through it, you cannot begin to imagine how difficult it is to kill yourself. If death were a passive thing, which occurred to those who couldn't be bothered to resist it, and if life were an active thing, which continued only by virtue of a daily commitment to it, then the world's problem would be depopulation and not overpopulation. Having been through the whole business, I would put the infrequency of suicide down more to the difficulty of it than to the undesirability of its objective. The date my mother chose for killing herself was June 19, 1991, because if she had waited longer she would have been too weak to take her own life, and suicide requires strength and a kind of privacy that does not exist in hospitals. That afternoon, my mother had been to see a gastroenterologist, who told her that large tumors were blocking her intestine. Without immediate surgery, she would be unable to digest food. She said that she would be in touch to schedule the surgery, then rejoined my father in the waiting room. When they got home, she called my brother and me. "It was bad news," she said. I knew what she meant, but I couldn't quite bring myself to say it. "You'd better come up here," she said. It was all very much as we had planned it.

I headed uptown, stopping to collect my brother from his office on the way. It was pouring out, and the traffic was very slow. My mother's absolutely calm voice—she used as logical a tone as if we were coming uptown for dinner—had somehow made the whole thing seem very straightforward, and when we arrived at the apartment we found her lucid and relaxed, wearing a nightgown with pink roses on it and a long bathrobe. "Couldn't you wait a little longer?" my brother asked, but my mother said that once her digestive system got blocked she might be unable to take pills. "I'd thought," she said apologetically, "that I could make it through your birthday"—which was three weeks off— "and do this immediately afterward. But it's really going to have to be now." It was too late to argue the logic of suicide; we had all agreed that it was a good logic. "So," my mother said, "if we've settled that, then we might as well get started."

I will say only that it might have been illegal for my brother to get her the glass of water she used to take the pills. It might have been illegal for my father to get the pills out of the medicine chest. I would have been within the law in focussing instead on getting her an extra blanket, because she was cold. My father had pretty much memorized the book, but we still consulted it. "It says here that you have to take the antiemetics first," he said. His voice was broken, but my mother's was even. "I've been thinking about this for so long that it's a relief finally to be doing it," she said. "The only thing I still fear is this not going smoothly." She finished taking the antiemetics and put down her glass. "What next?" she asked. My father consulted the book again. "You're supposed to try to have a light snack," he said. "It helps to keep the pills down." So we all went into the kitchen, and my mother toasted some English muffins and made tea. At dinner a few nights earlier, my mother and my brother had pulled a wishbone, and my mother had won. "What did you wish?" my brother asked her now, and she smiled. "I wished for this to be over as quickly and as painlessly as possible," she said. "And I got my wish." She looked down at her English muffin. "I got my wishes so often," she remarked. My brother put out a box of cookies just then, and my mother in the tone of fond irony that was so much her own, said, "David. For the last time. Would you put the cookies on a plate?" I think there is a certain natural drama to death from natural causes: there are sudden symptoms and seizures or, in their absence, the shock of surprises—of interruption. What was so curious about this experience was that there was nothing sudden or unanticipated about it. The drama lay in the very absence of drama, in the choking experience of no one's acting out of character in any regard.

Back in her bedroom, my mother apologized again for involving us all. "But at least you three should be together afterward," she added. Although "Let Me Die Before I Wake" suggested a minimum of fifteen Seconal, it recommended forty to be safe. My mother—who always believed in inventory— actually had twice as much Seconal as she needed. She sat up in bed and dumped forty pills on the blanket in front of her. "I'm so tired of taking pills," she said wryly. "That's one thing I won't miss." And she began taking them with an expert's finesse, as though the thousands of pills she had had to take during two years of cancer had been practice for this moment. I hadn't seen a Seconal since then, but recently I looked at one long and hard, and it was amazing to me how evocative that Day-Glo orange oblong was. I remembered that pile of pills on the blanket, and how my mother scooped them up, virtuoso, swallowing two or three at a time. "I think that should do it," she said when the heap vanished. She tried to down a glass of vodka, but said it was making her nauseated. "Surely this is better than your seeing me screaming in a hospital bed?" And, of course, it was better, except that that image was still only fantasy and this one had become reality, and reality in these instances is worse than anything.

Then we had about forty-five minutes, during which she said all the last things she had to say, and we said all the last things we had to say. Bit by bit, her voice slurred, and it was then that the drama of her death came, because as she became hazier she became also even clearer, and it seemed to me that the fact that she had long known what she wanted to say did not take away any of her words' immediacy, and that she was saying still more than she could have planned. "You were the most beloved children," she said, looking at us. "Until you were born, I had no idea that I could feel anything like what I felt then. Suddenly, there you were. I had read books all my life about mothers who bravely said that they would die for their children, and that was just how I felt. I would have died for you. I hated for you to be unhappy. I wanted to wrap you in my love, to protect you from all the terrible things in the world. I wanted my love to make the world a happy and joyful and safe place for you." She held my hand for a second, then my brother's. "I want you to feel that that love is always there, that it will go on wrapping you up even after I am gone. My greatest hope is that the love I've given you will stay with you for your whole life."

Her voice was steady at that point, as though time were not against her. She turned to my father. "I would gladly have given decades of my life to be the one who went first," she said. "I can't imagine what I would have done if you had died before me, Howard. You are my life. For thirty years, you have been my life." She looked at me—I was crying, though she was not— and her voice took on a tone of gentle reprimand. "Don't think you're paying me some kind of great tribute if you let my death become the great event of your life," she said to me. "The best tribute you can pay to me as a mother is to go on and have a good and fulfilling life. Enjoy what you have."

Then her voice became dreamily torpid. "I'm sad today. I'm sad to be going," she said. "But even with this death, I wouldn't want to change my life for any other life in the world. I have loved completely, and I have been completely loved, and I've had such a good time." She closed her eyes for what we thought was the last time, and then opened them again and looked at each of us in turn, her eyes settling on my father. "I've looked for so many things in this life," she said, her voice as slow as a record played at the wrong speed. "So many things. And all the time Paradise was in this room with the three of you." My brother had been rubbing her shoulders. "Thanks for the backrub, David," she said, and then she closed her eyes for good. "Carolyn!" my father said, but she didn't move again. I have seen one other death—someone shot by a gun—and I remember feeling that that death did not belong to the person who died: it belonged to the gun and the moment. This death was my mother's own.

It took my mother almost five hours to stop breathing. "Let Me Die Before I Wake" says that if the Seconal doesn't work you can smother the suicide victim. Waiting in the kitchen, my father and my brother and I had to discuss this possibility. I had begun to hate the air of secrecy and wanted to call my mother's friends, or my friends, but father said we had to wait until she was really dead. Every half hour, one of us would check to see how she was doing. Her breathing sometimes seemed slower, but it was hard to tell.

The discipline of not doing is usually more difficult than the discipline of doing, and, of all the not doing I have confronted, the most painful was the not waking my mother as she slid by slow degrees from sleep to death. To speak to her seemed absurd and theatrical to me; I have never spoken aloud to a sleeping lover or to a child who has dozed on my shoulders, and I felt that it would be affected and sanctimonious to go blathering on to my mother once she had said goodbye. In that room with her, I maintained a kind of empty silence, and wondered what stage of dying she reached—whether she had passed the point at which she could be fully revived. She had said that what she was most afraid of was waking up, and I didn't know whether I was most afraid of her waking or of her dying or of this uncanny, flat time of neither one.

Just after midnight, my brother, the most restrained and most reasonable of us, went to check and found that the breathing had stopped. An hour or so later, the doctor signed a death certificate saying she had died of ovarian cancer. Immediately after he left, we called the funeral home my mother had selected, and its staff came and collected her body. We were among the lucky ones: we did not have to resort to plastic bags, or to watch my mother vomit over herself. It was that ideal death which plays out in Hemlock Society publications: the gentle, easeful death.

By now, most of my mother's friends know that she killed herself, and I think they will have gathered that the rest of us were there. It is a measure of the general discomfort that the matter is almost never mentioned. No one's gentle amateur psychologizing has taken note of the Freudian or Sophoclean underpinnings here. Almost no one has asked me how we made the practical arrangements. Nor has anyone asked whether I wanted to be involved in the whole thing. I should emphasize that this is not discomfort with the larger subject of death: I have of late been drawn into as many conversations about cancer as any member of New York Hospital's oncology unit. Euthanasia, which many people I know support, is in its details a subject nearly as taboo as incest. If you do it, no one really wants to hear about it; people don't even know how to ask about it.

After my mother's death, I was the one who took on the cleaning up of my parents' apartment, sorting through my mother's clothes, her personal papers, and so on. The bathroom was thick with the debris of terminal illness: instruments for the care of wigs; salves and lotions for allergic reactions; and bottles and bottles and bottles of pills. Back in the corner of the medicine chest, behind the vitamins, the painkillers, the drugs to calm her stomach, the ones to rebalance certain hormones, the various combinations of sleeping pills she had taken when disease and fear conspired to keep her awake—behind all of them I found, like the last gift out of Pandora's box, the rest of the Seconal. I was busy throwing away bottle after bottle, but when I got to those pills I stopped. Fearful myself of both illness and despair, I pocketed the bottles, took them home with me, and hid them in the farthest corner of my own medicine chest. I remembered the October day my mother had said to me, "I have the pills. When the time comes, I'll be able to do it." In my grieving empathy, I went for an H.I.V. test, half hoping that it would be positive and I might find in the result an excuse to take them.

Ten days after I finished clearing out my mother's bathroom, my father called in a rage. "What happened to the rest of the Seconal?" he asked, and I said that I had thrown away all my mother's pills. I added that he seemed very depressed and that it disturbed me to think of his having ready access to the drug. "Those pills," he said, his voice breaking, "you had no right to throw away." Then, after a long pause, he said, "I was saving them for myself, in case someday I was ill also. So I wouldn't have to go through that whole process to get them." I think that for each of us it was as though my mother lived on in those orange pills, as though whoever possessed the poison by which she had died retained also some strange access to her life. It was as though by planning to take the remaining pills we were somehow becoming reattached to my mother—as though we could join her by dying as she had died. Our one comfort in the face of her loss was to plan to repeat its details on ourselves.

After my father and I spoke, I threw away those pills, to obviate the lie I had told him: each of us will have to start anew if the time comes. He and David and I have never sat down to discuss our own deaths, but I know that we all assumed (more or less consciously), from the day my mother took those pills, that we would die as she had died. If we are not hit by cars or stray bullets, if we do not suffer heart failure or fatal strokes, then, in keeping with our last inheritance from my mother, we will certainly all kill ourselves. Not one of us plans to go through the final agonies of terminal illness, and not one of us plans to live out the isolation of terrible age beyond the death of friends. We are signatories to a sealed pact of the conscious soul, a pact I entered into when I was so distracted by a more immediate grief that I hardly noticed what I was doing. That unwitting agreement governs all other conditions of my life. The terms of my own suicide are entirely clear to me; it is not something I plan to undertake anytime soon, but it would surprise me to die any other way. When the time comes, I will not have to seek farther than to obtain the pills themselves, because in my mind and my heart I am more ready for this than for the unplanned daily tribulations that mark off the mornings and afternoons. Having seen the simple logic of euthanasia in action and witnessed the comfort of that control, what astonishes me is how many people die by other means.

MOTHER'S LAST REQUEST

A Not So Fond Farewell

B. J. Nelson

Marie wanted to die. She'd been wanting to for most of her life, I think, and wasn't it time? She was asking me. She'd been thinking about how to kill herself for months, years, especially the last few weeks. Now she knew how she would do it and was simply focussing on when. She was eighty and a couple of her teeth had recently fallen out, her stomach was swollen, food made her sick; she was in pain all over, the worst pain she'd ever had, she said, though every pain throughout her whole life was always the worst. Over the years, the hundreds of times she was sick, each time she was "deathly sick." Each pain for decades had been "the most horrible pain" she'd ever felt. You never knew. She'd turn the least matter into melodrama, managing her life neurotically, even from the beginning, I've come to believe, by pretending, by living in a world of pretense.

Anyway, she might as well just go on and get it over with, didn't I think so, too? I told her that such a thing had to be up

"Mother's Last Request" appeared in *Harper's* magazine, March 1996. Copyright © 1996 by B. J. Nelson, reprinted with the permission of the author.

to her, no one else. But didn't I think she might as well? What did she have to live for? She had terrible noise in her ears and couldn't hear, she'd disconnected her phone, no one called anyway, she had no friends. She had lived for fifteen years as an almost total recluse, and other than a sister she hated and another son she hadn't heard from in thirty years, there was only me. She couldn't see her soap operas except as a blur, she was shaky, trembly, she got out of breath walking from her room to the front of the house, so before being too helpless, while she could still manage, wasn't it time?

She hadn't bathed or showered in a couple of years, I think she couldn't lift her legs enough to step in and get out of the tub. She sponged off, she said. But she was still able to go to the toilet on her own, she was still feeding herself, though lately only oatmeal, buttered bread, and a little yogurt; anything else made her vomit. She was weak and getting weaker.

"No, I'm not going to the doctor," she told me. "I know what he'd do, he'd put me in the hospital and I'd be kept alive for no reason or left in a nursing home, and I don't want that. I want to lay down right here in my own bed and go to sleep and not wake up. You don't know how many times I've prayed I wouldn't wake up. Every night I go to sleep praying, dear God, please, just let me die and not wake up. So I'm going to do it. But I can't by myself. You'll have to help me."

This was Wednesday noon. She was going to take pills. Years before, she'd saved a stash of pills for the purpose, but when she couldn't afford new medicine one year, she'd used the stash instead. Recently, though, she'd gotten a prescription for one hundred Xanax, a sedative. I called in the order for her and picked up the pills from the drugstore an hour later, a regular brownish cylinder with a white cap. Marie said she was going to take them that night at about eleven or eleven-thirty, her usual bedtime, when it was quiet and peaceful. I didn't know whether she really would. She had talked suicide too often. But the pills would put her right to sleep, then all I'd have to do was slip a bag over her head and wrap it airtight around her neck with a scarf. Not rubber bands. They might

leave telltale lines. She showed me the small plastic trash bag
and the blue silky scarf. She'd already tried the bag on to be
sure it wasn't too big. She said it wasn't. A large bag would
retain too much air and take longer. She'd read that in a book
from the Hemlock Society. She gave me the bag and scarf.

"Now, you just go on about your business," she said.
"Tonight when I'm ready I'll call you."

I went to my room and tried to think. If this was for real, if
this time she was actually going to do it, was there anything I
needed to consider? Feelings, emotions? My feelings for Marie
were fairly reconciled. I came into this world out of her body,
or the physical me did, so there was that kind of blood bond,
but I didn't like her as a person. I was ashamed of her as a
mother. I wouldn't miss her.

In a kind of gruesome test, I slipped the bag over my head
for size and found that it barely covered my neck. I could see
the scarf not quite grasping enough of it to completely cut off
the air and the final act getting messy. Marie would struggle,
even zonked on Xanax, and she would be clawing the thing to
get free, to breathe. The Hemlock Society book said that this
was common. I could see myself trying to hold her hands down
or, frozen, just standing there, watching. If she scratched herself
or I somehow bruised her, that might look bad to a coroner. It
might look like murder. And to some degree it would be. The
word hung in my mind. Murder. A vague image, the word itself
had no resonance. But helping to end someone's life, no matter
how sick and sad and miserable, is helping to kill a human
being. And in this instance, if it came about, I would be helping
to kill my own mother. Could I do it? More precisely, at the last
moment would I?

I drove to town and got a box of slightly larger plastic bags.
If it was going to be done, the bag should be the right size, not
too small. The last act should go smoothly, not with a struggle,
not with my hands fighting hers, the meanness of that. I
stopped at a liquor store and got a bottle of vodka. Might need
something to fuzz the edges afterward. It would be my first
drink in months.

It was now about three in the afternoon. I tapped at her door and went in, a rare visit. I'd been in her room perhaps three times in two years. She was sitting in her chair watching her daily soap operas. For the past two and a half years I'd provided this place for her in my house, a room perhaps twenty by twenty feet, also a sort of efficiency setup with cooking facilities, a refrigerator, and an adjoining bath. In this one room she stayed alone and kept to herself. She never left the house. She'd leave a list of the groceries and medicine she'd needed along with a signed check on the kitchen table, and I would shop for her. Her Social Security was just enough to pay for what she wanted. She'd show me her bank statement at the end of every month with only five or ten dollars left in her account. When we talked, it was usually when she was in the kitchen and I also happened to be there. But it wouldn't be a conversation. She might ask my opinion on the weather or some TV news item. Typically she'd say, "Do you think it's going to rain today?" I'd start to answer, "Well, no, I think—" and she'd immediately interrupt to disagree:

"That's what the weatherman says but they don't know. They said it was going to rain yesterday, there wasn't a cloud in the sky. I don't think they have any idea what the weather's going to be. I was going to make a salad, but I don't want to, I just don't have the interest. Nothing I fix tastes good anyway. I made a stew yesterday, it was like slop. I had to throw it all out. The arthritis in my hand is so bad, I took four of those pain pills, they didn't help a bit, I don't know what I'm going to do. I was going to make some macaroni and cheese but I don't even want that now. Those ratty kids next door were playing so loud, hollering and carrying on, I couldn't hear myself think. I wish that family'd move away, they're nothing but white trash. I saw the woman out in her yard yesterday wearing shorts, with big ol' fat legs, I'd be ashamed . . . "

She would talk like that forever if I listened. For about a minute I'd pretend to, then I'd simply walk away. If she began with a good word, her next word would qualify it and she'd end up carping. She didn't like herself or, worse, she hated herself, and the way it showed was depressing.

Now I stood in her room. "How 'bout a visit?" I said. She got up from her chair.

"Here, sit down."

"That's all right," I said; she only had the one chair.

"No, no, you sit here, I need to move anyway." She sat on the edge of her bed and I sat in the chair facing her. The room was dirty and cluttered. I'd offered to vacuum her carpet, but she said the noise drove her crazy and she didn't want me moving things around in there. I told her she didn't have to hear the noise, she could wait in the living room, but she said it was too bothersome. "Just leave it. I'll do it," she said. And never did. The carpet was spotted and matted where she'd spilled food.

"Well," I said, and that was all.

"It's going to be all right," she said. "Don't you worry."

She was decided. It was time. She was sick and it was probably a consumptive heart condition, that's what her father died of, and with that you don't get better, you just get worse. She'd read up on the symptoms in her medical book—it starts with a shortness of breath and your stomach, you can't keep food down. That's what was happening to her. Then it affected your kidneys and liver, they turned to mush, and you became bedridden and couldn't go to the bathroom or feed yourself— you couldn't eat anything anyway—and you'd just lie there in agony and finally die. So she was ready.

"Now, one thing I want you to do," she said, "I don't want you to tell my sister, or at least wait till you've gotten rid of all my stuff, 'cause she'll just be over here in a minute picking through all my clothes and taking everything, and I don't want her to have anything. Promise you won't tell her. Or I don't care, do what you want, but I'm telling you, I know how she'll do, you don't know how selfish she is."

And so on about how her sister had always taken and not given and had plenty of money and could afford to buy a new car every year and everything else she wanted. No forgiveness. About my brother and me, she said that she wished she'd made a home for us, that she knew she'd messed us up, especially

Billy, she knew he'd been the most hurt, but that it was too late now, she couldn't go back and change what happened, and she'd already cried herself out; she hadn't cried tears now in years. She'd made a mess of her own life too, but she couldn't change that either.

I'd heard it all before, the regrets, the bad times. I kept hoping she would finally declare some peace of mind or settled spirit. She didn't. I tried to remember some good moments we'd had together, some things I could mention so we could end with easier feelings. I couldn't think of one. She probably loved me the best she could, but if there was a time when I was small that she hugged me, that I felt the warmth of a mother's embrace, I couldn't remember that either. So I sat while she talked. She had lived a lifetime. But at the end of a life, after eighty years of awareness, hopes, desires, after only one chance at this world as we know it, shouldn't there be a final comprehension, a summing up, a point at least for having been? You live, for what? I wanted her to say what living had meant to her, but she was talking incidentals: her extra glasses, they were good prescription glasses someone could use, don't throw those away.

She had put a clean cover on the bed and she was going to dress in a nice clean gown. Should she wash her hair? No, she didn't need to. I could donate her clothes to charity or just burn them, but don't let her sister have any. She had already thrown away a bunch of junk and straightened the room all she could. Straightening tired her out. She said to tell Billy she was sorry but that she couldn't go back and make things different, and me, well, I could handle this, couldn't I? I told her truthfully that I didn't know. But she knew, she said, because I was always able to handle whatever came along, I never let problems bother me, did I? Well, problems are problems, I said. But she knew that I could help her die, that I wouldn't let it bother me. She was sorry she didn't stick with my father, but she just couldn't. She wanted to have fun, and then her life became such a mess. She never intended to leave us kids. She married other men so she could have a home for us, but it never turned out, she never got what she wanted, which was just to be happy and for us kids to be happy, but she couldn't help any of that now, she couldn't go back. She was just sorry about this and that and so on. She spoke, as usual, remorsefully, self-pityingly, but not exactly bitterly. It was as if she recited it all by rote: things happened, she could have done differently, but it wasn't always her fault either, and then it was always too late. After the fact, it was always too late. She voiced no new insight, no particular understanding. I felt depressed, and after about an hour I got up. I'd be back later, I said, and we could talk more then. Well, don't worry about me, she said, I'll call you when I'm ready, about eleven o'clock.

I went to my room and tried to read. It was five o'clock and I began to feel it was going to be a long night. She wouldn't do it, or she would fake it. She was involving me in another of her emotional dramas. I might have to call the EMS. She was only going to become more disoriented, more helpless. I should probably start thinking about placing her in a nursing home.

At six-thirty she was at my door.

"I can't think about it anymore," she said. "I want to just go on and do it, is that all right with you?"

"If you're ready."

"Well, I'm ready. I keep sitting back there thinking about it. Now, you've got the bag? And the scarf—don't forget the scarf."

"They're right here."

"All right, let's get it over with."

We walked through the kitchen. She was hobbling feebly. I asked her if she'd eaten.

"Not since this morning. I'm afraid I'll throw up."

"But shouldn't you have something on your stomach, to keep the pills down? How about a little buttered toast?"

"I don't know, not buttered, maybe just a piece of dry toast."

I put a slice of bread in the toaster and followed her into her room. She sat on the edge of the bed.

"Now, here's what I'm going to take," she said. A couple of pill bottles stood on her bedside table.

"This one's fifty Wygesic, they're my pain pills, they might help. These are Xanax, the ones you got today, and I had some more. There's a hundred and thirty-eight altogether. That ought to do it if I don't get too drowsy and fall asleep before I can take them all."

"You're going to take a hundred and thirty-eight pills?"

"If I can get them down. And the Wygesic too, if I can swallow enough water. I've got a pitcherful over there, you'll have to get that for me."

She was opening the pill bottles. I felt numb.

"Wait a minute." I brought the toast from the kitchen on a napkin. "Get this on your stomach first."

She forced herself to chew several bites slowly, sipping also at a glass of water. She ate about half the toast, then immediately poured a few pills into her hand and swallowed them with water. She took another handful and another, one after the other as if on automatic. She was concentrating solely on what she was doing and not looking beyond her hands. Then her glass was empty.

"More water, more water!" Almost panicky. I got the pitcher and filled her glass.

"Hey, go slower," I said. "Take your time."

"I don't want to fall asleep before I get them down."

"It's okay, okay? Take it easy."

She drew a breath and downed several more pills. She took off her glasses and laid them on the table.

"Don't throw those away, they're good prescriptions, somebody can use them."

She swallowed more pills. I was only sitting in front of her, watching. A terrible feeling came over me, a weight of darkness. Here was this old, lonely woman actually going to die, killing herself. This was the last moment she would ever know, a worthless, measly last moment in a dismal, cluttered room in central Texas. She would never again see the two squirrels in the tree outside her window. Or the sky, the sun, the rain. This earth, this great, beautiful earth around her would be no more. She was going to die and nothing would be all. I had no words for what I felt except pity. Poor old woman.

"Marie," I said, "let me hug you."

I stood and leaned down to put my arms around her shoulders, my cheek against hers. I think she sort of patted my arm.

"I love you," I said.

"I love you, too."

I sat back in the chair. It was the first time I'd hugged her in years, and even in those years a quick hug was a mere politeness. This time was almost the same. It had not been exactly awkward but neither had it felt natural. My words, I love you, had been what, perfunctory? Hers to me had sounded the same. There had been no clutch of emotion. She immediately went back to taking her pills, hurriedly, several at a time, one swallow after another, downing them with water. I filled her glass three times. She never looked up. We didn't speak.

Then she did. "Well, that's it."

She had swallowed 138 Xanax and 20 or so Wygesic. She started to lie back on her pillow and stopped.

"Turn your back. I'm going to put a towel between my legs. The book said people lose their bowels when they're going, and I don't want to make a mess."

I turned my head. When I looked again, she was lying on her back, the end of a towel showed between her knees. She had folded her hands on her stomach.

"Now I'm going to count," she said. "That's what I do to put myself to sleep. I read that once and it works. I start at a hundred and count backwards. I never get to one. I can get to twenty, fifteen sometimes, then I'm always asleep."

She closed her eyes and started counting in a normal voice. "Ninety-nine . . . ninety-eight . . . ninety-seven . . ."

She counted as if by seconds, steadily, correctly. By eighty-five, her count had slowed, and she was several seconds between numbers. After eighty, she said, seventy-eight, paused at length, picked up the slipped seventy-nine, and continued with seventy-eight, but more slowly. Her words were slurring. At sixty-six, I thought she was asleep. She'd stopped counting. Finally she managed to repeat sixty-six and that was it. She was breathing deeply and snoring intermittently with her mouth slightly open.

It was seven o'clock and beginning to get dark outside. I closed the curtains. I felt inept not to have closed them earlier. Then I didn't know how long to wait or if I should wait at all. I watched Marie breathing. If I touched her or shook her, would it rouse her? The Xanax might not have worked. She might suddenly wake. How long would it take before she was so absolutely doped there would be no chance of waking her? I imagined the moment I started to put the bag over her head, she would open her eyes. I waited perhaps fifteen minutes, then went to my room for the bag and scarf and came back. She had not moved. Her mouth was still slightly open, and she was breathing the same, softly snoring, her hands at rest on her stomach. I lifted one of them and it fell back. I nudged her shoulder. No reaction. I called her name, then louder, and shook her. No response. I walked through the house to shut the blinds and lock the doors. I took the phone off the receiver. If anyone knocked or called, I wouldn't be home. Did I need to think of anything else? I couldn't think.

The bag was not a difficulty. I lifted her head from the pillow and slipped the plastic over easily, in a single movement. I did it as gently as I could and felt no weight in her head at all. Her neck was limber, entirely relaxed. Lifting her head again, I overlapped the loose ends of the bag and wrapped the scarf evenly twice around. But not tightly. I felt an odd tenderness and sadness. Poor Marie, I thought, your whole life so damned unhappy. I felt sorry for her. I snugged at the scarf to be sure it was trapping the air.

I stood over her and watched the bag filling and being drawn back against the outlines of her face, and for a time there was nothing else. Her breathing appeared easy, but soon it was slightly harder and the bag was being sucked tighter at her mouth. Her hands started to lift and I stopped them. She didn't struggle. Her hands didn't resist mine and she didn't strain or move. There was no strength or force in her. She was only breathing harder and lying completely still. Then she quietly stopped breathing. I waited. In another moment, her chin ticked and she almost drew a half breath. That was all. The bag was collapsed and molded against her face. Her body had not convulsed or shuddered. There was no sudden absence in the room. It seemed only that she was no longer entirely present. She might have still been alive. I thought I felt a faint pulse at her wrist and under my palm on her chest the bare tremor of a heartbeat. I wasn't sure. But I needed to be sure so I waited. Perhaps five minutes. She remained absolutely inert. I loosed the scarf and pulled the bag from her head. Marie Brett had died at 7:25 in the evening, April 19, 1995. The big news that day was the bombing of the Federal Building in Oklahoma City.

I pulled the towel from between her legs. It was not soiled. I stuffed it and the plastic bag and the scarf and the pill bottles under a wad in the trash. There was nothing else to clear away.

I opened the blinds and unlocked the doors and put the phone back on the receiver, then mixed a vodka drink and sat in my room. It was 8:30. I would wait awhile to call the police. I needed to get set in my mind what I would tell them and how I would act. Anyway, it was over. I didn't feel easy. It seemed an oppressive weight might soon lift, but mostly what I felt was depressed. The drink made me lighter, but I was still tense. A friend called from Austin. I didn't mention Marie. We talked of nothing in particular, joked. After hanging up, I realized I had laughed too loudly. I would need to control myself better. I mixed another drink.

About 9:30 I called the police, said I didn't know if I should call them, but I thought my mother had died in her sleep. The police arrived within minutes and called in the coroner, a local justice of the peace. I told the coroner my mother had deteriorated rapidly the last weeks, that she'd had a consumptive heart condition, shortness of breath, stomach problems. He took a cursory look at her, pronounced her dead from natural causes, and called the mortuary. They arrived and Marie's body was taken away. I gave the mortuary man her birth certificate and Social Security number and told him cremation. He asked about embalming. I said no. How about a service? No, none of that, I said, just the simplest, quickest way.

Then they were gone. Marie was gone, and the whole last business was finished. The house was suddenly stone quiet. I felt an odd, distant loss. Or I can't say exactly what I felt. I needed to get drunk, I thought. I poured my drink out instead. My mother, I thought, the one person I'd known my whole life, she'd given me life. But I always only knew her as Marie. I never called her mother and she never called me son.

THE ACCIDENT

Daniel Oberti

From the *San Francisco Examiner*, Wednesday, June 24, 1953. The caption underneath a photo of a "Perilous Rescue of Mother from Cliff" reads:

"A woman near death from injuries was raised in a 'Stokes' basket stretcher from the rocky surf, 150 feet below Sutro Baths yesterday afternoon. The seriously injured mother of three lies in the stretcher as rescuers stand in the surf and others on the cliff's edge guide the ropes raising her to the top."

My mother was a very kind woman who never spoke of others in a negative way. She could always find a good quality to emphasize. She was, however, deeply troubled. My father, who operated a ravioli company in San Francisco, was a womanizing heavy drinker when I was young. After I was born my mother suffered two miscarriages and a stillbirth. All this was weighing on her when one day she left me home with the measles to shop for a model airplane to lift my spirits.

She never returned. Late that afternoon Dad came home and told my sister and me that Mom had had an accident. Shocked and fearful, we went to the hospital to see her. I'll never forget the smell of the place, the clanging brass gate on the elevator, the starched white nurses, the polished leather shoes of the doctors, the height of the bed. She had "fallen" off Lands End into the pounding surf of the Pacific Ocean. Her face had stitches over black and swollen eyes, her arm was in a cast, her leg in traction, her entire body jagged, her spirit muttering, "Oh God help me."

It was always called "the accident." Eventually she came home to a hospital bed set up in our TV room. There I remember talking with a stranger. I was nine years old, deeply wounded, and only wanting my mom back. We had house helpers who I detested.

I recall one evening that haunted me for many, many years. Dad was arguing with Mom as I lay in bed late one evening. He was so loud that I came down to stop him. Fearful, I stopped at the stair landing and crouched with my blanket. Thumb stuck in my mouth, afraid to go any farther, I listened and wept. The sharpness of his voice, the confusion and the terror, froze me in place, unable to go up or down the stairs.

From that moment on, a part of me hated my father. I blamed him and turtled up in a shell of insecurity. But life went on. In and out of institutions, Mom was diagnosed manic-depressive, suffered shock treatments, lithium, countless hours of therapy, and finally, under medication, was home and resumed a "normal" life.

Dad had gone into AA and never again imbibed. He kept a full liquor cabinet above the cooler and still hosted family dinners. It wasn't until my early forties that I realized that the dreadful evening of argument I clutched onto with such hatred was during my father's first few days of sobriety.

I was two years clean of alcohol myself when it occurred to me that he had been working through early sobriety. I forgave him. I forgave myself and began a glimmer of understanding which to this day still lifts my spirits and encourages me on a path of acceptance.

Dad passed on in the 1970s after a long struggle with cancer. Mom was shifted from one rest home to another. She

John and Linda Updike, Morgantown, Pennsylvania, 1988 (Carole Sherr)

LEFT: Peter Najarian's mother, Zaroohe, making patties (Karina Epperlein)

ABOVE: Peter Najarian's painting of Zaroohe as a young girl, based on her passport photo, circa 1920

Gus Lee's *mah-mee* Da-tsien Lee

Fannie, Norman Sasowsky's mother

Timothy Beneke between his brother
Richard and their mother, Lillian Beneke

Nick Davis and Johanna Davis, about six years before her death

Elsie Procter Matthews

Josephine (Josie) Duberman at seventy-four, in the last year of her life

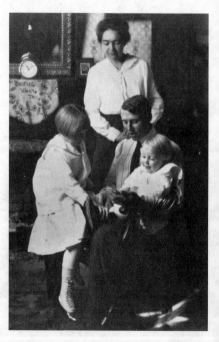

Allan Wheelis, one year old, with sister, June, mother, Olive, and father, A. B. Wheelis

Esther "Sunny" Blauner in her eightieth-birthday dress

Bob Blauner's two mothers, Molly and "Sunny" (Molly at left; "Sunny" at right)

Gary Young's mother, Jeanne Ewing, as a
girl in 1943; her sister is at left

Andrew Solomon's mother, Carolyn,
one week before her death

Daniel Oberti's drawing of his mother, Alice, on Christmas, 1989.

With love
mother.

Hilda Stegner, Wallace's mother

Samuel G. Freedman at a wedding with his sister, Carole,
mother, Eleanor, and father, David

Rafael Jesús González's mother, Carmen, the year of her wedding

Fred Moramarco's two mothers: Nina Moramarco and sister Nicolette

Nina Moramarco: a picture of innocence and romantic idealism

ABOVE: Peggy Wellman with
Vickie and David, circa 1954

RIGHT: Peggy Wellman looks on
as daughter Vickie signs her
son's cast, Detroit, 1956

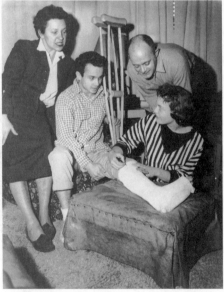

Lucha Quintana, the mother of Juan Felipe Herrera,
Chihuahua, Mexico, circa 1936

Mother and son, Helen and Mark O'Brien

Steve Masover bakes a cake for his mother Bonnie's fifty-fifth—her last—birthday

Margaret and John Boe

J. Herman Blake's mother, Lylace, and his grandmother
in their Mount Vernon home, circa 1956

Sheila and T. George Harris, Gardiner's parents, 1969

Carol Walter and her son Jess,
dancing at his wedding

would spend weekends with me on occasion. Her gentle manner was always present except for those bouts of wildness she would engage in until the doctors could subdue her.

The last ten years of her life she was under constant care. I visited her only sporadically. It was too painful. Little by little she began to fade. During the last two years she was extremely passive, detached. I would visit now more often and just sit with her. At times she didn't know who I was. Then I began to draw her. I would sit and sketch her and feel her presence. I knew her spirit was responsive. I felt closer to her now.

Somehow her inability to speak led us to a higher level of communing. I would feed her and simply watch her drift back to slumber. I knew somehow it was not for me to judge or assume I could reach her consciously.

She became smaller and more and more frail. My sketches embraced her skin. Each wrinkle had meaning, her hair, still silver, thinly covered her crown. Her breath still supporting, I paused.

Two days after I had listened to Ram Dass speak on the death of his father, the call came. When I arrived, her heart rate was extreme and her breathing was one gasp, followed by a deafening silence, followed by another gasp at life's essence. I held her feet, knowing that grounding her in the here and now would assist her. Her pulse regulated and her breathing became more metered. Ever so gently she calmed, gracefully she eased her way into a sublime moment of utter and complete peace. I was with her. I was with her through and beyond that moment for quite some time.

The next day I bought a beautiful white linen suit and wore it through the wake and funeral services. In a private moment I sang a hymn I had written, "Graceful Lady Tranquil Time." Feeling clearly, there were no burdens on my mind.

Two years passed and I still wondered about her fall. I went to the San Francisco Library and researched the frightful images that I had seen as a young boy. Rereading the newspaper coverage, I saw how some of the words and images must have struck me so profoundly that they had stayed with me over the years.

"Stokes" basket, the young firefighter William MacGurn who had gone headfirst to rescue her, the fact that the Coast Guard, the police and fire departments were all used had a powerful effect on a small boy. My father's words when he identified her at Mission Emergency reverberated with me also; I had pondered them for many years. "What has happened to you?"

Later that day I visited, for the first time, the cliffs at Lands End to sit and to meditate. To somehow put to rest the frightful memory. As I searched out the exact spot where she fell, I was taken by the awesome power of the vast Pacific Ocean entering the Golden Gate and the overwhelming beauty that Point Lobos provides its pilgrims.

I was a pilgrim on a path of understanding. Yet when I climbed closer to the edge, I was clear that my head would never fully comprehend what had happened. But into my heart there slowly entered compassion and understanding that the mystery of her experience is an event she shares with God alone.

Were I unstable and wrought with an overwhelming sadness and loss, I myself would seek such a place to pray. In the intoxication of sea spray, with the vista of eternal deep, with the cry of the lone seagull, the sound of the beckoning wave, my sincerest desire would be surrender of spirit, oneness with the cosmos and union with a Power so far greater than mine.

Vertigo. I could imagine how faint my body would feel. How simple and natural it would be to allow feeling to overwhelm the instincts of balance and control. The fear of falling simply would not exist in conscious mind and as I plummeted, fear would give way to complete trust in God, "free fall," absolute surrender, fulfillment and union in an instant of weightless experience.

Such a fleeting moment surely ended with the crashing reality of stone and rock, sea and wind, helpless delirium and physical terror. Yet the clutching hand of life desire brought words of gratitude and adoration to sustain this daughter's life.

Spirit provided the strength to carry her through the physical and I believe her heart was united with the oneness of wisdom, grace, and love.

PART 5

REGRET

After a loved one dies, feelings of regret are common, perhaps inevitable. There is always something we wanted to say or do, something in our life we wanted the deceased to live to see us accomplish. But regret is just one of the many feelings that are part of grieving. It is usually not as primary an emotion as it is for the five sons who tell their stories in this chapter.

Wallace Stegner's "Letter, Much Too Late" is laced with the guilt of his failure to express his love to his mother before she died, fifty-five years earlier, when the writer was twenty-five years old. Samuel G. Freedman also lost his mother fairly young. (He was nineteen.) Today he regrets "the selfishness and mean spirit of my imagined manhood," which compelled him to push her away, even during her final illness. Art Buchwald regrets the "matricide" he committed every time he told people his mother was dead, rather than in a mental institution—and above all the fact that he never went to see his dying mother in the hospital, nor did he attend her funeral.

For Rafael Jesús González it is the *way* his mother died in the hospital and was interred that he most regrets; both hospital deaths and contemporary mortuary practices are foreign to the rich Mexican Catholic tradition that was her heritage. Henry Louis Gates, Jr., has somewhat similar concerns: his mother chose to be buried in the new white cemetery, which the author finds soulless and sanitized. In the "colored cemetery," on the other hand, her death and glory might have been properly celebrated.

Regret. An emotion that is so much a part of life, especially as we grow older. As the poet David Ray writes, speaking for all of us, "If I had loved her enough, nothing else would have mattered."

SURROGATE

David Ray

On a visit to the hospice
I notice an old woman playing

the piano, and all the love lost
from my mother comes welling

back up, so long lost
I had forgotten I once loved her.

She never played the piano,
of course, and there's some doubt

how much love she ever could manage.
But I leave grieving. If I had loved

her enough, nothing else
would have mattered. I'd have taken

no note of her failures. I look back
over the years, seeking the date

of the great power failure, when our
    hearts
froze and were left in cold storage,
    forgotten.

Maybe it was the year we fled to the
    cellar,
the sky black with dirt and rubble.

Maybe it was one of those nights
when her sobs outlasted the rain

and I could not help her, this woman
who still tortures me by her absence

and by her ghost who has learned to play
the piano. And I cannot help her with that
    either.

LETTER, MUCH TOO LATE

Wallace Stegner

Mom, listen.

In three months I will be eighty years old, thirty years older than you were when you died, twenty years older than my father was when he died, fifty-seven years older than my brother was when *he* died. I got the genes and the luck. The rest of you have been gone a long time.

Except when I have to tie my shoelaces, I don't feel eighty years old. I, the sickly child, have outlasted you all. But if I don't feel decrepit, neither do I feel wise or confident. Age and experience have not made me a Nestor qualified to tell others about how to live their lives. I feel more like Theodore Dreiser who confessed that he would depart from life more bewildered than he had arrived in it. Instead of being embittered, or stoical, or calm, or resigned, or any of the standard things that a long life might have made me, I confess that I am often simply lost, as much in need of comfort, understanding, forgiveness, uncritical love—the things you used to give me—as I ever was at five, or ten, or fifteen.

Fifty-five years ago, sitting up with you after midnight while the nurse rested, I watched you take your last breath. A few minutes before you died you half raised your head and said, "Which ... way?" I understood that: you were at a dark, unmarked crossing. Then a minute later you said, "You're a good ... boy ... Wallace," and died.

My name was the last word you spoke, your faith in me and love for me were your last thoughts. I could bear them no better than I could bear your death, and I went blindly out into the November darkness and walked for hours with my mind clenched like a fist.

I knew how far from true your last words were. There had been plenty of times when I had not been a good boy or a thoughtful one. I knew you could no longer see my face, that you spoke from a clouded, drugged dream, that I had already faded to a memory that you clung to even while you waned from life. I knew that it was love speaking, not you, that you had already gone, that your love lasted longer than you yourself did. And I had some dim awareness that as you went away you laid on me an immense and unavoidable obligation. I would never get over trying, however badly or sadly or confusedly, to be what you thought I was.

Obviously you did not die. Death is a convention, a certification to the end of pain, something for the vital-statistics book, not binding upon anyone but the keepers of graveyard records. For as I sit here at the desk, trying to tell you something fifty-five years too late, I have a clear mental image of your pursed lips and your crinkling eyes, and I know that nothing I can say will persuade you that I was ever less than you thought me. Your kind of love, once given, is never lost. You are alive and luminous in my head. Except when I fail to listen, you will speak through me when I face some crisis of feeling or sympathy or consideration for others. You are a curb on my natural impatience and competitiveness and arrogance. When I have been less than myself, you make me ashamed even as you forgive me. You're a good ... boy ... Wallace.

In the more than fifty years that I have been writing books and stories, I have tried several times to do you justice, and have never been satisfied with what I did. The character who represents you in *The Big Rock Candy Mountain* and *Recapitulations*, two novels of a semiautobiographical kind, is a sort of passive victim. I am afraid I let your selfish and violent husband, my father, steal the scene from you and push you into the background in the novels as he did in life. Somehow I should have been able to say how strong and resilient you were, what a patient and abiding and bonding force, the softness that proved in the long run stronger than what it seemed to yield to.

But you must understand that you are the hardest sort of human character to make credible on paper. We are skeptical of kindness so unfailing, sympathy so instant and constant, trouble so patiently borne, forgiveness so wholehearted. Writing about you I felt always on the edge of the unbelievable, as if I were writing a saint's life, or the legend of some Patient Griselda. I felt that I should warp you a little, give you some human failing or selfish motive; for saintly qualities, besides looking sentimental on the page, are a rebuke to those—and they are most of us—who have failed at them.

Some, I suppose, are born unselfish, some achieve unselfishness, and some have unselfishness thrust upon them. You used to tell me that you were born with a redheaded temper, and had to learn to control it. I think you were also born with a normal complement of dreams and hopes and desires and a great capacity for intellectual and cultural growth, and had to learn to suppress them.

Your life gave you plenty of practice in both controlling and suppressing. You were robbed of your childhood, and as a young, inexperienced woman you made a fatal love choice. But you blamed no one but yourself. You lay in the bed you had made, partly because, as a woman, and without much education, you had few options, and partly because your morality counseled responsibility for what you did, but mostly because love told you your highest obligation was to look after your two boys and the feckless husband who needed you more even than they did. Your reward, all too often, was to be taken for granted.

Just now, thinking about you, I got out *The Big Rock Candy Mountain* and found the passage in which I wrote of your death. I couldn't bear to read it. It broke me down in tears to read the words that I wrote in tears nearly half a century ago. You are at once a lasting presence and an unhealed wound.

I was twenty-four, still a schoolboy, when you died, but I have lived with you more than three times twenty-four years. Self-obsessed, sports crazy or book crazy or girl crazy or otherwise preoccupied, I never got around to telling you during your lifetime how much you meant. Except in those moments when your life bore down on you with particular weight, as when my brother, Cece, died and you turned to me because you had no one else, I don't suppose I realized how much you meant. Now I feel mainly regret, regret that I took you for granted as the others did, regret that you were dead by the time my life began to expand, so that I was unable to take you along and compensate you a little for your first fifty years.

I began this rumination in a dark mood, remembering the anniversary of your death. Already you have cheered me up. I have said that you didn't die, and you didn't. I can still hear you being cheerful on the slightest provocation, or no provocation at all, singing as you work and shedding your cheerfulness on others. So let us remember your life, such a life as many women of your generation shared to some extent, though not always with your special trials and rarely with your stoicism and grace.

I have heard enough about your childhood and youth to know how life went on that Iowa farm and in the town where everybody spoke Norwegian, read Norwegian, did business in Norwegian, heard Norwegian in church. Though your father was born in this country, you did not learn English until you started school. You learned it eagerly. Some of our mutual relatives, after five generations in the United States, still speak with an accent, but you never did. You loved reading, and you sang all the time: you knew the words to a thousand songs. When I was in college I was astonished to discover that some songs I had heard you sing as you worked around the house were lyrics from Tennyson's *The Princess*. Maybe you got the words from *McGuffey's Reader*. Where you got the tunes, God knows. You always made the most of what little was offered you, and you kept hold of it.

School was your happy time, with friends, games, parties, the delight of learning. You had it for only six years. When you were twelve, your mother died of tuberculosis and you became an instant adult: housekeeper to your father, mother to your two younger brothers and sister, farmhand when not otherwise employed. All through the years when you should have had the chance to be girlish, even frivolous, you had responsibilities that would have broken down most adults.

Many farm wives had a "hired girl." You did not. You were it, you did it all. At twelve, thirteen, fourteen, you made beds, cleaned, cooked, sewed, mended, for a family of five. You baked the bread, biscuits, cakes, pies, in a cranky coal range. You made the *lefse* and *fattigmand* and prepared the *lutefish* without which a Norwegian Christmas is not Christmas. You washed all the clothes, and I don't mean you put lightly soiled clothes into a washing machine. I mean you boiled and scrubbed dirty farm clothes with only the copper boiler, tin tub, brass washboard, harsh soap, and hand wringer of the 1890s — one long back-breaking day every week.

At harvest time you often worked in the field most of the morning and then came in to cook dinner for the crew. You were over a hot stove in a suffocating kitchen for hours at a time, canning peas, beans, corn, tomatoes, putting up cucumber and watermelon pickles or piccalilli. When a hog was slaughtered, you swallowed your nausea and caught the blood for the blood pudding your father relished. You pickled pigs' feet and made headcheese. You fried and put down in crocks of their own lard the sausage patties that would last all winter. Morning and evening you helped with the milking. You skimmed the cream and churned the butter in the dasher churn, you hung cheesecloth bags of curd on the clothesline to drip and become cottage cheese.

I am sure there were times when you bitterly resented your bond-servant life, when you thumped your lazy and evasive brothers, or sent hot glances at your father where he sat reading *Scandinaven* in the parlor, totally unaware of you as you staggered in with a scuttle of coal and set it down loudly by the heater, and opened the heater door and lifted the scuttle and fed the fire and set the scuttle down again and slammed the heater door with a bang. Those were the years when you had unselfishness thrust upon you; you had not yet got through the difficult process of achieving it.

But however you might rebel, there was no shedding your siblings. They were your responsibility and there was no one to relieve you of them. They called you Sis. All your life people called you Sis, because that was what you were, or what you became—big sister, helpful sister, the one upon whom everyone depended, the one they all came to for everything from help with homework to a sliver under the fingernail.

Six years of that, at the end of which your father announced that he was going to marry a school friend of yours, a girl barely older than yourself. I wonder if it was outrage that drove you from his house, or if your anger was not lightened by the perception that here at last was freedom and opportunity. You were eighteen, a tall, strong, direct-eyed girl with a pile of gorgeous red hair. In the tintypes of the time you look determined. You do not yet have the sad mouth your last photographs show. Maybe the world then seemed all before you, your imprisonment over.

But nobody had prepared you for opportunity and freedom. Nobody had taught you to dream big. You couldn't have imagined going to Chicago or New York or winning your way, you could never have dreamed of becoming an actress or the editor of a women's magazine. They had only taught you, and most of that you had learned on your own, to keep house and to look after others. You were very good at both. So when you were displaced as your father's housekeeper, you could think of nothing better to do with your freedom than to go to North Dakota and keep house for a bachelor uncle.

There you met something else they had not prepared you for, a man unlike any you had ever seen, a husky, laughing, reckless, irreverent, storytelling charmer, a ballplayer, a fancy skater, a trapshooting champion, a pursuer of the main chance, a true rolling stone who confidently expected to be eventually covered with moss. He was marking time between get-rich-quick schemes by running a "blind pig"—an illegal saloon. He offended every piety your father stood for. Perhaps that was why you married him, against loud protests from home. Perhaps your father was as much to blame as anyone for the mistake you made.

You had a stillborn child. Later you had a living one, my brother Cecil. Later still, on a peacemaking visit back to Iowa, you had me. Then, as you told me once, you discovered how not to have any more, and didn't. You had enough to be responsible for with two.

Dakota I don't remember. My memories begin in the woods of Washington, where we lived in a tent and ran a lunchroom in the logging town of Redmond. By getting scarlet fever, I had balked my father's dream of going to Alaska and digging up baseball-sized nuggets. Then there was a bad time. You left my father, or he you; nobody ever told me. But Cece and I found ourselves in a Seattle orphans' home, put there while you worked at the Bon Marché. In 1913 you didn't have a chance as a husbandless woman with two children. When you found how miserable we were in that home, you took us out and brought us back to the only safety available, your father's house in Iowa.

I can imagine what that cost you in humiliation. I can imagine the letters that must have passed between you and my father. I can imagine his promises, your concessions. At any rate, in June 1914 we were on our way to join him in the valley of Whitemud, or Frenchman, River in Saskatchewan. Perhaps it sounded romantic and adventurous to you, perhaps you let yourself listen to his come-all-ye enthusiasm, perhaps you thought that on a real frontier he might be happy and do well. Very probably you hoped that in a raw village five hundred miles from anywhere we could make a new start and be a family, something for which you had both a yearning and a gift. If you went in resignation, this time your resignation was not forced on you. It was a choice. By 1914, at the age of thirty-one, you had finally achieved unselfishness.

Saskatchewan is the richest page in my memory, for that was where I first began to understand some things, and that was where, for a half dozen years, we had what you had always wanted: a house of our own, a united family, and a living, however hard.

I think you loved that little burg in spite of its limitations. You loved having neighbors, visiting with neighbors, helping neighbors. When it was our turn to host the monthly Sunday school party, you had more fun than the kids, playing crocinole or beanbag like the child you had never been allowed to be. You loved the times when the river froze without wind or snow, and the whole channel was clean, skatable ice, and the town gathered around big night fires, and skaters in red mackinaws and bright scarfs moved like Brueghel figures across the light, and firelight glinted off eyeballs and teeth, and the breath of the community went up in white plumes.

You loved having your children in a steady school, and doing well in it. You read all the books you could lay hands on. When your North Dakota uncle died and left you a thousand dollars you didn't let my father take it, though I am sure he would have found a use for it. Instead, you bought a Sears, Roebuck piano and you set my brother and me to learn to play it under the instruction of the French doctor's wife. Alas, we disappointed you, resisted practice, dawdled and fooled around. Eventually you gave up. But you could no more let that piano sit there unused than you could throw perfectly good apple peelings out to the pig. You learned to play it yourself, painstakingly working things out chord by chord from the sheet music of popular songs. How hungry you were! How you would have responded to the opportunities ignored by so many who have them.

Many good days. Also, increasingly, bad ones. Hard times. While you lived your way deeper into the remote and limited place where my father's enthusiasm had brought you, he felt more and more trapped in what he called "this dirty little dung-heeled sagebrush town." Eventually he got his way, and we abandoned what little you had been able to get together as a life. During the next fourteen years you lived in much greater comfort, and you saw a lot of the western United States. You continued to make a home for your boys and your husband, but it was a cheerless home for you. We lived in a dozen towns and cities, three dozen neighborhoods, half a hundred houses. My brother and I kept some continuity through school and the friends we made there, but your continuity was cut every few months; you lost friends and never saw them again, or got the chance to make new ones, or have a kitchen where women could drop in and have a cup of coffee and a chat.

You believed in all the beauties and strengths and human associations of place; my father believed only in movement. You believed in a life of giving, he in a life of getting. When Cecil died at the age of twenty-three, you did not have a single woman friend to whom you could talk, not a single family of neighbors or friends to help you bear the loss of half your loving life.

You're a good ... boy ... Wallace. That shames me. You had little in your life to judge goodness by. I was not as dense or as selfish as my father, and I got more credit than I deserved. But I was not intelligent enough to comprehend the kind of example you had been setting me, until it was too late to do anything but hold your hand while you died. And here I am, nearly eighty years old, too old to be capable of any significant improvement but not too old for regret.

"All you can do is try," you used to tell me when I was scared of undertaking something. You got me to undertake many things I would not have dared undertake without your encouragement. You also taught me how to take defeat when it came, and it was bound to now and then. You taught me that if it hadn't killed me it was probably good for me.

I can hear you laugh while you say it. Any minute now I will hear you singing.

A MOTHER'S PRESENCE

Samuel G. Freedman

I have never visited my mother's grave. I know, of course, where her body lies, in a cemetery along a road I have traveled hundreds of times in the nine years since she died.

And even now, I can see the burial. There is my grandmother, contorted and wailing, tossing herself on the coffin, seeming insane, insane. There is my father, little tears falling out of unblinking eyes and sliding down his cheeks; he does not wipe them. My brother looks dazed, numbed, and my sister topples into the arms of my mother's best friend, howls erupting from her like uncontrollable heaves.

I am there, too, with raccoon eyes, eyes ringed black—black for mourning, black from the night awake in a motel near an airport waiting for a morning flight home. My eyes are dry.

It is not for the lack of love or longing that I could not weep then, that I cannot visit the grave now, always promising I will, never keeping my word. But something remains confused and contradictory, the way, perhaps, it always must be between a man and his mother. Sometimes those two words—"man" and "mother"—seem mutually exclusive; with his mother, a son, even a grown son, remains somehow a child. And so to become a man I had to hurt and reject the woman who brought me into the world.

I realize that most acutely because my mother died when I was nineteen years old, on the cusp of manhood, in the midst of leaving home. Her illness tied me to home, yet I lived a thousand miles away. Duty and love called me home, yet I chose independence and distance.

Had my mother lived longer, there would have been time for discussion, explanation, reconciliation. We could have out-grown the roles of adversaries and, as two adults, renewed and strengthened our friendship, savored it for years. As it is, we are frozen in a moment without resolution, and I am stuck with choices that I see now as both necessary and shameful.

Those choices, as I think back, had their precedents. On my first day of nursery school, I had cried—even as my sister, a year younger, did not. And so on the day I was to begin kinder-garten, my mother decided to walk with me the three blocks to school. After a block and a half, I demanded she let me go on alone. Part of me, I think, simply wanted to show what a big boy I was. But another part, I am sure, wanted to leave my mother behind because she knew the little boy who had cried in nursery school, homesick only four blocks from home.

A few years later, in second or third grade, I brought home a painting I had done in art class. I was angry because I had had to rush to finish it before class ended. My mother looked at the painting and said it was nice. So angry was I with this unwarranted approval that I crumpled up the painting and threw it in the garbage. She rescued it and somehow straight-ened all the wrinkles. A few weeks later, she entered the paint-ing, without my knowledge, in a children's art contest sponsored by some local department store. It won for me the first prize, a silver dollar.

How could I not love my mother for her patience and her faith, salvaging that painting and saving me from my moods. Yet years later, I still had trouble accepting her approval—this

time for articles in my high school and college newspapers—
because approval from a mother seemed tainted, not suffi-
ciently objective and hard won.

Nevertheless, our relationship was good and strong. I can
envision a pennant of Chinatown from a day spent together in
New York, a birthday cake baked by her in the shape of a football field, the books in the den we both read and discussed; I
miss those talks, and I miss the sound of her voice more than
any aspect of her presence. I know that a certain number of
battles are normal with either parent, but I never had to rebel
against my father, as I did against my mother, just to grow up.

I can still see her, asleep at the kitchen table, her face resting on an opened newspaper. I am sixteen or seventeen years
old, and I am opening the front door quietly, because my friend
Mark and I have been out drinking, splitting a six-pack of beer
and a pint of Southern Comfort as we walked the streets of our
hometown.

"Why did you wait up for me?" I ask my mother. It is 2 A.M.
"I wasn't waiting up," she says. "I fell asleep reading the news-
paper." "You were," I say. "You were waiting up." I pause.
"C'mon. Go to bed. I'm home now."

I wait for my mother to climb the stairs, wait for her bedroom light to flick on, then off. I take some beers from the
refrigerator and go outside to meet Mark again.

I knew my mother did not want me to go away to college,
but I did. I knew she wanted to accompany me to the University of Wisconsin when I enrolled, but I would not let her. She
might have sensed how intimidated and worried I felt amid the
Norse farm boys and the bearded New York Jews; she might
have seen me homesick again.

All this time, she was getting sicker. She slipped on water
the dog had splashed out of her dish and pinched a nerve.
Reaching for towels on the top shelf of a closet, she lost her
balance and fell off a stepladder, breaking two toes. And
because of her cancer, nothing healed. I can never forget her
attending my sister's high school graduation in a wheelchair, a
virtual cripple, reduced and shamed in front of the people she

knew. As she sat in the wheelchair, a teacher walked past her and accidentally tipped it. I saw her begin to topple, and thought that if she did, she might simply break into pieces and I might lose my mind right then. Somehow, she righted the wheelchair in time.

All the following Fall at college, letters came from my father, invariably relating the latest diagnosis, the latest bad news of Mom. It seems those letters always came on a Saturday morning, right before I was going to a football game, dashing my pleasure, ruining my good time.

She decided to visit me at college that Fall. She took a motel room with two beds, just in case I wanted to spend a night. I did not. I hurried her in and out of my dormitory— what kind of guy has his mother visiting? She wanted to sit in on my classes, and I said fine, but she could not sit next to me. When I look back, I see myself walking out of the lecture hall at the end of class, putting distance between us, not acknowledging my own mother until we were a block or two farther along.

Such was the selfishness and mean spirit of my imagined manhood. I shrivel at the memory. I shrivel, and I can imagine it no other way. The twenty-eight-year-old I am would celebrate this amazing woman, his mother, show her off to friends; the nineteen-year-old I was tried to hide her as a vestige of childhood and dependence. And because she died soon after, there was never a time to change, or at least to apologize.

There was only one day, in Madison, Wisconsin, a few years after she had died. I was taking my girlfriend to dinner—a dressy sort of place, away from the campus—and on the way I remembered that it was the same restaurant at which mother and I had eaten one night during her visit. And I began to cry.

A FORM OF MATRICIDE

Art Buchwald

Shortly after I was born, my mother was taken away from me or I was taken away from my mother. This was done because she was mentally ill. She suffered from severe chronic depression, which required that she be committed to a private sanitarium. She never recovered and eventually, when my father ran out of money, she was placed in a state hospital in upper New York for thirty-five years—the rest of her life.

The medical facts, as provided to me by the Harlem Valley State Hospital in New York, are as follows:

My mother was born in Hungary in 1893 and came to this country in 1906, where, with very little schooling, she went to work in a factory. In 1918 she married my father and then had four children.

The report said, "She was jolly and friendly until the age of thirty, when she suddenly became suspicious and imagined people were poisoning her food. She was admitted to the Westport Sanitarium on June 4, 1925, and was released on August 20, 1925." (I was born on October 20, 1925, which meant that she was sick during the pregnancy.) "When her condition did not improve she was readmitted on February 18, 1926. She refused to eat and expressed paranoid ideas."

"The patient was transferred to Harlem Valley State Hospital, where she gradually regressed."

I never saw my mother, although she lived until I was in my thirties. When I was a child, they would not let me visit her. When I grew up, I didn't want to. I preferred the mother I had invented to the one I would find in the hospital. The denial has been a very heavy burden to carry around all these years, and to this day I still haven't figured it all out.

Early in life I had to explain her absence to strangers, as did my sisters. The easiest thing was to say she died giving birth to me. I don't know how many times I told this lie, but apparently every time I did I committed a form of matricide. She was dead as far as friends and strangers were concerned, but she was very much alive to me—sequestered away in a distant place I had never seen. The story was credible—but for most of my life I have lived in fear that someone would unearth my dirty secret and I would be severely punished for not having disclosed it.

When I grew up and I was in analysis in Washington, D.C., with Dr. Robert Morse, discussions about my mother took up quite a bit of our time. One of the reasons for this was that she turned up in so many dreams—watching me, following me, but never saying anything. I might escape her in the daytime but not when I slept.

In my dreams, she never helped. She just stared at me, as if to say, "Well?"

Although I had never seen her in person, I saw photographs. She looked very attractive, with brown hair, high cheekbones, and no-nonsense features. I perceived a stern look about her, though this could have been attributed to guilt. I sometimes felt that I would have been the recipient of a very disciplined, kosher upbringing had she not disappeared from my life at a very early age.

As the only boy in the family, I might have been spoiled by her. On the other hand she might have lowered the boom on me for trying to be a free spirit. I never knew what a mother was, so I couldn't imagine her holding me in her arms. Dr. Morse and I concluded that I was envious of people who did have real mothers, and when I acted out I wanted to prove that it didn't bother me.

During the various stages of my life, I often wondered if I was responsible for her illness and incarceration. After all, she was taken away at my birth, so who else could be blamed?

As with many children who never knew their mothers, I have been on a lifelong search for someone to replace her. The search has taken more time than my work, and although I know that I will never find a surrogate, I can't seem to stop looking.

In 1960, at age sixty-seven, she died. She had cancer of the liver. My sisters, Alice, Edith, and Doris, told me that they had gone to see her in the hospital when she was dying.

Alice said, "She looked very nice."

Edith's response was, "She didn't look nice—she looked awful."

"She looked a lot better than I anticipated."

"Well, you must have anticipated something really bad."

"She was dying of cancer. What did you expect?"

I asked them how long after that visit had she died.

"A month. I remember the hospital because a lot of patients were wearing crucifixes. Not little ones, big ones."

"I remember the hospital because it was so screwed up. Doris, who was a nurse, asked to see the records—and the doctor read from a document in front of him. It turned out he was reporting on a different patient. When Doris pointed this out, he didn't even apologize. He just picked up another folder."

"Did you say anything to her when you saw her?"

Alice said, "I remember saying to her, 'Mother, I just want you to know that Poppa has been good to us.' She gave me a funny look and a smile. I don't know what the smile meant, whether it was, 'Is that so?' or something else."

There was a funeral for her in New York. I didn't make it because I was in Paris at the time. My sister Edith wrote me a letter telling me about Mother's death, the services, and the difficulty in finding a burial plot. The rabbi, who didn't know her, gave the eulogy, and twenty-five of our aunts and cousins, mostly on my father's side, showed up for the funeral.

I was shaken by the news. Since the funeral had taken place a week before the letter arrived, it was obviously too late for me to attend, and there was no need to go home. So even when she was buried, I did not see her.

I asked my sister Edith why she hadn't called or cabled me in Paris.

"The funeral was the next day—you couldn't have made it."

"How did you know that?"

"We weren't thinking."

My wife, Ann, told me that I walked into our dining room in Paris and sat down. She said, "What's wrong?"

I blurted out, "My mother died," and immediately started to cry. Ann came over and put her arms around me and said, "Don't tell me that you expected to get through this without crying."

When we grieve, tears and guilt get mixed together. My sisters have always tried to console me by saying that, even if I had gone to see my mother, she wouldn't have known who I was. They said that I would have been as much a stranger to her as she was to me. This thought has helped, but sometimes, particularly at night, I think that I was a coward not to go and see her.

In spite of my never having seen her, she was very much a part of me. In 1963, I had a severe depression myself and was hospitalized. In my darkest moments in my room, I would cry, "I want my mommy, I want my mommy."

When I told my story to Dr. Morse the next morning, he said that he was not surprised. I had gagged up a whole lifetime of maternal deprivation.

FROM "MAMÁ"

Rafael Jesús González

My mother lies in the hospital in a coma, tubes in her nostrils and veins, fed oxygen and fluids, buzzers and blinking lights monitoring her heart and lungs, her head shrunken, face wrinkled and dry, gray hair lusterless and matted on her forehead, her breathing harsh in her throat. A woman of remarkable strength, her body, even now, fends off Death, kind Death.

My three brothers and I sit by her bed and admire the immense, gorgeous bouquet of flowers Ricardo's office has sent. She, for whom they are intended, who would have delighted in them, their florid abundance, will never see them. But the flowers, magnificent as they are, do not hold our attention as much as do the blaring sounds and frantic movements of light on the TV set facing her bed. (It is always on because, they tell us, the sounds help those in a coma; just how this is so I do not know.)

The only dignity I see in this attendance upon death is the kindness of the doctors and nurses who care for her. Even the flowers lack dignity, though certainly not beauty; arranged in the American, not the Japanese, mode, there are too many of them, too varied and multicolored. Amassed too densely and prodigiously, they inspire not meditation but astonishment.

Excerpted from an original essay commissioned for this volume.

Here sorrow is short circuited.

I look into her face, closed in a not-peaceful sleep, and try to recollect or imagine the passions that informed her living, this woman of so many passions and so many strengths, so many joys and so many sorrows, so much tenderness and so much rage, so much sweetness and so much bitterness. The gray residue of skin and bones sinking into the white expanse of the hospital bed belies it all. Mi mami, mi querida mamacita.

At the house from which, in the fifty-two years my family has lived here, she is absent for the first time, with little to do, I roam about the rooms, milking memories from the objects that fill them. I sort through her jewelry (most of which I gave her, much of which I made for her) which she never wore but singly, one at a time (having always made simplicity a corollary of elegance), and try to reconstruct the occasions on which she acquired it: mementos of my travels, celebrations of saint's days, birthdays, anniversaries, Christmases, Días de Reyes, Easters. An inventory of years, days, feelings—the single, common thread of love stringing them all.

If I feel a certain sense of transgression (though she would always let me go through her jewelry when I was home), how much more so when I hunt out from her dresser drawer her hoard of my father's love letters, thick bundles tied with ribbon. Yellowed, fragile with years, they document a love, a passion that created a world, many worlds, as each of the lives it touched, it created, attests. I read only a few, from 1934, the same year they married, and put them away, a little uneasily, a little guiltily, aware of a certain trespassing. I will wait.

All Hallows' Eve, almost a month later, I am at the mortuary to comb my mother's hair; she died three days ago. This last year it was I who cut her hair on my visits to El Paso. Going over the funeral items at the mortuary the day before yesterday, it seemed offensive to have a hairdresser for the dead do my mother's scanty, thin hair. The mortuary's cosmetician tries to be helpful and brings hairpins, curling irons, and gels, which I refuse. I simply comb Mother's thin gray hair back and try to make it look neat. Gilberto, red-eyed and choked up, waits for me in the mortician's office. It was he who used to comb Mother's hair, coaxing her to use her lipstick and saying, "A ver, enséñeme que tan bonita es," teasing a reluctant, indulgent, sad smile from her, the lipstick applied unevenly on her lips. To her death, my mother never went out of the house without rouging, powdering, and coloring her lips. In the coffin, the pain lines have been erased and the embalming has left revealed and stark the delicate, aristocratic bone structure of her face.

At Gilberto's insistence I have brought Mother's favorite scent, China Rain. My mother, always partial to White Shoulders and other even more expensive perfumes with the essence of tuberose predominant, some years back, on a visit to Berkeley, discovered China Rain in the Body Shop and had used it ever since. This bottle is last year's Christmas present from Gilberto. Before falling into coma last month, Gilberto tells me, she had taken to using the strong essential oil as a lotion on her stiff, surprisingly still graceful hands. I open the bottle and the scent, for a second, almost restores the soul to this shell of the body that bore me. When I apply the perfume essence to her temples and earlobes, I am shocked by how cold she is and how hard the embalming has made her flesh, the flesh which had always meant softness and warmth. Hours later, the trace of the scent is on my fingers and the house is strangely empty, soulless, without my mother. The laughter and excitement of trick-or-treating children playing ghosts and goblins in the street remind me of my childhood and my young mother's voice calling us in.

At 7:00 P.M. the next day, Día de todos los Santos, the brothers convene at the mortuary an hour before the rosary. The registry book lies open in the elegant anteroom, the recordatorios, focus of one of the several contentions among us, in a neat stack beside it. Before my arrival in El Paso the day of her death, my brothers had decided the remembrance cards were to be printed in English; I wanted them in Spanish, my mother's language, our first language. I convinced two of my brothers; the cards are printed in Spanish, on a variety of cloying images: Virgins, Good Shepherds, St. Josephs, St. Judes, St. Anthonys, St. Teresas. Not a single Señora de Guadalupe. I had wanted all the recordatorios to bear the Guadalupana image, Mom's focus of devotion. Not available, the mortuary had said.

Aunts, uncles, cousins, second cousins begin to arrive. Old family friends, old neighbors I have not seen in years. Friends of my brothers. My own friends from grade school, high school, college, my old college professors, compadres. In the seats to the side reserved for the immediate family, we four brothers sit and my nieces and nephew, Rebecca and Christelle and Richard, Arturo's daughters and son. Gilberto whispers to me that he wants me to talk to the deacon who has arrived. The deacon wants to know whether to recite the rosary in Spanish or in English. Spanish, I tell him, then, on second thought, suggest that he do it in both languages. I feel numb through the interminable evening.

Día de los muertos, morning of the funeral, the four sons and three grandchildren arrive early at the mortuary for a last look at what remains of Carmen González-Prieto de González, my mother. We sit or kneel before the flower-banked coffin, the body in it bearing but a resemblance to her. A young woman mortician comes in with white carnations to pin on our lapels. I refuse to wear one and place mine in my mother's hands just before they close the lid of the box.

The seven of us climb into the limousine and quickly arrive at St. Patrick's Cathedral a few blocks away for the funeral mass. As the casket is taken from the hearse, the children in the playground of the parochial school stop their play and stand in respectful silence until we have carried the casket up the steps into the vestibule. It is not an easy task; my brothers and I had decided that, as with our father, we would be the only pallbearers. The metal box is unbelievably heavy.

It is years since I had been in the cathedral; it has grown no smaller or less majestic since I served here as a young altar boy.

Now I note that the priest has no altar boys to assist him. He asks whether to say the mass in Spanish or in English; Spanish, I tell him. (Later I regret that I didn't tell him to say it in Latin.)

Arturo, Gilberto, Ricardo, and I escort the casket with our mother's body all the way to the altar. (Too heavy to carry by ourselves, we roll it on a wheeled trestle.) It is a long way down the aisle. Up on the front pew I find myself saying the old Latin responses under my breath. And when the time comes, I stand and go to the altar to receive communion. I do not know whether in memory of my mother or simply for old times' sake. The host still tastes like a wafer of fish food and sticks to the roof of my dry mouth.

On the drive to the old Evergreen cemetery, escorted by the police, disdainful of red lights, I see the city as I have never seen it before. Each corner, each house, each store, each land-mark holds memories of my mother and there is a cold stone rattling around in my chest.

At the open grave, we unload the casket for the last time. Nothing is memorable about the graveside ritual. Gilberto receives the brass crucifix from the priest, we receive words of condolence from relatives and friends, and just before leaving I pluck a red carnation from atop the casket to place before the Guadalupe on my mother's altar at home. As I go by, I glance at the gray granite headstone with my father's and my mother's names deeply carved in the stone; and the epitaph I had carved there fifteen years ago: LA VIDA ES LA CELEBRACIÓN DE LA TIERRA; LA MUERTE ES SU DESCANSO.

Back at the house, relatives and friends come by all day. There is a great quantity of food prepared by Debbie, Ricardo's compañera, and her mother—and beer, soft drinks, coffee. There is much laughter, tears (I remember my father telling us how, when he was a boy in Torreón, the sugarcane vendors would hawk their goods on the Day of the Dead, crying, "Llo-rando y comiendo caña, llorando y comiendo caña"). Tears and laughter, águila y sol of the peso of grieving.

Two days later, after lunch and on our way to the house to pick up my luggage, Arturo, Gilberto, and I drive by the cemetery and, on impulse, Arturo drives in just to see how things are. The mound is fresh, and still so are the flowers strewn on it; the rain and the cold have kept them fresh. We pick a handful of carnations to place on the home altar.

At the house, I place the carnations in a vase at the feet of the Virgen de Guadalupe, and as my brothers load my baggage to take me to the airport, I make the sign of the cross before her image. It will be the first time I will ever have left home without my mother's blessing.

The last time I saw my mother before she went into the coma, she told me that the joy had gone out of life when my father died. I have not been able to forgive my mother her lack of joy, her talent to ferret out the sadness in any story, the grief in any situation, the lament in any song.

A complicated woman, my mother; she and I always had difficulty tracing the mazes of the labyrinth we traveled, we created. I am too old to believe in blame now, but the great love I have for her is tainted with resentments. Along with the family closeness we learned distances. I love my brothers and I know that in need we will always be there for each other, but we cannot talk to one another. All of us are wounded, harboring our own grief and rage. There are tight, choked-off silences between us, judgments, closed and locked chambers I yearn to open to the blessing of air and light, but cannot find the key or the crowbar to do so.

My mother's has been a strongly woven spell, difficult to disentangle, the threads hard to distinguish one from another. Now that she is gone I am filled with a great grief for all the joy that might have been. And also thankful for all the joy that was. And awestruck by the immense complexity of it all. And infinitely sad for all that will be left unsaid.

THE COLORED CEMETERY

Henry Louis Gates, Jr.

It was 1986 and I had been at an out-of-town conference, when I got the news. I'll never forget that slow walk down the corridor to the hotel door. From a distance, I could see the pink message slips taped all over my door. It had to be death or its imminence, I thought. It had to be Mama. Messages from the dean, from the police, from the department, from my wife, my father, from the hotel manager, from the police again. CALL HOME.

She had been in the hospital for a checkup, and seemed to be doing fine. The white lady sharing the room with her said she was talking one minute and slumped over the next. They kept her alive on a machine.

She's up, she's down, she might not make it through the night. She's a little better? She's worse? She won't . . . not even through the night? I flew out to Pittsburgh, the nearest airport, at dawn, then rented a car from there, weeping all the way. Sharon and the kids drove down from Ithaca.

At the hospital, Mama kept looking up at me, then at the big blue-gray machine, trying to ask something with her eyes.

She'd be fully awake and conscious, then they'd have to jump-start her heart again. She'd come back as if she'd just been asleep, asking that same question again with her eyes. We'd go, we'd come, over the course of the day, till my family finally got there, at about nine that night. She'd waited to say goodbye.

It was about midnight when we agreed not to shock her heart anymore. Rocky [*the author's brother*] by now an oral surgeon, had assumed charge. I had told her how much I loved her, and she had smiled that deep-down smile, something to take with her on the road.

Nemo [*the author's mother's brother*] and Mama are buried near each other, in the new, highly esteemed, and otherwise white cemetery just outside Keyser, behind the mill overlooking Mr. Bump's trailer park. It probably bothers Mama to be looking down at Nemo every day, unless she has forgiven him for not calling her to say goodbye when Big Mom [*Nemo and Mama's mother*] was dying.

It's the kind of cemetery that seems fake to me, with all the headstones bronze and flat, exactly the same size. We got the "deluxe" model and jazzed it up as best we could. It's got a little poem on it, and a bas-relief flower. Maybe it should have just said "Miss Pauline," because everybody'd know who that was.

I hate that cemetery. Not because of the lack of aesthetic appeal; not because it's integrated; but because what Nemo called the Power isn't there. When you go up on Radical Hill, up past where Sherry Lewis used to live, enter the gate, and take the dusty road to the colored cemetery ... now, that's a *cemetery*. All the markers have different shapes, and the graves are laid out whopper-jawed. Upkeep varies, so some graves look pretty disheveled. Not Daddy Paul's [*Big Mom's husband*], of course, and not Big Mom's, either.

This is where the old souls come to hide, resting till the Day of the Lord. Falling out over graves, like I once saw Mr. Bootsie do when I was a boy, listening to Mama perform her eulogy. Please, please—just one more look, don't take her yet, just one more look, was all he said, shouting and whooping and hollering and falling out all over his mother's grave.

You had a chance, in a colored funeral. You had a chance to work out your grief. You didn't have to be in a hurry with it, either. You could touch it, play with it, and talk to it, letting it work itself up in its own good time. Mama said she didn't want one of those tearjerkers, with crepe-hangers sitting in the mourners' pew and then crowding around her grave. She wanted a closed casket, ten minutes at the max, and don't let Nemo officiate. That was when she was younger. She'd pick out her dress and wig hat, the jewelry and the shoes, when she got old. By the time my mother died, at the worst of her dejection and alienation from herself, her family, the Colemans, seemed to be coolly distant, somewhat embarrassed by her eccentricities and depression. They were tired of her, it almost seemed, and she was tired of life. I think by the end she wanted to die. Nor did she believe in an afterlife. She just wanted release.

Instead of the modern Episcopal Milquetoast service we had for Mama, I passionately wish that her funeral had been like the one for Miss Minnie, or the one for Papa Charlie—or the one for Uncle Boke, which happened back when I was five. That was a nice one.

The sermon was long and loud, demanding that you break down. He's with the Lord today, walking in grandeur past brooks and fountains, hand in hand with his mother, Miss Lucy Clifford, and his kind old father, Mr. Samuel. I know you want him back, but the Lord had need of him up there. Maybe it was to sing the tenor parts of the spirituals, or maybe to tend the fires. Maybe to polish the silver up nice, or to keep the gold real shiny. I *know* you'll miss him; we'll miss him too. But we'll meet again soon at the Pearly Gates. On that Great Day of the Judgment, when we cross over, he'll be waiting there for you, welcoming us into the fold.

Oh, man, did those sermons feel *good,* sad-good, and hurting. And then they'd sing that killer song, people falling out all along.

> *When I'm gone the last mile of the way*
> *I will rest at the close of the day,*

And I know there are joys that await me
When I've gone the last mile of the day.

Then Mama had risen to read her piece, looking all good and sounding all fine.

At Mama's funeral, I wanted to fall out like that, too. I wanted that blue-black preacher who had substituted that time for Reverend Monroe and had blown his tired ass away. I wanted him to get up on that pulpit and preach the Sermon of the Dry Bones, like he'd done for Uncle Boke. People *still* dated things by that sermon: Hey ... that was two years, three months, fourteen days, seven hours, and five minutes after Brother Blue Gums preached the Sermon of the Dry Bones.

I wanted the Heavenly Gospel Choir to sing a lot of long, sad songs, and wanted people to fall out. I wanted the church to be *hot*, with the windows closed, those paper-colored funeral home fans spreading the steam rather than cooling things down. I wanted starched collars to wilt and straightened hair to kink up and "go back." I wanted the kitchens crinkling up in that heat, crackling loud and long, before our very eyes. I wanted the whole world to know my mama's death and her glory while alive. I wanted to cry and cry and cry, so I could tell her how sorry I was for not being a good enough son. I wanted her to know that I could have tried to do more, I could have tried to understand better, I could have come home more. I wanted her to know that I had tried, and that I loved her like life itself, and that I would miss her now that she was gone. I wanted to be sad in that dark, holy place, and I wanted that sadness to last.

PART 6

ALIENATION

As they grow old together and come closer to the time of death, have the son and mother been able to overcome the conflicts, the distances, the alienations, that came between them earlier in life? The alienation that the death of Samuel Freedman's mother (in the last chapter) froze in time. How well these perhaps inevitable differences have been transcended may be the central question to be asked of every mother-son bond, looking at that bond as a trajectory, a relationship that changes over the years.

In this book we've seen many different outcomes, many different answers to this question. The most desirable would seem to be when son and mother are able to let go of their mutual grievances while the latter is still alive and thus become free to enjoy fully the last years of their time together. The narratives of Updike and Najarian in chapter 1 are good examples.

But this happy state is not always arrived at. Some of the most famous writers in this anthology were alienated from their dying mothers, their anger and bitterness remaining long after her death. This is true for the three literary giants we read in this chapter: John Cheever, Henry Miller, and Nelson Algren. Granted that each of them may have had a particularly difficult mother, they still are unable to forgive her. Unresolved grief remains the legacy of an alienated mother-son relationship.

MOONSET, GLOUCESTER

Charles Olson

Goodbye red moon
In that color you set
west of the Cut I should imagine
forever Mother

After 47 years this month
a Monday at 9 A.M.
you set I rise I hope
a free thing as probably
what you more were Not
the suffering one you sold

sowed me on Rise
Mother from off me
God damn you God damn me my
misunderstanding of you

I can die now I just begun to live

WHEN I THINK OF MOTHER

John Cheever

She is Mrs. Fuzzy-Wig; she is the noncomformist. She lives in a little house on a back street and paints lampshades. Her five children are married and scattered, and does not want to visit them all. They dread the time when she will become so infirm — she is in her eighties — that she will be forced to live with them. But they do not dread it nearly as much as she does. I will not go to live with them — she thinks, of her children; I will die before I go to live with them. I will die. Now she is obsessed with impressing onto every surface that she touches the image of a rose. The hall carpet — all the carpets — represent roses. The hall is papered with a galaxy of bloodred roses that are all as big as lettuce heads. The effect is confusing. But you are not through with roses in the hall. Every chair and stool and sofa in the living room is covered with cloth that is stamped with roses. Here they are bigger — they are as big as cabbages, and those on the chair seats are repeated in the wallpaper, just as big but of a slightly fainter shade of red. Step into the dining room, and the situation is the same. There are roses on the bedroom carpet, roses on the bedspread, roses on the wall, and roses have been painted on the pin tray, the lampshades, the wastebasket, and the matchbox. It is with things like these last that she is now occupied; there are still plenty of surfaces in the house that lack a rose. She has covered all of the lampshades and many of the chair backs, but there are still plenty of cannisters, boxes, etc. that present bare surfaces. She is very happy.

All her children, looking to her for the graceful discharge of affection, have been rudely discouraged. She has arbitrarily, now and then, laid claim to their affections. . . . All of this is past for them and yet, because she did not conform at all, they will all, for the rest of their lives, laugh uproariously when they see a woman of her kind slip on a banana peel—with that unhealthy mixture of tenderness and loathing that she has implanted in them.

After I had driven all day through a tiring light, there was the restless night in Quincy, the smell of smoke. Then a break-fast with the umbilical cord seeming to have been cut but to lie, ragged and bleeding, on the table between us. *(1952)*

When I think of Mother, I think of the streets of Quincy, where she spent most of her life. It appears to be a small place, dark, a sphere among larger and more swiftly turning spheres; and to go from one to the other meant the severance of many moral and emotional ties. It was the common situation of having to break with one's origins or live in despair. She is a woman of many excellent qualities. She seldom spoke of her numerous friendships without hinting at the power of loneliness. It was a powerfully sensual world; the smell of fires and flowers and baking bread and peaches cooking for jam and autumn woods and spring woods and the hallways of old houses and the noises of the rain and the sea, of thunderstorms and the west wind. This is a red-blooded and a splendid inheritance. *(1954)*

Quincy Journal. On the train downriver from Scarborough, much speculation. . . . The sky and the water are overcast. At

Tarrytown I saw a boat that had been sunk by the autumn rains. Drank some whiskey in the diner with a cheerful businessman. The diner smelled of spoiled food. The linen was sordid; the waiters sullen. . . . Outside, the autumn countryside; the brooks risen over their banks, and the sea, which seems, along the coast, to relate a sad, sad tale. I have made this journey thousands of times, and I suppose it is only natural, considering the past, that I should feel anxious; that I should revert to childish things; that I should be afraid not of any image but of shades, of that creation that lies in the corner of my eye. Back to the diner at the end of the trip for some more whiskey. . . . Only after drinking a little whiskey do I feel the simple pleasures of travelling through the tag end of this rainy day.

To Quincy on the local; the flat industrial coast. This poignant, debauched countryside; street lights, mud puddles, and the evening star, and these sodden people—all but the pretty girls and the wild boys. Mother in bed with a stroke. Her speech thick, but her mulishness, her hearing, her appetite, and her intellect unimpaired. *(1953)*

Quincy only deepens my depression. Why should I, a grown man, be thrown back so wildly into the unhappiness of the past? *(1954)*

Pain in the chest. Rowed with Mary [*Cheever's wife*] about lingering glances; very depressed; practically insane. A call from Quincy to say that Mother is very sick. Emotional hurly-burly; some tears. Got a room on the Owl for Boston. The atmosphere of all such places seems to me to be the atmosphere of erotic misdemeanor. This may be a subjective projection. Rainy dawn in Boston; rainy Sunday morning. The unregenerate slums of Boston on a dark day. How lasting they seem; unassailable. Found mother very withered now, weary (she says of life). Her wits and her hearing are sharp. "I shout at Mrs. Bacon and she doesn't mind. Other people don't like to have me shout at them. She was talking on the telephone—she was telling someone about her cardiograms. I shouted at her, 'Nobody wants to hear about your cardiograms? She didn't seem to mind." Old and feeble and alone and helpless as she is, I still seem to lay at her feet the sense of a tragic misunderstanding. "He's a *regular* boy," she says of someone and I still flinch. Home on the 1:00 and up the banks of the Hudson after dark to this warm and comfortable house. I have my troubles, but they do not seem to be insupportable. *(1956)*

Mother died on the 22nd, and I do not note this any more than I note the walls of the chalice full of wine. The A.s' antic house. This strong emotion as we follow a path to the grave. Norwell covered with old snow. *(1956)*

On our knees in church (even in the cathedral) we are face-to-face with the bare facts of humanity. We praise Him, we bless Him, we adore Him, we glorify Him, and we wonder who is that baritone across the aisle and that pretty woman on our right who smells of apple blossoms. Our bowels stir and our cod itches and we amend our praise for the spiritual life with the hope that it will not be too spiritual. The door at our back creaks open and we wonder, Who has just come in? *(1956)*

I walk and walk. I say a prayer on Fifty-third Street. I have lunch and see the ballgame. I come home on the train, drink some gin, and study Italian. I wake at three in the morning, paralyzed at the thought of what I have left undone, such as my teeth. And then I think I see clearly that passage in human relationships where the line between creativity and light, and darkness and disaster, is a hair. And I think this is an inherited burden, one that Mother carried much, and that, as in everything else, light will triumph. *(1956)*

Fred [*Cheever's brother*] comes.... he looks like Mother, a painful and bewildering memory, and I remember our conversations—my desire to put one idea after another, to sort out good from evil, while she skipped, or so it seemed to me, from one wild half-truth to another, from one larcenous prejudice to another. The aim never seemed to be to communicate but to confuse, obstruct, and dismay. *(1962)*

I get up at half past six to get breakfast—in a fair humor, I think, but while I am shaving, so to speak, Mary also rises, scowls, coughs, makes small noises of pain, and I speak meanly. "Can I do anything to help you, short of dropping dead?" I am offered no breakfast, so I have none—but that we, at this time of life and time of day, should reenact the bitter and ugly quarrels of our parents, circling angrily around the toaster and the orange-juice squeezer like bent and toothless gladiators exhaling venom, bile, detestation, and petulance in one another's direction! "Can I make a piece of toast?" "Would you mind waiting until I've made mine?" Mother finally grabbing her breakfast plate off the table and eating from the sideboard, her back to the room, tears streaming down her cheeks. Dad sitting at the table asking, "For Christ's sake, what have I done to deserve this?" "Leave me alone, just leave me alone is all I ask," says she. "All I want," he says, "is a boiled egg. Is that too much to ask?" "Well, boil yourself an egg then," she screams; and this is the full voice of tragedy, the goat cry. "Boil yourself an egg then, but leave me alone." "But how in hell can I boil an egg," he shouts, "if you won't let me use the pot?" "I'd let you use the pot," she screams, "but you leave it so filthy. I don't know what it is, but you leave everything you touch covered with filth." "I bought the pot," he roars, "the soap, the eggs. I pay the water and the gas bills, and here I sit in my own house unable to boil an egg. Starving." "Here," she screams, "eat my breakfast. I can't eat it. You've ruined my appetite. You've ruined my day." She thrusts her breakfast plate at him and drops it on the table. "But I don't want your breakfast," he says. "I don't like fried eggs. I detest fried eggs. Why should I be expected to eat your breakfast?" "Because I can't eat it," she screams. "I couldn't eat anything in an atmosphere like this. Eat my breakfast. Eat it, enjoy it, but shut up and leave me alone." He pushes the plate away from him, and buries his face in his hands. She takes the plate and throws the fried eggs into the garbage, sobbing horribly. She goes upstairs. The children, who have been waked by this calamitous and heroic dialogue, wonder why this good day that the Lord hath made should seem so calamitous. *(1961)*

Casting around drunkenly for some explanation of my grief, I think perhaps I sought out and married a woman who would treat me as capriciously as my mother did, but a woman with whom I could quarrel as I could not quarrel with my mother. *(1966)*

I dream that I see my mother, leaving the state capitol in Boston, where she has gone to defend some good cause. She wears a long black coat with a fur collar, a tricorne hat. The flight of steps that separates us appears to be the steps of a Spanish church up which the last of a wedding procession is moving. When the procession has gone I go to my mother. "I'm very tired," she says. "I'm terribly tired." Her voice is small, a little cracked. Before I can reach her she falls. Her body begins to roll down the stairs, and I think with horror that she may go all the way, but the fall is stopped; she lies sprawled on the lifts. *(1963)*

I have been a storyteller since the beginning of my life, rearranging facts in order to make them more interesting and sometimes more significant. I have turned my eccentric old mother into a woman of wealth and position, and made my father a captain at sea. I have improvised a background for myself—genteel, traditional—and it is generally accepted. But what are the bare facts, if I were to write them? . . . My parents were not happy, and I was not happy with them. *(1961)*

UNHAPPY MEMORIES

Henry Miller

Even the earliest memories of my mother are unhappy ones. I remember sitting by the stove in the kitchen on a very special kind of chair and talking to her. Mostly she was scolding me. I don't have pleasant memories of talks with her. Once she grew a wart on her finger. She said to me, "Henry," (remember I'm only four years old) "what should I do?" I said, "Cut it off with the scissors." "The wart! You don't cut off a wart!" So she got blood poisoning. Two days later she came to me with her hand bandaged and she says, "And you told me to cut it off!" And BANG, BANG, she slaps me. Slaps me! For punishment. For telling her to do this! How do you like a mother who does that?

My sister was born mentally retarded; she had the intelligence of a child of about eight or ten. She was a great burden in my childhood because I had to defend her when the kids called, "Crazy Loretta, crazy Loretta!" They made fun of her, pulled her hair, called her names. It was terrible. I was always chasing these kids and fighting with them.

Reprinted from *My Life and Times,* by Henry Miller. Copyright © 1971 by Henry Miller and Germini Smith, Inc. Reprinted by permission of Bradley Smith Productions, La Jolla, California.

My mother treated her like a slave. I returned to Brooklyn for two or three months while my mother was dying. My sister was down to a skeleton. She was walking around with pails and brushes, mopping the floor, washing the walls, and so on. My mother seemed to think that this was good for her, that it gave her something to do, I suppose. To me it seemed cruel. However, my mother had put up with her all her life and there's no doubt but that it was a heavy cross to bear.

You see, my sister couldn't attend school because she was so backward. So my mother decided to teach her herself. My mother was never meant to be a teacher. She was terrible. She used to scold her, crack her, fly into a rage. She'd say, "How much is two times two?" and my sister, who hadn't the faintest idea of the answer, would say, "Five, no—seven, no—three." Just wild.

BANG. Another slap or crack. Then my mother would turn to me and say, "Why do I have to bear this cross? What did I do to be punished so?" Asked *me,* a little boy. *"Why is God punishing me?"* You can see what kind of woman she was. Stupid? Worse than that.

The neighbors said she loved me. They said she was really very fond of me and all that. But I never felt any warmth from her. She never kissed me, never hugged me. I don't ever remember going to her and putting my arms around her. I didn't know mothers did that till one day I visited a friend at his home. We were twelve years old. I went home from school with him and I heard his mother's greeting. "Jackie, oh Jackie," she says. "Oh darling, how are you, how have you been?" She puts her arms around him and kisses him. I never heard that kind of language—even that tone of voice. It was new to me. Of course, in that stupid German neighborhood they were great disciplinarians, really brutal people. My boy friends, when I'd go home with them, would say, "Defend me. Help me. If my father starts to hit me, grab something and let's run."

I had no real contact with my mother when I was grown. I saw her briefly when I came back from Europe after being away ten years. But after that I had no contact with her until she became ill. Then I went to see her. Still the same problem—

we had nothing in common. The horrible thing was that she was really dying this time. (You see, once before I had gone to see her when she was supposed to be dying.) She lasted three months before passing away. That was a terrible period for me. I went to see her every day. But even when dying she was that same determined tyrannical person dictating what I should do and refusing to do anything I asked her to do. I said to her, "Look, you're in bed. You can't get up." I didn't say, You're going to die, but I implied it. "For the first time in my life I'm going to tell you what to do. I'm giving the orders now." She rose up in bed, thrusting out her arm, shaking her finger at me. "You can't do that," she yells. There she was, on her deathbed, and I had to push her down with my hands around her throat. A moment later I was in the hall sobbing like a child.

Sometimes now in bed I say to myself, You have reconciled yourself with the world. You don't have any enemies. There are no people you hate. How is it you can't conjure up a better image of your mother? Suppose you die tomorrow and there is a hereafter, and you encounter her. *What are you going to say when you face her?* I can tell you now she'll have the first and last word.

A weird thing happened when we were burying her. It was a freezing cold day with the snow coming down thick. They couldn't get the coffin angled right to lower it into the grave. It was as if she was still resisting us. Even in the funeral parlor, before that, where she was on view for six days, every time I bent over her one of her eyes would open and stare at me.

THE CHILD

Nelson Algren

Q: How did you get along with your father?

A: Oh, I was contemptuous of him.

Q: Why?

A: Well, in the first place, he was incredibly simple. He couldn't understand a movie without seeing it three times *and* having it explained. And he always told the same jokes, year after year. I really liked him, but I'd get awfully impatient with him. He was too simple.

Q: How about your mother?

A: My feeling about her was a little more complex. I always thought she should be more dignified. She was always on her knees, scrubbing, something like that. She was clumsy, a clumsy woman. I wanted a graceful mother. I wanted somebody to be elegant, I guess, I don't know. She was always climbing, sponging the walls. I'd bring someone home, some kid home from school, you know, some kid whose mother was always well-dressed, or had a servant, or something like that. I'd bring him home and my mother would be in the middle of the floor with a scrub bucket. Oh Christ, you know. Oh Jesus, you know. I'd be really bothered. And it bothered me when she mispronounced words. I wanted her to say words right. She'd refer to somebody: "Oh, he was elexecuted." I'd say, "Elec*tro*cuted, Mother." Elexecuted. Elexecuted. And I never knew anyone else who would get *m*'s and *n*'s mixed. When she wrote she wrote "moon" for "noon" and she couldn't say "aluminum." I don't know why. I would get impatient about that. Then I'd get impatient with the old man. He had a tire and battery shop on Kedzie Avenue, and I used to help him. There was Johnson's, a big gambling joint about half a block away, upstairs, and we did a lot of tire changing for the gambling people, the guys who worked in the block joint, and the cops used to play up there. So I told the old man. He knew I went up there and I said there was a horseshoe bar in the place. I was about seventeen and I liked to gamble even then. The place was once called "Hunting House Dancing Academy." The cops used to come in the restaurant and then go upstairs. And I told the old man that. He said, "Well, that's crazy." He said, "A cop can't do that; they'd put him in jail. That'd be dishonest." I said, "Cops, Pa, cops take money, cops steal." "Oh," he said, "I don't want to listen to crazy talk like that. A cop, a policeman is made to defend the law! That's why he is a policeman. If he doesn't do that, then he gets put into jail." I said, "Don't act like that, Pa." I mean I said, "Aw, come on . . ." You know he was too gullible to believe.

Q: Are they alive?

A: The old man died the year after Bernice [*Algren's sister*] died, in 1940. Then nobody died until 1960, when the older sister died. Then my mother died in July of 1961. She was eighty-six, I guess.

Q: Where was she?

A: In a nursing home. There's a whole continent of nursing homes for all the old vegetables, for people you don't want around the house any more. Oh, it's a fantasyland. If you get a license for that and a doctor's connection to send them and you get twenty-five of those people there at eighty-five or a hundred bucks a week, and hire half a dozen nurses to lift them, you will have yourself a great money-maker. It's a real unnatural sight.

Q: Who paid for it?

A: I paid for it. I got some money from the Welfare people. You're supposed to split it. I didn't get a full claim, but I would go along with them. I got her in there. I had to get her in there right away because she started just falling down. She was all right but there was no one to take care of her. If I don't get her into this nursing home, then she's got to go to County Hospital and she's too alert not to be humiliated by that because she has spent her whole life try-ing not to take charity and she had succeeded in that, so I put her in this nursing home. But I put her in there without a dime. The first day I didn't even have the dough to pay the ambulance. "Do everything, get her in there," I told the ambulance, "and you can send me the bill." After she was in there I talked to them.

Q: How many years was she in there?

A: Oh, it wasn't a matter of years. I put her in one when I went to Europe and she walked right out of it. She saw the signs: right to the graveyard. She got out of there. She's been liv-ing over on Lawrence Avenue all alone for years and she just put on her clothes and got out of there. But she had to go back. She gave in and went back. The people running the place went along with me. When I got five hundred bucks I'd give them two or three hundred. I didn't pay attention to the bills. I was being nice, you know, just giving them enough so they'll keep her there. I said to them, "I'll fight with you later." We're killing each other with kindness. They got plenty out of it. And they got money from the Wel-fare people, too. Then I had to get hold of the undertaker. So far as I know, that nursing home still feels I owe them money. I don't pay no heed to that. And the undertaker—I just don't know. He still wants about thirteen hundred dollars and I think I am going to give him eight hundred when he's willing to take it. "We don't do things in that way," he said, and "We had a great expense with your mother, you know." I said, "I understand, but you must realize that my loss is greater than yours." And there was a silence on the other side. He's the funniest guy. They turn that love into money. You can't argue with them. You can't say, "How much are roses going to cost?" You can't say, "Can I get any of the material cheaper?" You have got to go for the thirteen hundred dollars, and that is what I went for. Then after the funeral I dismissed it all from my mind.

PART 7

RECONCEIVING THE MOTHER

A theme that appears in many of our narratives is the effort of a son to arrive at a more "conscious" attitude toward his mother, one not as driven by unconscious conflicts, repressed longings, and old wounds. In other words, to see her in what psychologist Paul Olsen calls "her infinite complexity," as a human being with strengths and weaknesses, rather than as all good or all bad. Without such a consciousness, men will blame their mothers for everything that is wrong in their lives and often will transfer such feelings to all women.

Achieving a conscious attitude can take years, if not decades, and as we've seen in the last chapter, it is not an inevitable outcome. During our twenties and early thirties, we rarely have the depth and the distance to view our mothers with the love and compassion necessary for acceptance. And during our late thirties and forties, we often remain stuck in the pain of a difficult relationship with her. Struggling with feelings of grief and loss, it may not be until our fifties that a more seasoned consciousness emerges.

To change a mother-son relationship, it is often necessary for a man to change the way he views his mother, in other words to *reconceive* her. Sometimes this work of reconceiving takes place when the mother is still alive, sometimes not until she has died. But whether she is dead or alive, the impulse to enter into the mysteries of a mother's being can be very powerful. Part of it is the need to understand why she is or was the way she is or was, to learn about the forces that shaped her. This may involve actual research on the son's part: Gus Lee's lawyerlike investigation of his *mah-mee* (chapter 2) is a good example. In this chapter's first selection we read how Fred Moramarco began the project of puzzling out the meaning of his mother's life twenty years after her death. He scrutinized old photographs, visited her hometown in Italy, and talked to relatives for clues to her character. Finally he came to see Nina Moramarco through a complex multidimensional lens, rather than simply as his "crazy mother."

In this way a mother becomes more than just our mother and more than just a link in our family history. She becomes a central actor in a historical and social drama. Hilton Als portrays his Barbadian mother, an immigrant to Brooklyn, as a "Negress," an exemplar of the complex sociological category he calls "Negressity." And in doing so he turns on their head common stereotypes about poor black women. David Wellman, whose story follows Als's, reconceives his mother politically, interpreting Peggy Wellman's mothering style no longer in terms of her difficult personality but instead through the historical framework of her having been a communist during the years of McCarthyism.

In writing these stories, in placing their lives squarely in the path of their mother's histories, our authors move beyond the patriarchal assumption that it is through the histories of their fathers that men define themselves. They assert the centrality of their mother's family lineage and thus reclaim a maternal legacy.

THE ROUTINE THINGS AROUND THE HOUSE

Stephen Dunn

When mother died
I thought: now I'll have a death poem.
That was unforgivable

yet I've since forgiven myself
as sons are able to do
who've been loved by their mothers.

I stared into the coffin
knowing how long she'd live,
how many lifetimes there are

in the sweet revisions of memory.
It's hard to know exactly
how we ease ourselves back from sadness,

but I remembered when I was twelve,
1951, before the world
unbuttoned its blouse.

I had asked my mother (I was trembling)
if I could see her breasts
and she took me into her room

without embarrassment or coyness
and I stared at them,
afraid to ask for more.

Now, years later, someone tells me
Cancers who've never had mother love
are doomed and I, a Cancer,

feel blessed again. What luck
to have had a mother
who showed me her breasts

when girls my age were developing
their separate countries,
what luck

she didn't doom me
with too much or too little.
Had I asked to touch,

perhaps to suck them,
what would she have done?
Mother, dead woman

who I think permits me
to love women easily,
this poem

is dedicated to where
we stopped, to the incompleteness
that was sufficient

and to how you buttoned up,
began doing the routine things
around the house.

THE MOTHER
I CARRY WITH ME

Fred Moramarco

Robert Johnson has written:

> If a man has a disturbed relationship with his actual
> human mother, it is very easy for him to contaminate his
> anima, that life-giving interior femininity, with his
> mother's demands and expectations. A mother-hungry
> man (and that hunger can dominate a man for his whole
> lifetime if he has been inadequately mothered) can have
> the mother image stamped on his life expectations in
> areas one would not dream of. [He] can find himself fac-
> ing mother in the form of the university he attends, the
> corporation he works for, the church he attends, the
> political party he espouses, his nation.

My mother. The words come haltingly; their very sound is a
muffled moan within me. My mother. For me, so much pain
seems to flow from those two words: My sense of the sorrowful
nature of life. My troubled relationships with women. My anxieties and disappointments. My fear of going crazy. I don't mean
that I *blame* my mother for all of the difficulties of my life, but

my conception of her—the mother I carry with me—seems to have been weighted with a heavy negative load. I want to try to get some perspective on this—get some fuller understanding of who my mother was and how she differs from the mother I carry with me.

Lately I have become more and more aware of what a large psychic presence my mother has been throughout my life. As I write this, she's been dead nearly twenty-five years, but still she looms large above my life's landscape—in all of her aspects, for I have come to know her differently than I knew her as a child; I have come to discover the various faces of woman within her—faces she did not show me as I was growing up, but which have emerged as my own knowledge of life deepens, as the distance from my childhood widens, as she becomes a more realistic, less iconic presence.

I was born on July 13, 1938, to Stephen and Nina Moramarco in St. Mary's Hospital in Brooklyn. My parents were from a small village in southern Italy called Gravina di Puglia. My father immigrated first, as a teenager, with one of his brothers. They worked as ice deliverers, and after he saved some money, he returned to Italy to marry my mother and bring her to the New World. On a recent visit to Gravina I learned more about my father and mother's courtship from his sole surviving sister. My mother's family, the Toriellos, were local "nobility," condescending and very autocratic. They absolutely forbade my mother to have anything to do with my father, who came from peasant stock and lived on the wrong side of the tracks. My aunt remembered being the guardian of my mother's "hope chest"—a trunkful of linens, tablecloths, and towels that prospective brides accumulated in those days—because my mother could not keep it in her own house for fear her family would discover it. So theirs was a *West Side Story* sort of a romance. When my father left for America, the Toriellos thought they were rid of him, only to be absolutely nonplussed when he returned to elope with his darling and take her back with him 4,000 miles across the sea. With his brother he started an ice delivery business and the two bought brownstone homes one block apart in Brooklyn. My father and mother started a family; a son, Federico (Fred), born around 1919, then three daughters in fairly rapid succession: Lucretia, Nicolette, Philomena.

Around 1928, in the midst of the Jazz Age, tragedy strikes. The eight-year-old Fred is hit by an automobile and killed. My mother's life is shattered and the blow resonates throughout the lives of all of my sisters. And although I never knew the brother they always referred to as "the First Fred," he has resonated through my life as well. A few years ago I wrote about him for the first time:

THE FIRST FRED

I can see him in the large oval photograph above my bed. I am eight years old, looking up at the brother I never knew, the "first" Fred killed by a rare auto in a country with few of them, thirteen years before I was born. The picture is sepia, under convex glass. He wears a sailor suit, a ribbon dangling at the collar. He looks like me and there are pictures of me that might be mistaken for him. But they are smaller, less importantly positioned. His is an icon, an altarpiece, and on Palm Sunday my mother always slides a sliver of palm between the glass and its frame, a sacred gesture of her enduring grief. At eight, I am also hit by a car, my mother hysterical, pushed toward the edge of a permanent madness. She has three daughters, but her sons seem doomed by the machinery of the twentieth century. I survive, the only reminder a forehead scar tracing its indelible mark on my skin. My mother is never the same to me. *Jesu, Giuseppe, e Maria,* she recites daily like a litany in the days and nights and weeks and months and years that follow until she is in and out of hospitals with Jesus, Joseph, and Mary offering even less consolation. Suddenly all this makes a whole of my life—father and mother long dead, two of my three sisters dead also, the other lost in a madhouse—and my

surviving soul drifting more and more loosely in the
colossal free-floating everywhere of the universe. Closer
to the first Fred every day.

Year after year, I watched her become more and more fren-
zied, more and more weighted with grief, and I watched my
three sisters follow in her path, each spending time in mental
institutions, each eaten away by the "cancer" that my mother
suffered from as well. We spoke of the "Toriello illness" in my
family, the weeping melancholia that afflicted several of her
brothers and sisters. And no doubt there was a genetic element
involved. But on that trip to Gravina when my Zia Maria told
me the story of my mother and father's courtship, I began to
think of her illness differently. I began to experience what it
must have been like for this woman to be disavowed by her
family, to leave them for the love of her life, to travel to another
continent where she did not know the language, to be suddenly the mother of four children in a city that could hardly
have been more different from the little town of Gravina, and
then, just as she is becoming adjusted to being a wife and
mother in the New World, to have her firstborn cruelly and
accidentally taken from her. And yet she rebounded from that,
and late in life—she was forty-two when I was born—had yet
another son as World War II erupted and the world seemed
such a treacherous and dangerous place. I began to think of
her, not so much as a crazy woman, a sick woman, as I had
thought of her for most of my life—but instead as a courageous
woman, a remarkable woman, with amazing resourcefulness
and energy. And I began to unearth buried memories that
reminded me her life was not all weeping and moaning.

There is a picture of her—one I love because I so rarely saw
her like this, but when I did, it was manna, blue skies, and
magenta sunsets. She is standing with my Zia Maria in front of
St. Mark's Cathedral in Venice. The picture is dated by her
handwriting in back, *23 Luglio, 1952*. If that's right, I am fourteen and back in Brooklyn—not with her in Venice. My father is
not with her either. She is jubilant, smiling, feeding the pigeons

tourist style, a bird fluttering from her outstretched hand. I remember this trip she took back to Italy; I remember being relieved by her going. She would never let me bring my friends into the house because she was obsessive about order and cleanliness, and they might mess things up. Now that she was gone I knew my father would be a soft touch and bend the rules. I remember showing up with a group of friends and being stunned when my father said, "Just because your mother's gone, that doesn't mean you can do whatever you want to." I felt betrayed by him that day, because I had always thought of him as an ally against my mother's craziness.

But here in Venice she is not crazy, and this is how I would like to remember her—or, I should say, how I would like to conjure her at this particular time in my life. For when our parents are no longer living, they become phantoms in our head that still shape and direct our lives. As Robert Anderson wrote in *I Never Sang for My Father,* "Death ends a life, but it does not end a relationship, which lingers in the mind of the survivors toward some resolution which it never finds." I will probably never resolve my relationship with my mother; I still want her to be happy, to carry that Venice smile into the rest of her life. It's not that I felt responsible for her unhappiness, but rather that I felt helpless to do anything about it. When she would pace up and down the first floor of our Brooklyn railroad flat weeping and trembling, after one of what were then called "nervous breakdowns," I could not stand to hear it or see it.

During the summer my mother was in Italy, the second-floor tenants moved out of our brownstone house. When she returned, she asked my father to move upstairs and live separately in his own apartment. In this way, she explained, we could all have our own bedrooms, and she could sleep peacefully and not have to put up with his snoring. She insisted he take the old furniture upstairs and she completely refurnished the downstairs apartment, replacing the dark, worn, mahogany dining room set with a beautifully appointed French Provincial fruitwood. And the deep burgundy and green living room gave way to a pink-and-beige-brocade Louis XIV sofa and chair. A round marble-top table sat in the center of the room. This was her "good period," a time when she took control of things and arranged her life the way she wanted it, but for me it meant trouble because it made the house even more unapproachable, and she worried that things would get dirtied and ruined. For a while she seemed energized by the new arrangement, but soon the old melancholy asserted itself again, and I remember her sitting by the window, rocking back and forth as her face and body lost its robustness. She stared through the wooden venetian blinds into the street and chanted her litany: *"Jesu, Giuseppe, e Maria."*

Unlike my friend Gary Young [*see section 4*], I never heard my mother singing—at least I can't remember her singing, which amounts to the same thing, since she exists for me in the inter-section between memory and imagination, where most of the distant past resides. It's a crowded place, and she's probably less happy there than she was in life, because although life treated her erratically, it also bore her some gifts—a romantic love life, children, a home of her own, a neighborhood with friends and relatives nearby, a chance to travel. It's been my tendency to stress her grief rather than her triumphs, her weeping rather than her laughter, which I have trouble remembering. I don't remember *doing* many things—hardly *any*thing—with my mother. I would go fishing with my father and uncle; my sisters would take me to zoos and parks; I would play with my friends and cousins. Specific memories of being in my mother's presence during my youth are vague and almost all negative. In early ado-lescence when I would come home later than I should have at night, she would dead-bolt the door so I had to wake her in order to get in. I distinctly remember the sinking feeling of turning my key in the lock, then twisting the doorknob and hav-ing the door not budge because of the dead bolt. Then I would knock loudly and eventually wake her up. She would begin her tirade before opening the door, making me wait in the hallway listening to her ranting.

My father died in 1967 while I was in graduate school. I remember my mother in the funeral home, leaning over and kissing his forehead, all the while quietly chanting her litany in

Italian. She wore a blue lace dress, not the traditional black for mourning. She looked frail and withered—and she herself had only a year more to live at the time. But there was a peculiar stoic dignity about her that day, and I remembered it when I returned again to New York that summer after the funeral to sell my family's house and move my mother and my sister (also in precarious mental health at the time) to Long Island where they could be close to my sister Nicolette, who at the time was raising a flourishing family. It was a terrible summer, going through the house I grew up in, selling things for a song, virtu-ally giving away the house, which was located in the Bedford-Stuyvesant section of Brooklyn. This was the year of the riots that followed the death of Martin Luther King. Needless to say, property values had plummeted.

After I returned to Salt Lake City I would call my sister Nicky to ask how Mom was doing. I was amazed to hear that she was experiencing a dramatic recovery. Suddenly she seemed her "good" self again, going out in the world, wearing clothes she liked to dress up in, smiling the Venice smile. It startled me to hear this because when I left she seemed so frag-mented and depressed. She had just turned seventy and so it was remarkable to think about her "reviving," getting her old creative energy back. With hindsight I look back at the trip to Italy, the impulsive purchase of new furniture, and the rebirth she experienced after my father's death as related moments of lucidity and energy in her life. And all of them had to do with acting on her own, without living in the shadow of my father. It's amazing to think of my own sad and weeping mother as a woman who might have flourished in a feminist age, but that just might be the case.

Somehow I feel that the meaning of my life has something to do with the meaning of my mother's life, and that this has to do with my awareness and understanding of women, who have always been a puzzle and mystery to me, as they are to so many men. Why did my mother show me so much of her pain and so little of her pleasure? Or is it that she showed me both, but I only responded to the pain? Why am I still drawn to suffering women? If a woman is not suffering enough, or in enough pain, she seems uninteresting to me—she seems to be not showing me her true self. If I can put a smile on a woman's face I feel a surge of power that I can only attribute to my powerlessness because I could not do that for my mother. Why does a mother become all women, and specifically the women I have slept beside, I have lived with?

I met Sheila Sobell in 1963, shortly after her own mother had died. She had been engaged to someone else, and that had broken off, and I saw the sadness in her eyes and knew that unlike my mother's sadness, which seemed eternal, this sadness I could do something about. We would have long late-night telephone conversations filled with laughter and energy. *I could turn her pain to laughter!* I remember how powerful that made me feel, so powerful that I married Sheila, because I needed that laughter and vibrancy in my life. My mother died a few years after we married, but she loomed large in our relationship, especially after we became parents. Because our children were boys, I tended to identify with Stephen and Nicholas rather than with Sheila whenever she attempted to discipline them. When she insisted that they clean up their rooms and help wash the dishes, I flashed onto my mother's compulsiveness about keeping the house clean and neat. When she told them to be home at a certain hour, I remembered the dead bolt and my sinking feeling in the hallway. And whenever she raised her voice to them, even in the slightest way, I heard my mother's shrieking and hysteria. This took its toll on our marriage, which ended in divorce the year our first son went off to college.

> *There has been a great deal written about the need for young men to separate from their mothers, but much less has been said about the need to understand the mother, to assimilate her sense of the world rather than to reject it outright. We don't want to remain overly dependent upon our mothers, but we can't attribute all of our insecurities to the things*

she didn't give us. We remain psychically connected to the mother for all of our lives; wouldn't it make sense to get inside that connection? What have our mothers to give us that we have been unable to take?

Because my mother is now within me and not out there in the world, I want to know her better. And although she is long gone, I want her to know me better as well. So I need to tell the mother inside of me the one thing in my life that I am the most ashamed about, and that is *that I did not attend her funeral.* This fact haunted me for years, although the circumstances of her death conspired to make a return trip to New York from Salt Lake City difficult at the time. I was in graduate school and relatively poor. I had been back twice in that last year. When my sister called less than six months afterwards to say that my mother, right after her brief period of recovery and lucidity, had had a sudden and fatal stroke, the emotional shock was just too much for me to handle. At that time, I didn't have a clue about how to deal with strong feelings or emotions and I knew that another trip back home to attend my mother's funeral would devastate me. But after she was gone and buried, these reasons seemed empty. They still do, though the guilt and shame I felt has subsided. So I whisper intimately to the mother I carry with me that if I knew then what I know now, if I were not so afraid of feeling then, I would have found a way to have joined my sisters in expressing our family's grief. It's ironic that at the time I was writing my doctoral dissertation on the work of Edward Dahlberg, a man who wrote beautifully and tenderly about his relationship with his mother in *Because I Was Flesh.*

Dahlberg ends his book with the word *Selah,* a mysterious Hebrew word whose derivation and exact meaning is unknown. But it is a lovely musical word that evokes mystery and peace, like the ancient Sanskrit *Shantih* with which T. S. Eliot ends *The Waste Land.* So I would like to move out of the wasteland of distortions I have associated with my mother throughout my life and reconceive Nina Toriello Moramarco, a woman of many facets, who I am just now beginning to know, though her body has long since melded with the elements. One recently discovered photograph shows my mother as I never knew her: a beautiful young woman artfully posed to bring out her innocence and romantic idealism. It's time I celebrated and paid tribute to this adventurous and complex woman from whose loins I sprang into this world, whose body conceived and nurtured my own, and who I carry with me wherever I go. *Selah.*

THE WOMEN

Hilton Als

———

For years before and after her death, I referred to myself as a
Negress; it was what I was conditioned to be. And yet I have
come no closer to defining it. In fact, I shy away from defining
it, given my mother's complex reaction to Negressity for herself
and me. I have expressed my Negressity by living, fully, the prescribed life of an auntie man—what Barbadians call a faggot.
Which is a form of kinship, given that my being an auntie man
is based on greed for romantic love with men temperamentally
not unlike the men my mother knew—that and an unremitting
public "niceness." I socialized myself as an auntie man long
before I committed my first act as one. I also wore my mother's
and sisters' clothes when they were not home; those clothes
deflected from the pressure I felt in being different from them.
As a child, this difference was too much for me to take; I buried
myself in their clothes, their secrets, their desires, to find myself
through them. Those women "killed" me, as comedians say
when they describe their power over an audience. I wanted

———

them to kill me further by fully exploiting the attention I afforded them. But they couldn't, being women.

Being an auntie man enamored of Negressity is all I have ever known how to be. I do not know what my life would be, or if I *would* be at all, if I were any different.

To say that the public's reaction to my mother's being a Negress and my being one were similar would be egregious. My mother was a woman. Over the years in Brooklyn, she worked as a housekeeper for a relatively well-off Scotsman, as a housekeeper for a Jewish matron, in a beauty salon as a hair-dresser, as an assistant in a nursery school. My mother responded to my being a Negress with pride and anger: pride in my identification with women like herself; anger that I identified with her at all. I could not help her react to any of this any differently than she did. This failure haunts me still. I have not catapulted myself past my mother's emotional existence.

Did my mother call herself a Negress as a way of ironically reconciling herself to her history as that most hated of English colonial words, which fixed her as a servant in the eyes of Britain and God? I don't think so, given that she was not especially interested in Britain or history. But "Negress" was one of the few words she took with her when she emigrated from Barbados to Manhattan. As a Negress, her passport to the world was restricted; the world has its limits. Shortly after arriving in New York in the late forties, my mother saw what her everyday life would be; being bright, a high school graduate, and practical, she looked at the world she had emigrated to, picked up her servant's cap, and began starching it with servitude. In her new country, my mother noticed that some New Yorkers retained the fantasy that in writing or speaking about the "underclass," or the "oppressed, silent" woman, or the "indomitable" stoic, they were writing about the kind of Negress she was, but they weren't. My mother was capricious in her views about most things, including race. As a West Indian who had lived among other West Indians, my mother did not feel "difference"; she would not allow her feelings to be ghettoized; in her community, she was in the majority. She was capable of giving a nod toward the history of "injustice," but only if it suited her mood.

I think my mother took some pleasure in how harsh the word "Negress" seemed to the citizens in her adopted home. I have perhaps made more of the word "Negress" than my mother meant by it, but I saw and continue to see how it is used to limit and stupidly define the world certain women inhabit. I think my mother took pleasure in manipulating the guilt and embarrassment white and black Americans alike felt when she called herself a Negress, since their view of the Negress was largely sentimental, maudlin, replete with suffering. When my mother laughed in the face of their deeply presumptive view of her, one of her front teeth flashed gold.

My mother disliked the American penchant for euphemism; she was resolute in making the world confront its definition of her. This freed her mind for other things, like her endless illness, which was a protracted form of suicide. From my mother I learned the only way the Negress can own herself is through her protracted suicide; suffering from imminent death keeps people at a distance. I was so lonely knowing her; she was so busy getting to know herself through dying. When my mother became ill with one thing or another, I was eight; by the time my mother died, I was twenty-eight. When she died, I barely knew anything about her at all.

My mother killed herself systematically and not all at once. Perhaps that is because, as a Negress, she had learned stamina, a stamina that consisted of smiling and lying and maintaining the hope that everything would eventually be different, regardless of the facts. Until the end, my mother avoided the facts; she was polite. She would not die. She became ill, and for a long time, which is difficult to cope with; illness silences the well, out of respect. My mother knew that. Being somewhat generous, she acknowledged her children's helplessness in the atmosphere of her dying by allowing us to live with it so that we could see her physical dissolution (clumps of hair, one leg, a few teeth, eventually all gone) without delineating any of its mysteries. Being children, we could only see her imminent death in terms of our imminent loss; we failed to understand what her dying meant to her. She imposed her will by not telling anyone what was really "wrong"; this kept everyone poised and at her service. She would not speak of the facts contributing to her death; nor would she speak of the facts that contributed to her wish to die in the first place. She was quietly spirited, functional, and content in her depression and love; not for the world would she have forfeited the will she applied to disappearing her own body, since it took her so many years to admit to her need for attention, and being ill was one way to get it. The reasons my mother chose to disappear herself, slowly, are manifold. Perhaps she chose to destroy her body out of a profound sadness at the eventual dissolution of her thirty-year romantic relationship with my father; perhaps she chose to disappear her body out of her interest in the discipline inherent in self-abnegation. Perhaps it was both.

My mother first became ill at the end of her love affair with my father. As with most aspects of my parents' relationship, it is unclear whether or not my father dictated the course their relationship would take. The difference between my mother and the woman he became involved with after my mother was significant: she consented to live with my father whereas my mother had not. After my mother refused to marry him, my father never asked her to again. My mother encountered my father's girlfriend once, on the street. My father's new girlfriend was in the company of one of my father's sisters. My mother saw a certain resemblance between my father's new girlfriend and herself; they were both homely but spirited, like Doris Day. It was clear to my mother that his new girlfriend was capable of withstanding my father's tantrums, his compulsive childishness, and his compulsive lying. It was perhaps not as clear to my father's new girlfriend as it was to my mother that my father lied as much as he did because of his need to rebuild the world according to his specifications while being ashamed of this need. Just like a woman.

I think the resemblance my mother saw between herself and my father's new girlfriend shattered any claim to originality my mother had. And, being a woman, she chose to be critical of this similarity rather than judge my father. Shortly afterward, she was made sick by a mysterious respiratory illness. In the end, I think my mother's long and public illness was the only thing she ever felt she experienced as an accomplishment separate from other people. And it was.

When diabetes cost her one of her legs, she said, politely: Oh, I'm dying now. When they removed a gland in her neck as a test for whatever, she said, politely, Oh, I'm really dying now. When one of her kidneys failed completely and a machine functioned in its place, she was still polite. She said: Well, I'm dying. When she lost her vision in one eye, she said she was dying; eventually she could not breathe without stress, and she said she was really dying; her blood pressure was abnormally high, her teeth were bad, she could not urinate or take sugar in her tea or eat pork or remember a conversation, but she remembered these two things: that she was polite and dying.

After they cut off one of her legs for diabetes' sake, she often experienced phantom pain. The world twitched and throbbed. For my mother, experiencing physical pain became a perspective she could own. In pain, she wasn't anything but ill—not a Negress, not a mother of six, not a lover, not a patient. Pain has its own meaning. She passed life by long before she died. When she died, the things she wore in her casket—a wig made of a synthetic fiber colored brown; a white polyester shawl—didn't look as if they belonged to her at all.

LOYALTIES
AND BETRAYALS

David Wellman

M̲y mother, Peggy Wellman, died as she lived: on her own terms, tough and independent. My father, Saully Wellman, was away again, this time in China. After battling congestive heart failure for a couple of years, and keeping it mostly to herself, Peggy was finally hospitalized. But she had her way before going into the hospital. She spent the last day with my sister Vickie and her kids. She dug in her garden. And she had a night out with "the girls" (her waitress buddies), drinking, smoking, eating high-cholesterol foods.

"I'll fly right back," I told her that evening.

"It's not necessary," she said. "I'll see you in a couple weeks when you're finished grading exams. You have a job to look out for."

I insisted she hear me out. "You know, Mom," I said self-consciously, "it's okay to tell your son you'd like him to fly home if you feel that way."

"I know," she said. "I will."

That was the last time I spoke with her. She was gone before the sun rose.

Peggy's death was no liberation. I did not feel relieved. Nor did I look forward to completing the separation process that psychologists theorize between mothers and sons. Separation was not something Peggy and I strived to achieve. Since she and her husband were public communists, leaders of the Michigan Communist Party during the period of McCarthyism in the 1950s, most of the time we worked hard so she wouldn't be separated from us by the government. So when I first came across the concept of separation in the literature about men, I thought that didn't apply to me.

I'm not so sure any more. It's true I didn't have the option to separate from a typical mother. But like men who do, I've devoted considerable psychic energy to separating from a construction of "mother" which makes it difficult to be an adult male in today's world.

Because managing McCarthyism and surviving state repression had been seen as heroic, and being tough and showing no emotions had been so thoroughly idealized, I elevated Peggy to sainthood when she died. My narratives became Saint Peggy stories. I also reinterpreted my own survival of her harsh discipline as heroism. And the farther I got from it, the more heroic my stories became.

I could never admit how hard it was for me to be loved by Peggy, that her toughness made her a difficult person to love. So I made her into a hero. It was so much easier to love the idealizations than the realities.

Separating idealizations of Peggy from realities is difficult. Choosing between them was impossible in the 1950s. Growing up Red meant we had no choices. Everything we did was supposed to be necessary. Having choices was a luxury other kids had, kids whose parents were not "public enemies." I would get angry with friends who had choices and chose not to make them. I thought they were incredibly lucky (spoiled rotten!) when they complained about having to choose between options.

My buddies thought Peggy was real good-looking. Some even said beautiful. That's not how I saw her. Built low to the ground (she was barely four foot eleven), squat (between 120 and 140 pounds), with a muscular and powerful body, I thought she looked like a human fireplug. There was nothing graceful about Peggy. Her hands were strong and round, her fingers stubby. Her legs were short and thick; she had odd-shaped feet, tiny but wide across the toes, narrow at the heel. How could she be beautiful, I wondered, when her body and mine were virtual duplicates of each other?

She was the opposite of 1950s femininity. She smoked, could "drink any man under the table" and "curse like a sailor" (her words). A waitress most of her life, she had transformed biting wit, a devilish sense of humor, and brilliant repartee into high art. She was also particularly skilled at using all three to her advantage—often to my *disadvantage.* "What are you?" she'd joke as I learned how to verbally joust with her, "a wise guy or a truckdriver?"

She didn't come close to the 1950s fantasy of mother/ woman. She wasn't kind, saintly, forgiving, sympathetic, or long suffering. Born in 1912 and brought up in a tough Tacoma working-class neighborhood by a single mother who had immi-grated from England to Canada and who preferred making IWW soapbox speeches in downtown Seattle to raising three kids, Peggy didn't have much time for such "luxuries." Independent when it wasn't yet fashionable, she left Washington on the back of a lover's motorcycle headed across the continent for New York. She was sixteen years old. Having dropped out of school two years earlier and already raised two brothers while working as a waitress, Peggy waited until she was "legal" before leaving an unhappy home and a troubled relationship with her equally independent mother. Three years later she was elected secretary of the Boot and Shoe Workers Union in New York.

She didn't see her family again for eight years. By that time she and Saully had met, lived together and broken up. It was 1936. He was in Spain with the International Brigades. They got back together when he returned, but it wasn't until 1942—two years after I was born and Vickie was on the way—that they asked the state to recognize their relationship. Saully had volunteered to be a paratrooper and Peggy insisted they get married. If she had to be a widow, she needed survivor's benefits.

I thought Peggy was not only too independent to be beautiful, but also too tough. Damn, was she tough. Especially on me. Somewhere between a Marine Corps drill sergeant and a tough-love therapist, Peggy "took no crap" from rebellious teenage boys.

"You want something to cry about?" she told me, an adolescent, trying to hold back tears after being smacked. "I'll give you something to cry about!"

And sometimes she did. But it wasn't enough to keep from crying. I was also expected to not show how I felt about it.

"And you wipe that look off your face!" she said when I allowed myself a rebellious glance.

Peggy's toughness was crucial to our survival. As an increasingly hostile government penetrated our everyday lives, she taught me and Vickie to control our emotions and mask our feelings. Her lessons became critical survival skills.

As a twelve-year-old, I remember watching Saully being escorted into court by federal marshals. Charged under the Smith Act with conspiring to teach and advocate the violent overthrow of the government,* he was draped in chains. I couldn't control the lump in my throat, but I worked hard to fight back the tears as Peggy squeezed me tightly. She smiled insincerely and said under her breath, "Not here. No tears in public."

Two months later at the same federal building, Peggy was arrested for violating the Walter-McCarran Act.† Finding she had been a member of the Communist Party, the government

---

* The government did not need an overt act to arrest him under the Smith Act. This legislation punished political activists for the probable consequences that might result if they tried to put their ideas into action.

† Passed in 1952 over President Truman's veto, the Walter-McCarran Act provided that noncitizens could be deported for any one of more than one hundred "offenses." Membership in organizations proscribed by the United States attorney general, e.g., the Communist Party, was one of those offenses and therefore grounds for deportation.

ruled she was an "undesirable alien" and ordered her deported to Canada.

Surrounded by agents of the Immigration and Naturalization Service, she winked when she caught my eye in court. I somehow managed to cover the pain with a silly grin.

While that neither stopped the hurt nor the uncontrollable fear, I knew better than to say out loud what I felt inside. Feelings had become suspect, especially feelings about Saully going to jail or Peggy being deported. Peggy called that kind of talk "belly-button gazing"; it was "self-indulgent." Sometimes I felt like stomping my feet and screaming at Peggy, like other kids did when they were frustrated. Allowing myself to realize I was actually mad at her was unthinkable. It was never an option.

And when I sometimes doubted that things would, as Peggy insisted, "work themselves out," or seriously questioned whether there really would be a "revolution," I also learned to keep that to myself. "Keeping things to yourself" was one of Peggy's most important rules. When I wondered if the "revolution" was worth all this pain, I kept that to myself too.

When security became crucial, Peggy instituted a new set of rules.

"When's Saully coming back?" I asked after he had disappeared yet again.

Peggy put an index finger to her lips, looked around the room and said, "The walls have ears; we'll talk about that some other time." I had no doubt the walls had ears. I could see the government's eyes, always at least two sets of them, twenty-four hours a day inside the FBI cars parked outside our house.

The wrong kind of phone talk could be a serious security breach. "Don't say someone's name when you answer the phone and recognize their voice," she told me in her I-mean-business tone, when I innocently announced that so-and-so was calling. Or, "Don't ask, 'Who is calling?' That just makes the FBI's work easier." It seemed as though we were never safe, never alone.

Idle curiosity was not an option either. When someone said good-bye, you didn't ask, "When will I see you again?" That was another Peggy rule: There were no "innocent" questions.

What we didn't know couldn't hurt us. We had a limited episte-mology: We knew only what was "necessary" to know.

I knew the world was a treacherous place. Family friends came and went. They usually went, frequently to jail. Some-times they went for good. Some of Peggy's friends were deported for allegedly being communists. Gone for good, like a lot of her friends who had died fighting in Spain or during the Second World War.

I also knew about betrayal. When the House Un-American Activities Committee held hearings in Detroit in 1951, a woman who baby-sat Vickie and me and ate dinner with us, someone we called "Grandma Bernice," turned up as a "friendly witness." "Stool pigeon" is what Peggy called her, and we never saw her again. A couple of years later, when the government was having trouble deporting Peggy because they could not prove where she was actually born, Peggy's mother—Grandma Hobson—was forced to testify against her own daughter. Facing the possibility of being deported herself, and threatened with indefinite imprison-ment for perjury and "contempt of court," Grandma—after refus-ing three times—testified that Peggy had been born in Canada and brought to the U.S. when she was a few months old. And though no record of this entry could be found, on October 20, 1954, Peggy received a letter from James Butterfield, district direc-tor of the INS. "You are hereby directed," he wrote, "to appear in complete readiness for deportation to Canada on November 2, 1954. Be in possession of all your personal belongings."

That was the only time I saw my mother cry. She was out-side, on the porch with Saully. I never told her I saw her crying. I kept that to myself.

Because betrayal was a regular feature of everyday life, loy-alty and self-reliance were golden rules in Peggy's house. She didn't permit "ratting," "snitching," or "telling on" anyone. Even as I write this, years after her death, I ask myself: Can I talk about Peggy honestly without betraying her?

We were also expected to be self-sufficient. She insisted we take responsibility for what we did. Noble motives were never acceptable substitutes for plans gone bad. "The road to hell," she liked to say, "is paved with good intentions." Peggy was concerned strictly with outcomes, she wouldn't accept excuses. "Tell me how you're going to deal with it," she'd say, "I don't want to hear why you did it."

Self-reliance meant being independent and tough, being able to take the government's best shots without flinching. It meant not being dependent on anyone, knowing how to take care of yourself. Not just emotionally. Physically too. So when Saully was in jail, Peggy taught me how to fight, how to protect myself. She tried to teach me how to be in control of myself, how not to act spontaneously, but always to think through consequences. I never completely learned that lesson though.

We lived in a binary world. We were the "good guys," the government was the "bad guys." Not surprisingly, my relationship with Peggy had its uncompromising moments.

"In or out," she demanded one freezing Saturday night in February as I sat on the doorstep of our second-floor flat on Clairmount Street. I'd been tobogganing with buddies, standing up, backwards. The sled flipped over midway down the hill and landed on my ankle. It was so swollen now I literally could not walk. Bobby Rowlson had carried me up the stairs, and knowing Peggy's temper, deposited me and ran.

"I think I broke my ankle," I said. "I can't walk."

"Where did you get your medical degree?" Peggy asked from behind her newspaper. She had just gotten off work and was still wearing her waitress's uniform.

"I can't walk."

"You should have thought about that before horsing around on that hill."

"I can't walk."

"What do you expect me to do? Carry you?"

I did, but I didn't have the nerve to say so.

"I can't walk," I repeated.

"Then you'd better crawl."

But she did carry me—the next morning. After a night's sleep, she put me on her back, took me to the car, and then to the hospital.

I knew we were different. But I never thought Peggy was extraordinary. Nearly all of my buddy's mothers were tough women. Even though she had lost one lung to TB, George's mom worked every day cleaning people's houses. When Woody and Jim's dad was killed in World War II, their mom worked as a waitress. Almost everyone got yelled at a lot. Guys who were spared public verbal humiliation were the exceptions. And we made fun of them. We were all expected to take care of ourselves. Most of us had jobs by the time we were thirteen. Even Maurice, whose father was a doctor. We were supposed to be able to handle any wild cards life dealt us.

If I allowed myself to complain, Peggy's response was consistent: "Things are tough all over. Deal with it." And my friends' lives seemed to confirm her. Most were learning to manage feelings, hide emotions, keep secrets.

My black friends also lived in a dichotomous world. Theirs was racial, not political. But it was equally either-or. Their options were even more limited. The government had deeply insinuated itself in their lives, especially the Detroit police with its unofficial racial codes. Betrayal was also an experience we shared. They knew how to protect themselves too. And they usually learned that from their mothers.

At the time I thought my experience wasn't terribly unique. But I've come to realize that Peggy managed state repression by normalizing its awful consequences. She transformed methods for handling a harsh and difficult world into principles for living.

She also managed state terror by rejecting victimhood. We didn't see ourselves as victims. Instead my family, especially Peggy, was idealized in communist circles as heroic. When she was arrested, a Peggy Wellman Defense Committee produced mountains of material maintaining her innocence and re-creating her as a larger-than-life figure. Mother-wife-activist. The heroine of an unfolding American family tragedy.

I made my contribution to this re-creation by regaling friends with amazing tales of how Peggy once tripped an FBI agent who followed her too closely on a New York bus. One of my favorites recounted Peggy driving seven hundred miles between New York and Detroit without stopping except for gas. She forced the FBI agents following us to drive all day, long after they were supposed to be spelled by a fresh set of escorts.

I never admitted how uncomfortable I was sitting in the car all day. And I never talked about the terror I felt.

Because my parents normalized circumstances that were clearly abnormal and constructed their experiences in heroic terms, Vickie and I were unable to openly discuss our feelings about the situation. Don't take it "personally," we were told as the government relentlessly hammered our parents. And when we rejected that notion—it certainly *felt* very personal, especially when FBI agents followed us back and forth to school each day—they would tell us not to be so "subjective." While too young to know the difference between objectivity and subjectivity, we came to recognize that "subjectivity" was subversive.

I never felt very heroic. But I never thought of myself as a victim either. Even though the world was harsh and treacherous, it had complexities. I broke Peggy's survival rules. I found it impossible to keep everything to myself. I shared intimacies, especially with her. I kept very few secrets from Peggy.

Some questions *were* innocent. And I insisted on asking them. So when a couple of eleven-year-olds in my sixth-grade class at Brady Elementary exchanged stories about "getting pussy," I asked Peggy if something was wrong with me because I was still a virgin. She smiled a very warm, wise smile and assured me I was quite normal.

"You know, sweetie," she said softly, "those who say, don't know. And those who know, don't say."

That was not reassuring.

"But, Peggy," I said in absolute horror, "I don't say, and I don't know either!"

I trusted Peggy. Profoundly and implicitly. I felt perfectly comfortable discussing my emerging sexuality with her. I thought that was normal. I thought that was how it is with sons and mothers. Later in life, when I shared this experience with male friends, I discovered it was not.

When Peggy insisted I take consequences into account before I acted, she made it possible for me to take responsibility for myself. Taking responsibility meant I actually did have options. I could exercise judgment. I didn't have to be a victim. Peggy's rules therefore helped me discover options in a world that seemed to exclude choices.

Peggy's rules were not one-dimensional. And they were not applied inflexibly. Loyalty was also a code for honor and integrity. Being responsible meant taking risks as well as accepting consequences. Taking risks meant doing things because it was "right" to do them, even when it was inconvenient, possibly painful, and there was little chance for success. Peggy's principles gave me a set of values to live by.

She insisted I be "principled" in my relations with young women. We spent many long evenings exchanging heated words as we debated, defined, and deconstructed the meaning of that code. She allowed me to dispute her rigid Victorian morality. She reluctantly allowed me to question monogamous relationships. But one thing she refused to discuss. "Respect," she called it. That was her limiting principle and she applied it consistently and persistently.

She called black people Negroes when sometimes black people still called themselves colored—and white people called them worse. She would not allow the word *nigger* to be spoken in her house. And years later, when a couple of my black friends used the word in what they considered an affectionate manner, she told them to please not use it in her presence.

To Peggy, toughness meant more than being tough. It meant having principles and living by them. Even when that hurt. Toughness meant being idealistic, especially when idealism was neither fashionable nor profitable. Given the 1950s popular image of Communists as opportunistic agents of a foreign enemy, Peggy's version of toughness was remarkably principled and idealistic.

Peggy was an irreverent comrade who used a mischievous sense of humor and wit to rebel against—and get in trouble with—humorless C.P. bureaucrats. She rebelled against party dress codes. She loved to tell stories of her youthful defiance of party discipline, how she and her closest friend Ernesta would "dress up," wear nylons and makeup, go out dancing and drinking while party stalwarts like Saully were busy organizing the working class. When she could afford expensive food, she would justify the purchase by paraphrasing Mother Jones, an American communist heroine: "Nothing's too good for the working class!" She didn't take orders easily and would use her colorful waitress language when she disagreed with the party's message. "Mind your own damn business," I heard her tell a dour national party officer when told that it didn't look right for a male comrade to be renting a room while Saully was in jail.

She also took too much pride in her capacity to consume large amounts of alcohol to match the public image of a bolshevik. And who can conceive of a revolutionary who loved to cook? On those rare occasions when she didn't have a meeting, or wasn't working, she would put together elaborate, elegantly crafted dinners that were delicious. She also loved to garden and nurture houseplants. She could make flowers grow in nearly any climate. A homeopathic doctor with plants, she cured her sick green friends with tender loving care and friendly talk. She may have cherished her green thumb more than her Red politics. She was also an accomplished tailor who made many of her own clothes. She enjoyed knitting a complicated sweater. When something went wrong around the house, she fixed it. One time she took an upholstery class so she could reupholster our living room couch and chairs.

Peggy's kitchens, gardens, irreverence, and practical skills were emotionally safe, protected places where I could ignore the angry world outside. They were dependable intermissions from the mean-spirited drama I had not volunteered to star in. I was proud when she stood up to C.P. heavies. I admired her rebelliousness and tried to emulate it. I loved to watch her cook and listen to her laugh and tell stories. I enjoyed working with her, even if it meant staying home Saturday afternoons. Her smile could disarm anyone—even me.

Being tough didn't preclude love. Peggy created deep, profound relationships and sustained them throughout her lifetime. "She loved beauty," her dearest friend, Lydia Mates, wrote when Peggy died, "and found it wherever it was: in children, flowers, and comrades. Where it wasn't before, she pitched in to create it." What I experienced as being too tough, her friends felt was strength and intense loyalty. She had an especially deep love for Lydia and three other women comrades who were like sisters to her: Lil Green, Annie Shore, and Margie Watt. The love they shared enabled them to manage a particularly difficult set of experiences in Cold War America.

She loved me too, in her own special way. But I didn't always know that. It was not easy to be loved by Peggy. The government was partly responsible, making it difficult for her to tend to my emotional needs. But not entirely. If you were a boy, Peggy made it very difficult to be loved by her. She seemed to be so much easier on Vickie. When Vickie got stubborn, she was cajoled. More often than not, I'd get slugged. And when Peggy caught the two of us fighting, she always assumed I had started it.

I've only recently been able to figure out why Peggy was so tough on boys. Even though she loved men—some of her closest, dearest friends were men—she had serious grievances with people occupying that category. And in retrospect, I can see that she had good reasons to be angry at men. Her father abandoned her before she was two. Saully and his male comrades left her regularly: to fight in Spain, to fight in Europe during World War II, to go underground, to be in jail. Each time they went off to pursue the good fight, she was left alone—the last three times with two kids to raise.

And there may have been an even deeper reason. Men in the prefeminist Old Left—and some women too—talked at, or down to, women and children. They didn't listen. They lectured. And they were always right. Comrades didn't discuss, they debated. The debates were polemical verbal contests with no middle ground and only one winner. Saully had mastered this style.

Most of her life Peggy was either being abandoned by men, covering up for them and making excuses for their absences, or being lectured at and talked down to by them. But she didn't always direct her anger at the men who made her miserable. While Peggy and Saully had a volatile, acrimonious relationship—especially near the end—she often aimed her rage at me. The physical confrontations, the roundhouse punches and open-handed slaps to the face, didn't stop until I was twenty-two years old.

The last time she tried to hit me I was washing dishes. I had made some insolent remark and probably sounded like Saully. But instead of taking the blow, as she wound up to smack me, I grabbed both her hands.

"Don't you hit me again!" I demanded.

"Let me go!" she responded, resisting.

"Don't hit me again," I repeated, holding her hands tighter.

"Let me go!" she replied, continuing to struggle. I did. And she immediately began to tickle me. She didn't stop until I was rolling on the floor and begged for mercy. We had both saved face.

I always normalized Peggy's anger toward me. I told myself it was necessary preparation for dealing with harsh realities. Didn't most mothers discipline their sons with physical force? I blamed the government for her ugly temper. But I never thought of myself as the recipient of misdirected rage. And it never occurred to me that Peggy was unhappy. In my eyes she was an emotionally healthy, heroic woman.

Peggy's principles had a lot to do with my involvement in the New Left. But not in ways the FBI would have expected. In fact I had moved to California in part to get away from politics. I wanted to make it on my own, be known for what I did, not who my parents were. And I knew that radical politics could have devastating consequences. I wasn't willing to pay the personal price Peggy and Saully had paid. So I kept my history secret. And I didn't go South in 1963 like I thought I should.

Peggy did. She helped her union organize a caravan of buses to the March on Washington. And she marched from Selma to Montgomery with Martin Luther King.

I agonized over what to do. I worried that because my parents were Reds, my involvement would discredit the movement. Should I be discreet instead of publicly involved? I felt an ugly, self-defeating kind of self-censorship. And once again I broke Peggy's cardinal rule for survival: I didn't keep the fears to myself. I shared them with her. "Stop belly-button gazing!" she exploded over the phone one afternoon. "Do what you think is right. But *do* something!"

When I joined Berkeley's Free Speech Movement in 1964, she wasn't convinced that disrupting the campus and going to jail was the way to get "free speech." She thought Students for a Democratic Society was a group of spoiled middle-class college kids. She liked my Student Nonviolent Coordinating Committee friends better, but asked why they were "so damn intense." When my SDS and SNCC comrades came through Detroit, she was less taken with them than Saully was. Though she marched against the war in Vietnam and organized her union to oppose it, she also thought my friends went too far, especially when we flew the Vietcong flag.

We had heated political arguments. Peggy didn't think the Equal Rights Amendment was progressive: it undid union work she had put a lot of energy into. Progress was getting employers to sign contracts that recognized differences between men and women, contracts that allowed waitresses to carry less than waiters, and guaranteed them longer breaks than men. She thought the ERA would end all that. So she led a sit-in protest of waitresses at Michigan's capitol in Lansing.

Though Peggy's ideological politics did not move me to be political, I could not help being moved by the principled ways she maneuvered through life, being principled even when that was unpopular. Watching her taught me about loyalty, taking risks, idealism, a sense of humor, and irreverence. Her sense of morality, what she called being principled, did not recognize distinctions between ends and means. For Peggy, ends never justified means. The way in which goals were accomplished was just as important as the goals. Because of her, I found the New Left critique of the Old Left compelling. Ironically, then, values

I still cherish, values typically associated with the New Left, I learned from my communist mother.

I still live by those principles. But sometimes I wish I hadn't learned her lessons so well. She never taught me how to compromise. That gets me in trouble. At the university some colleagues equate principled behavior with "rigidity" and confuse consistency with "inflexibility." Like Peggy, I'm usually in the minority, even on the Left.

One of my favorite Peggy stories is based on a conversation we had the weekend after Martin Luther King had been murdered. It was 1968. I had just passed my doctoral exams in Berkeley and was back in Detroit visiting. The two of us were sharing a drink late one night.

"You know," she said, "I was proud when you graduated from high school. You were the first one in our family to do so.

"I understood why you wanted to go to college. That made more sense than going into the Army or working in a factory. And I was pleased when you graduated.

"I didn't completely understand why you went to graduate school, but I knew you wanted to avoid the Army and that was a good idea.

"I knew you were happy to finish your master's degree, and I was pleased for you. I read your thesis. It was hard going for me, but I tried to understand it." (The thesis analyzed civil rights leadership in San Francisco. And although I struggled with the writing, I actually thought it was relatively easy to read.)

"Now you've passed your orals and you plan to write a dissertation that I'll never be able to read. I don't understand that. Why do you want to be better than me?"

"I don't," I said, taken aback by the formulation. "I just want options."

"Don't you think I want options? Do you think I like being a waitress or a business agent?"

"It's not about being better than you," I tried to explain. "It's options."

But no matter how I tried to explain my choice, the justification was always unsatisfactory. She kept asking why I wanted to be better than her.

I finally said: "I'll show you. I'll write a dissertation you'll understand. That way you'll know it's not about being better than you."

But I never showed her. She died six years later, two months and one chapter before I finished.

I always loved that story, but more and more I'm finding it sad and painful. I now hear in Peggy's comments a fear that her son was abandoning her and adopting that arrogant, inaccessible way of talking she associated with maleness. I now realize that Peggy saw independence also as being disloyal. The men in her life usually abandoned her when they exercised the option of independence. When Peggy asked, "Why do you want to be better than me?" that meant she didn't trust me to be independent and male.

Peggy's legacy is both a blessing and a curse. I feel privileged to have experienced a mother who gave herself so completely to an ideal, who devoted so much of her life to principled beliefs, who actually thought she could build a better world than the one she inherited. I seriously doubt that I will see idealism of this quality again in my lifetime. But I'm also left feeling that I can never measure up, that I can never be what she was, do what she did, face down what she faced up to. I sometimes feel that my success is her failure, that I've gone over to the "other side."

My encounter with Peggy over the dissertation is painful because now it also makes me feel angry. Anger that she died before I could prove independence did not mean disloyalty. Anger that perhaps, in some ultimate way, she had betrayed *me*, because her death betrayed the possibility that I could ever be independent *and* loyal, one man who would not abandon her, an intellectual son who could write for his working-class mother, one man who would not talk down to her.

I've only recently permitted myself to feel angry at Peggy, to call it that, and to sometimes even say it out loud. My walls still have ears, they always will. And I'm still pretty good at concealing my emotions. But though I know that once again I'm violating Peggy's rule about keeping things to myself, I'm beginning to think I need to say it. "Only the silence and emptiness following a moment of forgiveness can stop the monster of deadly anger," writes Mary Gordon.

I don't feel such a silence yet. Does that mean I have not yet forgiven? By voicing the anger I do feel some peace. But I don't feel the silence. There's still a lot of hollering in my head.

PART 8

HER SPIRIT LIVES ON

The far-reaching impact of mothers on the souls of men is a classic theme of literature and psychology. There are innumerable famous men who would have been disparaged as mama's boys had they been lesser mortals: Franklin Roosevelt, Dwight Eisenhower, and George Patton, among many others. Then there is César Chávez, whose illiterate mother's *dichos* and *consejos* (proverbs and advice) were a more important source of his philosophy of nonviolence than were Gandhi or St. Francis. And for a writer or an artist, a mother may be a personal muse.

This is the case with Juan Felipe Herrera, who sees his mother's love of language as the fount of his own fascination with words and writing. For the migrant farmworker Lucha Quintana, poverty and patriarchy conspired to stifle the possible expression of her many creative talents. In his life and work her son fulfills her unrealized potentials. Herrera saw so much pain in his mother's life that in his mourning he searched for moments of joy, finally realizing that he, her only child, was that joy.

For twenty years the mother of Mark O'Brien lovingly lifted him out of his oxygen tent so that he could get some glimpses of a world outside. Writing after her death, O'Brien, in a moment of epiphany, realizes that like his mother, he too bites his lip to cover up pain and frustration. This suggests a larger realization, one that many sons come to only in the course of decades: the understanding of how much we are like our mothers. We don't see this early in our lives and many men will never see it. The larger culture, as well as modern psychology, instructs us to "separate" from our mothers—psychically as well as physically—and to identify instead with our fathers. The idea behind "Like father, like son" seems self-evident. Not so its cognate: "Like mother, like son."

Writing about his mother after her death from cancer, Steve Masover came to realize how much he resembled her, how her gifts had enriched his life and would continue to do so. The next two selections are rich in oedipal overtones. John Boe evokes his erotic attachment to Margaret Boe through the image of her white slip and the sensuality of slipping into bed at night next to that white slip. And Herman Blake finds his mother's spirit in the lilac flowers for which Lylace Blake was named and in the women he tries to help in his work as a university administrator, women who, in their poverty, their obesity, and their stressed-out lives, remind him of her.

Gardiner Harris's mother died when her son was thirteen. Shortly after, he wrote about his experience in a prose poem; "What Am I: I Am My Mother's Spirit," the title of which, incidentally, inspired the title of this book.

Gardiner's poem is full of feeling, but twenty years later he berates himself for shutting down his emotions rather than feeling the enormity of his loss.

In our final essay, "Holding Ava," Jess Walter recapitulates a number of recurring themes about the death of mothers. Like so many others, his mother is dying of cancer. Now it's her son's turn to care for her, a mother who had comforted him through a childhood of bruises and pain.

Jess and his wife named their newborn daughter after her grandmother, thus Ava will carry on her father's mother's spirit in this parable of death and rebirth.

DELIA REXROTH

Kenneth Rexroth

California rolls into
Sleepy summer, and the air
Is full of the bitter sweet
Smoke of the grass fires burning
On the San Francisco hills.
Flesh burns so, and the pyramids
Likewise, and the burning stars.
Tired tonight, in a city
Of parvenus, in the inhuman
West, in the most blood drenched year,
I took down a book of poems
That you used to like, that you
Used to sing music I
Never found anywhere again—
Michael Field's book, *Long Ago*.
Indeed it's long ago now—
Your bronze hair and svelte body
I guess you were a fierce love,

A wild wife, an animal
Mother. And now life has cost
Me more years, though much less pain,
Than you had to pay for it.
And I have bought back, for and from
Myself, these poems and paintings,
Carved from the protesting bone,
The precious consequences
Of your torn and distraught life.

LUCHA IS SHORT
FOR LIGHT

Juan Felipe Herrera

Not long after my mother died, I have begun to unravel some of her things that I keep bundled in two old sports bags. In one tiny envelope I find a miniature burgundy-colored address book, the kind that was popular in the fifties, almost the size of a postage stamp. The minivolume in my palm, I rub my thumb over its rouge colors. Phrases from poems emerge, short stanzas from songs she remembered are written sideways against the flow of the tiny blue lines. This is the place where she felt free to express her thoughts, this atomic compendium, one of the secret reservoirs for her voice and the spin of her creative life. Again, I am halted by my mother's love for language. Language, the little book, my inheritance. Even after her death, she alerts me in her familiar manner.

Small in stature, Lucha Quintana—maybe four feet, six inches, diminutive as her belongings. Yet her life, words, and insights loom over my horizons and continue to reach out to me. Lucha still envelops me as much as she did in the early years, as her only child. During the summer, my father, Felipe Emilio, was usually away in New Mexico, visiting his grown children by another marriage. We were bonded by her miniature womb, which only gave one living child, as much as by the spaces left by my wandering and starry-eyed father. "We've got to move," he would say, "there's good water up in the hills, clean water from natural springs." Soon he would leave and scout the scorched valley of California or jaunt to Santa Rosalía, in the heart of Chihuahua, his birthplace, in search of thermal springs. We lingered behind, in the quiet and coppery outskirts of small *migrante* towns, like Vista or Ramona or Fowler, where I was born.

I was my mother's first address book. As we walked to town in the afternoons, after school, she would recount the places where she had lived: the old shanties in the barrio of "El Niño Perdido" in Mexico City, where "the floors were dirt and the pillows were bricks." Or, "Overland Street, El Paso, Texas," she utters, "this is the house where your grandmother Juanita died of a stroke." Later, in a lighter mood: "This is the same yard where my dog, Picho, would arrive barrel-chested from eating mounds of handouts at the local *mercado* butcher shop." Segundo Barrio, Frutas Street—another address; she lifts her eyes and speaks—"Here, I helped your uncle Chente make toys out of wood. He became an artist out of necessity and later exhibited his work in the streets of New York. 'I want to go to Europe,' he would tell me, 'that's where the art is.'" Her voice changes again: "I made love over there, hiding in the night alleys. Afraid of my mother." She reflects. "I don't want that for you, Juanito, I want you to be free and full of life."

Every day was inscribed with memories of times gone by, deep lessons from tiny and solitary places like the one-room apartment my mother shared with my grandmother in El Paso in the late thirties, a few years before my grandmother died in 1940. When the pain of my last weeks with my mother comes to me, I return to her last moments with her mother; I imagine my mother waiting in line at the *panaderías*, after a hard day scrubbing and toweling dry the floors, waiting for *pan dulce* to take home to the little brick house in Segundo Barrio. She switches on the radio, throws off her shoes, and lies on the bed, exhausted.

My grandmother's severity also punishes me. I recall my mother's story of how my grandmother Juanita pulled her out of third grade for stealing candy with her girlfriend Chava. "I was never allowed to return to school; all I had left were a few songs in English and a spelling medal that I won that last year. From that point on I worked as a maid and housekeeper." As much as my mother lauded her with praise and honor, never speaking ill of her, I always sensed that this was a devastating blow to her at such a young age. She spent the rest of her life making up for the severed years of school learning. I learned her repertoire of school songs, poems about autumn, and teachers' names; I read her newspapers and collection of *Reader's Digest* and *Life* magazines. I retraced her steps. In sixth grade in San Francisco, while my mother baby-sat for my older cousins in the Mission District, I would cruise down Mission Street with a couple of my friends from school and pilfer key chains, shirts, and toys until we reached Woolworth's at Fourth and Market. Her words were kept close to my heart: "In those days my mother worked hard as a maid, I was her only companion, me and a little kitty I had . . . until she died." I was her opposite, I thought to myself, floating at free will across the city streets. Yet I carried on with ancient tasks tucked neatly inside my closed fists.

Somewhere in my mother's self-sacrifice for her mother and for me, her own true moments arise, her ease in the small pleasures of being alive, whether in the open fields of Delano picking grapes and drying peaches or in a second-story apartment building in the Mission District caring for a neighbor's child. My own sense of loyalty has also often overtaken me. In my own fight to keep her close, I have wanted to battle and reshape her life; I have denied her choices and her own transformations as she lifted herself through the limits within her bounds. "How could I leave her?" she would say to me. "It was my duty to care for her in her old age." On the day of my grandmother's death, my mother was thirty-six—the same age I was when she died.

Our intimacy and inner connections burn inside me; addresses, numbers, and names blend into stories and kind ghost shapes. My grieving tempered by our closeness, I talk to her every day as I touch her small box of ashes, which I keep in my bedroom. Then I breathe out and ask for her blessings as I walk into the flat streets of the city; I go teach at Fresno State, eleven miles north of Fowler, that little raisin town where forty-five years ago my father had to stop his wandering short because the hour had come for my mother to give birth to her only child.

In her last days, while staying in San José, California, with me and my wife, Margarita, my mother rose to the occasion as I played one of my favorite pieces by Takanaka, a Japanese rock guitarist and disciple of Carlos Santana. A few feet from the small kitchen, my mother danced, her left hand up leading an invisible partner across the sound waves. This was the last time I saw her lightness and her love for music come alive. Was I the invisible partner? Four months later she died quietly, at the age of seventy-nine. What followed were thin attempts at reconciling with her death and life: therapy, journal-writing, aerobics, muffled screams. I follow the therapist's advice—to turn myself inside out, to pull out my pain. Almost ten years later, I find that my pain has just begun to quell; the first hurdle, the rage-hurdle, crosses under me, the one made of resentments and denials.

Our closeness smothered me. I knew too much about her tribulations. Where was her joy? I asked myself at the time of her death. What joy was possible in the hard ranks of scrub-woman work, with sliced-open cans begging for food in the trim stucco houses of Mount Franklin in El Paso? Standing with outstretched hands, my mother and grandmother stop at each door and ask for leftovers and housework. "Keep this a secret," she said to me. She worked for Sarita, a middle-class Mexican woman in the city. *"Atasca la hacha,"* Sarita howls to my mother, signaling her to wipe the batter bowls with her hands and finish the remains of the swirled delicacies. We joked about this often. *"Atasca la hacha, Juanito,"* she says as I spooned a thick bowl of cooked oatmeal spiced with cinnamon, butter, and brown sugar. Once she and my aunt Aurelia lost themselves in Mount Franklin and wandered for hours in the burning heat. "We were so exhausted; all we could see was the sun coming down." Her first job away from washer-work came in her early thirties at the El Camino Restaurant on Paisano Drive in central

El Paso. The stay was short; she married Pedro Garcia, a brooding man who would check her eyes as they walked downtown
and kick her to the ground to reprimand her for looking at
other men. By the mid-forties Pedro worked as chef and she as
a "salad girl" at the St. Francis Hotel in San Francisco while the
Lawrence Welk Orchestra played in the lobby. By '47, in a
drunken stupor, Pedro met his fate in front of a truck rolling
toward him full speed. A year later she met my father, an older
man in his sixties, a soft-spoken man with fine handwriting and
starry tales.

"My joy came when I met your father," she tells me. "He
never hit me or spoke harshly to me, he never told me what to
do or how to do it. Once he threw his dinnerware down on the
table, when we were living in a trailer in Deming, New Mexico.
You were one year old. 'Where's my food?' he said. I told him
right there, 'Don't you ever throw your fork down like that. I
will leave.' He knew I meant business. I wasn't going to stand
for it." This moment stands out for me, it carries the weight of
her bruised past transformed into her choice to free her life at
its most intimate channels. My parents' life together was calm
and buoyant. Yet, her joy slipped from me as much as I wanted
to grab it and hold it up so I could see it and taste it. What
kind of joy was it if my father died when I was sixteen? What
kind of life did she live if she had to die with straps, tubes, and
needles fixed in her for days on end? I mix my father's death
with my mother's life, I shorten her life sphere by the hard
edge of her final ten days. Braid two deaths, shorten one life—
leave a little room for the life in-between. There was joy, I say
now—the grieving has taken me this far.

The clear awareness of her past difficulties smothered me
as a child and as an adolescent: her extreme poverty as a girl, of
being Mexican in the border towns of Texas and in the migrant
labor camps of central California. I did not note the simplicity
of our lives, the care for each other, the deep sense of respect
my mother and father had and how they raised me with the
ideals of freedom and love. Now I sense the number of gifts
that my mother possessed, the ones that I took for granted: the

power of poise and calm through harrowing encounters, the knowledge that the formula for song was the same as for cooking—you create as you go, you stay light on your feet and give without expecting to receive. And more: her power of insight into people and their hardships, her ability to forgive others, her high energy and adaptability and her love for drama and instantaneous change. My mother's only sister, Aurelia, was her opposite. In San Diego, in the fifties, my aunt screws her mouth and peels her eyes, then forces a nickel out of her pocket as my mother urges her to give alms to a blind man by the Goodwill store where we shop. My aunt Aurelia scolds, "Why are you so nice to people, Lucha? Can't you see, they are taking advantage of you, can't you see? Don't give them the little money you have. Let them work for it, let them get a sense of accomplishment. Save your tears for our mother, Lucha." My aunt Aurelia was not a listener, not gentle, nor was she forgiving. She was there to remind my mother that the world was harsh and that bitter hearts roamed the boulevards in search of do-gooders. My aunt Aurelia died six years after my mother. Her own closed world fell upon her: a cold single room with an uncaring husband who laughed at her, even after a number of strokes that went unreported until my wife and I took her to a hospital for the warmth that my mother would have given if she still lived.

As a teen, I began to rebel against my mother's stories, against my own furious versions. Like my father, the time came to wander, to race away on Saturday mornings, go down Broadway Avenue—sailor shops, tattoo parlors, pool halls; walk for miles to the waterfront of San Diego; sit on the piers and gaze out into the bluish skyline. Navy cruisers and battleships refresh me with their lack of sentiment; they cannot wail or remember or grieve about what could have been, they sway alone in their armed elegance and stoic silver. At the age of seventeen I was accepted into the University of California at Los Angeles. I kissed my little mother at the door of our little apartment at 1846 B Street; I held her warm hands in mine and never returned. This was my first flight away from her and my beginnings.

That same year, she moved to San Francisco a few doors from my aunt Aurelia. At times she moved a block or two into one-room studios where there was more light. We always talked about the light, "la luz." Her birth name was Maria de la Luz, Mary of the Light, "Lucha" for short. She would joke about letting the light into the room as *Luz la chaparrona*. Naming herself as that "small light." I was too busy to listen to her lightness; I mumbled back. Rushed through haphazard relationships—married at nineteen to a Jewish girl of seventeen that I met the first year at UCLA. We had a child, Joaquin. Less than a year later, we separated; neither one of us was prepared or focused. Living the life of a grass-smoking, long-haired, would-be revolutionary for the Chicano Movimiento was more sensible than sifting through my child-pain bundles, more relevant than dealing with my deep cultural differences with a young Jewish woman from New York. Within a short period of time, I became involved with a Mexican woman with three children. Another child came and so did the separation while I was at Stanford in the late seventies.

Mother Mary of the Light was patient. She listened to the little I would disclose to her. She knew I was afraid of letting her into my pain. "I can read your face," she would tell me. The role of a listener was more familiar to me, more secure; since childhood I had been her audience, I had received her bright suffering through stories and songs. To speak about my inner self was almost an impossible task; even in our last years and months together, the words were nervous stones lodged inside my chest. When I did manage to utter a word, she would acknowledge me and let me discover on my own that she had been waiting for me to speak. She seemed to know my stories ahead of time. This eased my stiffness. Why had I carried such guilt and regret over my choices to break out of myself? *Luz la chaparrona* entered with care into my difficulties and let me unravel at my own pace the puzzles and personal workings that belonged to me. She was aware of my deep melodies.

As a child, my mother rocked me in her arms singing Mexican lullabies from El Paso. We sang *corridos* as soon as I was old enough to talk and later, in my teen years in San Diego, she helped me purchase my first guitar, a Stella steel string. In El Paso, she had learned the popular songs played on the radio and danced in the Teatro Colón, a dance club downtown. The guitar still rests in my study. *La guitarra* has become a symbol of the achievements of my uncles and in some ways, in its umber hollowness, it is a sign of the unfulfilled dreams of my mother. In the thirties, as my uncle Roberto organized *"El barco de la ilusión,"* his first radio show, in Juarez, he cut short the role Mother would play with members of Los Pirrines, a popular theater troupe that combined acrobatics, songs, and dance into their portfolio. "This is not good for a young woman," he said. "This is going to stop," he told my grandmother Juanita. "Lucha must think of other things." My mother quickly ended her association with the group and walked back to the drill of floors and the clap of houses filled with foreigners living on the eastern hills of Mount Franklin. She carried a veiled resentment for my uncle Roberto that was only apparent in the way she talked about her other brothers. His assertive role as one of the older sons mitigated her own position as the fiery and youngest child. She preferred the first-born, Uncle Geno. "He had such beautiful writing, you should have seen his letters to my mother. It was his idea that we come up North, to Texas." My mother's voice trails off with a mix of consolation and wariness, "Los Pirrines had a tragic fate, you know; years later, the leader of the troupe committed suicide."

In many ways my mother's stunted desires and longings for theater, song, and dance enter into my own longings. I take on the unfinished dramas. For the last twenty-five years, theater, poetry, and art have been at the center of my enterprise. The story of Los Pirrines became my story of political *teatro* since 1968, the first time I saw El Teatro Campesino. Her tale of my uncle Chente's desire to be a painter and to someday arrive in Europe with his beret and easels became my multimedia project through the years. The entire collection of oral histories and family scenarios has become my literary story-chart. Part of this transfer of unfinished business has to do with the love I have for what she taught me, the other part has to do with wanting to fulfill her dreams, to assuage her wounds and keep her close. This I work on: In this set of notes I go over the words, I look for where they cross over into her terms, I fall in between and seek my way, take stock of where my own language begins.

In the mid-fifties, in Escondido, as we settled from *migrante campesino* labor in the central valley of California, my mother stops in a thrift store and purchases instructional books for me. We walk through the city sidewalks echoing the alphabet to each other. Spanish into English, then back again as we go another block. By the time I entered first grade, I had a fondness for words, illustrated stories, riddles, word games—for letters. On one occasion, she found an old primer in Spanish, printed in the early 1900s. Not long after that, I mastered reading in Spanish—with the accent of colonial Mexican society. The story-lessons were illustrated with metaphors on morality; one of her favorites was the one about the boy and the tree. "In time, with careful attention," she explains, "the tree flourished. Think on that tree, Juanito, you must watch what you do and how you do it—be kind, open. An abandoned tree breaks, becomes crooked."

My mother's love for learning and teaching was also part of her own quest for knowledge at a metaphysical level. Her incessant meditations and questions had more to do with deeper striations of meaning. The notion of hunger was one of her recurring subjects. "What is hunger?" she would ask me. "Why do we have to eat, why is it so?" Does this question have more to do with spirit than with food? I ask. On a visit to her studio apartment in San Francisco in the mid-eighties, she recited a short poem for me, on "emptiness." What was the groundwork of our existence, our lives? The questions float over these notes.

Next to my Dalí calendar on the wall, an old photo a few feet above my computer: My mother holds me in her arms in the middle of a farmworker camp. Her arms are thick and her hair is pulled back, dark and luminous. She squints hard into the camera as the day burns over her. Our old army truck is parked behind us in the middle of a *campo* somewhere in the dreamy vined flatlands of a small town in the valley. Holds me close, tight. Her words resound: "Those were great days. Out in the open. I was an active woman, always doing something, Juanito. When I was pregnant with you I was still picking hops, imagine." Still, the joy escaped me; for years I could only think of her arduous struggle as a *campesina* woman with few if any resources. Her story about almost hemorrhaging to death in the fields shortly after her cesarean stalks me. My own name is my omen—I was Juanito to my mother. "I should have called you Cesareano," my mother jokes. Being born cesarean was a gift. I was alive, yet I was not aware of her own gift to me. I had escaped the jaws of forceps lurking in the tiny boned cavern of my mother. I was an unexpected detour into life. I did not fully realize this. The tragic fate of two of my mother's earlier child-births with Pedro García was my subject—shadows that ran after me, beyond their own fragile sources. One child was crushed by forceps, the other stillborn. As a young boy, I raged against the doctors who ran their arms through my mother's tiny river. The nurses at my birth were gargoyles, the ones that left my mother screaming in the recovery room in the Fowler hospital. If only I could have given her the morphine for the vertical wound, I would have, I thought to myself. What could I do against the powers of the past?

Slowly, I let go. I begin to acknowledge the possibility of joy; my mother's full life, her passage through family strictures, abuse, poverty, and her emergence into songs, her agile move-ment and wisdom. The old Stella guitar in my study lies ready outside of its worn black case. My mother's tiny address libretto stays with me; the photographs she took as I grew up in the small towns of California speak of her office, her love for light and images of the heart. Lucha, the photographer, the self-made poet, the storyteller, the compassionate seeker and loving wife, the small-framed philosopher. As I write these notes, approach-ing my forty-sixth birthday, I begin to accept my mother as she was. Where was her joy? I ask in the morning as I walk over to her small box of ashes. I burn incense and ask, "What was it?"

"You are the joy," the light says.

A TALENT FOR LOVE

Mark O'Brien

Helen Agnes Kelly O'Brien
August 10, 1926 – September 4, 1994

On a Friday in September 1994, my brother Ken spoke his words and my words at her funeral. Post-polio syndrome had weakened me so much that I was unable to attend, so I was grateful to Ken for asking me to contribute to the eulogy and thereby giving me a way to participate. I lay in my iron lung in Berkeley, a hundred miles from her funeral near Sacramento, trying to remember the last time I had seen her. I knew it had been July. She and my father had visited me in my apartment, where we ate sandwiches and talked. It had been an unexceptional visit. I couldn't recall any details: what she said, what she wore, the last time she kissed me. Guilty for not being able to recall these final details, I tried to picture Helen as she was now—dead, stiff and rotting in a coffin on a hot Sacramento day.

Suddenly, I felt she was okay. I didn't have a vision of Helen in heaven. No, it was just a feeling that she was okay, that she wasn't that body in the coffin, she was something more, a spirit. And that spirit was okay. Freed from worry, she would want me to know so that I wouldn't worry.

Helen was my mother and of course I loved her. But she was also the woman who fed me, washed me, and lifted me every day for nineteen years. After I got polio in 1955—I was six then—all my limbs were paralyzed and I lived in hospitals for two years. Both Helen and my father, Walter, wanted me to live with them again, so in 1957 I returned home to Stoughton, a suburb of Boston. That's when she began the extraordinary task of taking care of me.

She would lift me from the iron lung into the ambulance cot early on weekday mornings. She would take me to the TV room where I'd watch cartoons and Laurel and Hardy with my younger brother, Ken, and my younger sister, Karen. After Ken left for school, Helen would take me back to my room, lift me into my bed, feed me breakfast, wash me, and exercise me. My father helped on weekends, but she did most of the work of keeping me comfortable, happy, and alive. Perhaps she loved me so much that she wanted to help me in every way she could. Her lifting me established between us a solid relationship of trust.

She was with me for almost every day between my return from the hospital in 1957 and my departure in 1976. She had two breaks from the task of taking care of me. The first came in the early sixties after she burned her hands while deep-frying clams. The second time was in the mid-seventies when she flew back to Massachusetts for her father's funeral. All the other times she had been within a shout. When we were living back east, she would lift me and take me outside to see the snow after a Massachusetts blizzard. Later she would lift me and take me outside so I could watch children play in the schoolyard that was across the street from our first Sacramento home. She continued to lift me when she was pregnant with Rachel, her fourth and last child. She didn't tell me she was pregnant until the eighth month, perhaps because being a woman of her times and an Irish Catholic to boot, she felt embarrassed to talk about sex and childbirth with her children.

I depended on her for my daily needs until I was twenty-seven, perhaps too long, some would say. But there were very few exits for disabled children growing into adulthood in those days. The last time she lifted me was in September 1976, when I left home, headed for a journey that would eventually take me to Berkeley, where I would earn a B.A. and begin my new life.

My encounter with polio was only the first in a series of tragedies Helen would face. In the winter of 1961, my sister Karen, who was Helen's first daughter, died of pneumonia at the age of seven. When the snowdrifts melted in the spring, it was easier for the women of the neighborhood to meet. All of them asked Helen about Karen's death and Helen always told the story in the same way, precisely, in chronological order, her voice becoming softer, her tone more subdued as she neared the end. It is her version I remember most clearly, even more than my own. The details—coma, oxygen tent, the collapse of Karen's stomach—always culminated in a shrug of the shoulders. Whenever another woman expressed admiration for Helen's courage, she would respond, "What else could I do?" It was as though she couldn't conceive of any other way to respond to the death of a daughter than with grace and dignity.

But Karen's death exacted a price. She would continue to laugh at my father's wisecracks and enjoy herself at parties, but she would no longer burst into song. Those songs she had first heard on Broadway, such as "Oh, What a Beautiful Morning" and "I'm Going to Wash That Man Right Out of My Hair," would be heard from now only from our hi-fi. She kept her life going, but she was no longer young.

She had other occasions to grieve. In 1975, my sister Rachel, then twelve, was diagnosed with juvenile diabetes. By 1983 my own health had begun to decline and post-polio syndrome forced me to quit graduate school. In 1992 Rachel's husband Jeff died. Yet Helen kept on loving life and the people around her. She saw each of us as the distinct people we were and are and treated us accordingly.

When my brother and I were twelve and thirteen, our father asked us one Saturday morning why we weren't watching cartoons.

"Oh, Walter," she said, laughing, "they'd rather watch Zsa Zsa Gabor on the Jack Paar show."

She saw me and everyone else as we were, not as sentiment might have decreed. I felt embarrassed, but she was right; I could no longer pretend I was a child.

I wish I had asked her more about her youth. I wish she had offered more about who she was. Once she showed me a picture of herself taken before she had married my father. Waterskiing in a dark one-piece bathing suit, her long straight dark hair flying back in the wind, she looked young and care-free. I had trouble reconciling that image with the one before me daily, the one who bit her lower lip when she was worried or embarrassed.

In order to get into Kaiser rehab, I had to have a doctor document how disabled I was. So my father got a doctor to come to the house and take pictures of my curved spine with a Polaroid camera. I lay naked on my bed while the doctor, standing on a chair, took more than a dozen pictures and my mother bit her lip.

I fought with her two or three times. Once I was trying to figure out square roots as she took my dictation. I changed my mind several times about the correct method and she got angry and stormed out. Later she returned and taped a charcoal pencil on my mouthstick and set up a pad of paper on my book-stand so I could figure it out myself. I felt bewildered by her anger. We never discussed it.

Another time she was having trouble adjusting my portable TV. I suggested she wait for my father to get home so he could do it. She said, "You could have a little patience!" I replied that I did, that I was patient enough to wait for my father to do it. She stormed out. Again, I felt bewildered and angry. Again, we never discussed it.

I think she channeled her grief and anger, as well as her underused intelligence, into worrying and cleaning. I wish she hadn't worried so much, especially about "what people would think." When her friends came to visit, she would hide my mouthstick in a drawer. My mouthstick, a wooden dowel inserted into a round Tinkertoy and covered with a piece of an old rubber glove, was encrusted with dried saliva and bits of food. It wouldn't have won any prizes for aesthetics. But it was the only way I could do anything—read a book, turn the radio on and off. So her removal of the mouthstick made me completely helpless. When her friends left, she'd give it back.

She vacuumed every room and washed our clothes twice a week. Once when my father found her vacuuming the garage, he told her to stop.

My leaving home gave Helen the freedom to travel. She flew back to Boston, where she was born, to visit her sisters and friends. Her brothers, both Coast Guard officers, had sent her silks and perfumes from their stations all over the world. Now she could see those places herself. Traveling with my father, she visited the Irish port city of Cork, where her grandfather had grown up. Every two or three summers, my parents would fly off to new destinations: Spain, Hawaii, Romania, France, Hong Kong, and China. After returning from each journey, she'd show me her photographs and talk excitedly about the cities and villages she had seen, the food she had eaten and the people she had met. After a Caribbean cruise, she told me she and my father had dined on the ship with a couple who had dined with Jimmy and Rosalyn Carter.

This essay has been the most difficult thing I've ever written. I want to describe her more fully, her laughter, her figures of speech, the enjoyment she took in meeting people. But I've forgotten so much of her because I took her for granted. She was always available to me, so asking me to describe her is like asking a fish to describe water or an eagle to describe the air. She is a part of me, a very large part. Perhaps that's why I've worried so much about writing an account of her that is both loving and truthful. Like her, I worry too much.

In recent years, my legs have hurt me terribly whenever I'm lifted. Not wanting to frighten myself or the people lifting me, I've developed a habit of biting my lip. It keeps me from screaming.

SPEAKING IN SILENCES

Steve Masover

In May 1987 my mother's doctor found a suspicious lump in her right breast. Phrases like "surgical biopsy," "possible malignancy," and "chance of metastasis" sounded clearly through the phone lines, but I could hardly hear my father's voice from the removed and hidden place to which I retreated as he spoke. How was I to incorporate news of Mom's cancer? Despite the conflict and distance of recent years, despite the fact that I rarely reflected on what Mom really meant to me, she remained the most constant and stable element in all my life and world.

In my dependent years it had been Mom who loved me, fed me, and clothed me, who taught me to talk and to read and to be a good boy, whose praise was always my most sought-after reward. Later, as I grew into a life I gradually understood to be my own, into the calamitous world of the late sixties and early seventies, where every conventional idea and relationship was subject to critique and reevaluation, she remained immersed in the particulars of family. I longed for her empathy and support as I ventured further from the safety of home, but there seemed only a widening gulf, a cleavage of the once-common language, vision, and gesture by which we inhabited our diverging worlds. I earned Mom's attention and approval by my success outside the family, by fulfilling expectations that seemed to require I turn away from her. Feeling bitter and abandoned, I attempted to propel myself entirely out of her orbit via a relentless succession of achievements, intending to leave her filled with pride for a son she could no longer reach.

Leaving home to attend Berkeley in 1978 gave me some measure of perspective on the previous years' convoluted attempts to simultaneously gratify and punish my parents. I realized that frantic pursuit of success in the sciences promised me no personal reward, and developed a vocal and radical critique of the scientific culture I'd been poised to embrace. I abandoned a field not too different from my father's, and turned instead to the study of literature. Mom balked at my change of direction, seeing no secure future in either my increasingly polemical posture or my vaguely articulated ambition to write. I belittled her concerns, and after graduating remained indifferent to finding a career. At about the same time, I began to explore my long-suppressed attraction toward other men, and took care to make no secret of my emerging orientation. Mom was deeply troubled by my leaps leftward along the political spectrum, my aversion to professional success, and the diverse threats she saw in my sexuality. But it had taken a decade of anxious dissimulation before I was finally able to come out, so I had little patience for pretending to live in the space Mom had mapped out for her oldest child. Shallow and wary formulae governed our infrequent contact; and though the tension between us masked both love and need, we continued to grow ever further apart.

How, then, was I to absorb the news of her cancer? Mom's disapproval of my bearing had become a fixed point from which to navigate toward discovery and definition of self. But, midway through my twenty-ninth year, a lesion in my mother's flesh threatened the entire precarious structure of resistance and trust that comprised my relationship to her. I felt stunned, afraid, and completely at sea.

The tumor was malignant, and Mom went under the knife. We anxiously awaited the results of the lymphadenectomy, another of the harrowing medical terms Dad spoke into the

telephone as if to smother the truth that lay coiled and ven-
omous in the breast from which I'd once fed. I couldn't bring
myself to visit her in the hospital, couldn't face the thought of
my proud, dispassionate mother vulnerable and afraid.

When the lymph node biopsy showed that the tumor had
spread, Mom began a six-month course of chemotherapy. She
and Dad put aside the differences that had grown between
them to deal both medically and logistically with the cancer,
and to make as much as possible of the time left to her. Mom
called on the resolve and strength she'd cultivated all her fifty
years, distilling from them a profound determination to will the
cancer into remission. Her fortitude, along with her circumspect
and optimistic phrasing, helped me to ignore the almost certain
expectation of recurrence. I remained distant for a long while
after her operation, rationalizing my measured contact with
Mom by denying the gravity of her illness, and by deprecating
my ability to communicate through the rubble that despair, left-
ist politics, and queer sexuality had made of our once happy
and intimate interdependence. I wanted to hide from the truth,
so I buried my feelings in long hours at work, in political meetings and demonstrations, and wallowing in my inability to find
a man I could love.

My relationship to Mom had become so encumbered by
artifice that I couldn't break through to my real feelings. Nevertheless, motivated by a sense of urgency that reshaped her life
despite her refusal to openly acknowledge that the cancer
might prove fatal, she persisted in trying to close the rift
between us. Over time I made myself more approachable. Our
conversations and correspondence remained superficial, or so it
seemed to me; but I slowly grew to accept something less than
Mom's perfect understanding and wholehearted embrace.

Rigid and impossible demands each of us had made of the
other began to fade in importance, and Mom dared to peek
into my "real" life. There were vast expanses of my world about
which she'd remained deliberately ignorant, so that any dialogue between us first required an explanation of the perspective from which I approached her illness. I told her how David,

a man with whom I had very recently been lovers, was suddenly hospitalized with pneumocystis pneumonia three weeks after her cancer was first diagnosed. He hadn't known that he was infected with HIV; nor had I, frightened as I was by the epidemic, dealt honestly with my proximity to it. I felt helplessly caught up in a hurricane of grossly premature illness and death. Yet Mom's cancer, I told her as we walked through the quiet streets of her neighborhood, made me afraid in a place deeper than had ever been sounded before. In seeing her vulnerable to death I abruptly discovered in myself a myth of personal immortality, a myth that had somehow endured despite the prevalence of AIDS among friends and peers; and in her illness there was also proof of the myth's deceit: if Mom wasn't immortal, I too would die someday.

She really listened. For the first time she let herself hear me speak of a man I'd cared for and slept with, and about what it was like to be part of a queer community. And for the first time, as we turned the last corner toward home, she admitted that she'd "read some books about being gay." I was surprised and grateful to learn that, despite her adamant rejection of my sexuality when I first came out, she was trying in her own silent, private way to come to terms with me. As the import of what she'd told me sank in, I realized that her admission changed the whole terrain of our relationship. Not long after, in a gesture of resonant significance, Mom allowed me to invite Stuart, then my lover of a little less than a year, to dinner at her house in Menlo Park.

We began to spend a few hours together every several months, just the two of us. Once when she visited me in the East Bay after lunch at an Indian place she particularly liked in downtown Oakland, we stopped for coffee at the Italian restaurant where I had recently become a cook. Our common love of good food had been one of the few safe subjects between us for years, and she was impressed by "my" restaurant's menus and reviews despite the fact that the job paid next to nothing. Over cappuccino and biscotti I told her I was thinking of having a child with Susan, my friend, housemate, and comrade of seven years. I explained how all of my housemates and "family"—Michael, Joanie, Vera, Susan, and I—planned to raise our children together.

Acknowledging how hard it was for her that my life so thoroughly confounded her expectations, I joked that if I ever was to have a child I might easily have the same problem: perhaps my daughter or son will want to run a major corporation, or join the staff of a right-wing senator. She laughed, and said she'd never thought of that possibility. Even if there was to be a turkey baster between Susan and me, Mom was excited to think she might become a grandmother. As we got up to leave, she said she wanted to get to know Susan better.

A few months later, I invited my parents to a housewarming party in our neighborhood. They came, they mingled, and Mom began to appreciate the family we had made for ourselves outside the traditional structures of intimate relationships and marriage. She invited my housemates to her seder that spring, and we hosted Thanksgiving in the fall. Little was said to mark the gradual integration of our worlds; but, despite the gulf that remained between us, tremendous barriers had been crossed.

Toward the end of 1990 Mom developed an intense pain in her leg. After blood tests and bone scans, the doctors decided to perform a bone marrow biopsy; there was little doubt what the diagnostics would show.

My sister Laurie called from Seattle to talk about what might happen and what might be needed, and she let me know how it had hurt Mom when I didn't visit her at the hospital in 1987. Laurie made me ashamed to understand how Mom must have thought me so brutally indifferent when the cancer was first diagnosed. I fought down fearful reluctance to ask whether she'd let me come with her to the clinic for her biopsy. A few days before the appointment, sitting in a café down the street from my house, I wrote:

In the background of everything these past four days is Mom, the fear of a new tumor, the biopsy on Thursday to which I will accompany her. My mother, who despite everything and because of everything, despite and because of history, I love.... I imagine her standing here, straight as she always stands, her eyes alive and worn, loving and wary both at once. She's careful not to give too much away, afraid I'll refuse her gifts as I have so often these dozen years since leaving home. And a voice whispers in my ear, over and over again like a mantra or a chant: Mama's gonna die.... Layered over, under, and through everything I do and think is a growth in my mother's pelvis, a touch of death I feel in the marrow of my bones ... not some other mother, some other child, but this son's mother is chilled by the looming shadow.

The clinic visit was horrible: gleaming surfaces and aseptic smells, empty wheelchairs arrayed ghoulishly inside the lobby door, a fluorescent, oppressive certainty of sickness and death. Mom was anxious behind her businesslike manner, and my head ached with tension and constraint. It seemed she was with the doctor for hours. Afterward, she leaned on me to favor the hip from which an oncologist had wrested a core of flesh and bone with a needle the diameter of a pencil lead. That night I slept terribly, tossing and turning in tangles of sheets, sweating, aching, cold.

Five days later we heard the results of the test. "A tumor mass," the doctor called it, but Mom resented any talk of inevitability, let alone death. Minutes after Dad finished telling me what Dr. Rogoway had reported, Mom phoned me back to tell the story from her perspective. She maintained that the problem was localized and treatable, and remained determined to beat back the disease until a cure could be found. But despite the taboo she created around the inescapable conclusion suggested by Dad's survey of the medical literature, we all realized that death was approaching irrevocably. There were so many things I wanted to ask her about, and to tell her, but she never allowed me to steer our discussions into deep water. I couldn't even consider speaking explicitly about the end of her life. To Mom, acknowledgment meant surrender.

I began to write a poem I'd promised her eleven years before, when she'd asked for one to match the piece I'd recently written for my father. For her birthday in February 1991, I finished a lengthy poem in ten parts, a tapestry woven from the images, associations, and emotions that had begun to surface in my journal when I first learned of her cancer. I wrote what wasn't possible to say to Mom: how it was she who had made the world safe for me; how I longed to know who she was behind the habitual silence with which she shielded herself; how her approaching death filled me with fear and a bottomless grief; how she herself is my link to all blood, memory, and history that came before me.

Mom called to thank me for the poem after she'd read it, saying she would "need to think about it a lot." I know she did, because Dad told me how she kept the hand-sewn book I'd made by her bedside, and that she looked at it often. "I cloak myself in words and absences," I had written. "You and I, we speak in silences." We never spoke about the poem after that single phone call, but I felt a great weight had lifted from my shoulders nevertheless. I'd found a way to tell Mom how much I loved her.

Over the subsequent year she began to show unmistakable evidence of strain and sickness for the first time, only then and gradually losing her youthful beauty. To my friends and housemates she looked far healthier than my concern and depression implied. They missed the significance of the subtle signs, how any tiny expression of tiredness or hurt signified numbing exhaustion and racking pain underneath what she showed. Dad, Laurie, my brother Dave, and I began to discuss more openly among ourselves her approaching end, though there still seemed no way to broach the subject with Mom.

On December 30, 1991, no one at the office where I was working as a temporary secretary knew it was my thirty-third birthday. I felt glad of the anonymity and desperate to be alone. I rushed home at five o'clock, shed my office drag, and scribbled a quick note to my housemates. I fled before the phone could ring, and drove up into the hills that circle the San Francisco Bay. At a spot overlooking the city, I stood feeling the night breathe cold against my face, smelling the faint, salty damp from the darkness beyond the Golden Gate Bridge. The week before, I had looked across the dinner table at Mom, and had seen clearly and concretely for the first time, from her pallor and the sagging of her skin, and especially from the weariness in her eyes, that time was growing short. I knew that was the last birthday I'd ever celebrate while she was alive, and wondered how I had never realized before that my birthday is as much her day as mine, how it commemorates that she gave birth that day at least as much as that I was born. I huddled against the car on the downhill side, by the cliff edge of the turnout so passing cars wouldn't see me there, sobbing until my stomach ached. I begged her out loud, raw and desolate, "Mommy, don't go away from me," conjuring out of vast and inconsolable grief a hallucinatory vision: my mother looking down on me, serene and immortal, from the dark clouds towering over the bay.

After a long keening, cold and spent, I came home to find a message from Mom on my phone machine. I'd left the house partly because I couldn't brave talking with her that night, but still felt crushed that I hadn't been home to receive her call. It was too late to call back, but I played the message again and again, listening to the sound of her voice; and the next morning yet again, listening to her wish me happy birthday for the very last time.

In the first two weeks of March Mom seemed to age twenty years. I found her hunched over like an ancient crone at the dining room table when I visited, she who had always carried herself with the posture of a yogi. It was all I could do to keep from crying out when I saw her. When she stood, with Dad's help, it seemed she'd shrunk six inches in height. In the following weeks she rose from her bed only with assistance. Dave, out of work and living with our parents since the beginning of the year, became Mom's principal caretaker. He and Dad attended her around the clock. I began to come down to Menlo Park twice a week, often bringing groceries to cook dinner. Though I wanted to be with Mom, I felt ashamed that I couldn't even imagine living so close to her dying as the rest of the family.

In early May, dependent on a morphine pump to stave off pain, Mom grew weaker and less coherent. She had finally acknowledged to each of us alone that the end was approaching, though it was not a subject she wanted to talk about. We spent hours sitting with her, mostly silent, holding her aged and shrunken hand. Delirious in the nights, my mother cried out as if in a childhood fever for her "mommy"; but in the days, for Grandma, she wore her brave and stoic mask. She struggled fiercely to maintain dignity in the face of helplessness and pain, allowing no one but her mother, husband, and children at her bedside.

She refused to relinquish her wry sense of humor. As I sat beside her one evening while she spoke to Laurie in Seattle, after dialing the phone because she was too exhausted to dial for herself, I was struck to the core by her profound beauty. She suddenly appeared so wise and kind to me, so gentle and strong and familiar, like a deep river I'd watched, listened to, and swum in for so many years it had become part of me. I felt as though I'd never really seen her before. When she handed back the receiver to be set down I told her how beautiful she'd seemed as I watched her talk to my sister. She looked away for a moment, then raised her eyes impishly, coquettishly, to meet mine. "Why don't you hand me that phone again," she whispered.

She ate little solid food, making the effort to sit at a table set up in her room only twice a day, then just once. On a Thursday evening I prepared her last meal. Laurie had flown down to the Bay Area the previous morning, after waking up suddenly certain it was time to come home. Mom was almost unable to speak. When she tried, she spoke in disjointed streams of consciousness from which we had to infer meaning. Barely managing to hold a fork, she pushed my carefully cooked dinner ineffectually around the plate. She was embarrassed by her lack of coordination, but still seemed so grateful for what she was able to taste. As we cleared the dishes away I thought of how she had relieved my earliest hunger so many years before, of how she had taken such pleasure in nourishing me since before I was even born. The wheel had turned, and it was we, the children, who provided for her in those last weeks of her life. In that moment, as Dave reached out tenderly to help her up from the chair and she thanked me with her eyes for that last culinary pleasure, I felt we had finally come full circle.

On Friday evening Dad made a beautiful talk for her, telling her she had fought the best fight possible, but that it was time to say good-bye. Later, as I sat by the bed holding her hand, she mouthed the word silently to me, watching from behind a veil of morphine and pain to be sure I understood. I wept as I hadn't in her presence for as long as I could remember. By Saturday she couldn't swallow. We rubbed ice on her chapped lips to moisten her mouth, laid wet compresses on her forehead to cool her fevers. She had lain nearly immobile for two days. That evening Mom spoke the only coherent sentence of the day. "I just want to die, Jer," she told my father. She had never before spoken the word *death* in reference to herself. She had finally surrendered.

Throughout the night her breathing became increasingly irregular. At four o'clock I woke to the sounds of my father, brother, and sister moving urgently back and forth between the rooms upstairs. I knelt silently under my blankets on the hideaway bed, praying that she be taken mercifully and easily home. I was afraid to go up. It was my role, Joanie consoled me later, to see her only as she wished to be seen, beautiful and whole. It was what she wanted, Stuart said, so that I wouldn't be haunted by the last hour's agony. Whatever prevented me, I couldn't go upstairs. Dave came down at ten minutes of five on Mother's Day morning to tell me she had gone.

As I prepared to write this essay some sixteen months later, I thought of how I had spoken to Mom as she began to slip away, two or three days before the end. I told her that we, her family, would continue to carry her with us into the world, that the qualities she gave to us were expressions of herself that would extend beyond the years of her own life. I thought of how she often figures so vividly in my dreams since her death that I wake to think I really ought to call, it's been such a long time; and how I suddenly remember.

I see her still in the lines of my face, hear her in the inflections of my voice and in my introspective silences. She surfaces in my sometimes too severe morality, and resides in the empathy that hides underneath. She remains with me in her recipes that I continue to prepare for my family, friends, and lovers, and in particular dishes of mine that I taste remembering how she loved them. I watch the world with her eyes. She lives in my deepest and least articulate places, the parts of me that lie many fathoms beneath words, in the bedrock of my self. That is her, my mother, there in the bedrock on which I stand.

My Mother at the Piano

John Boe

My mother didn't tell me traditional nursery tales; rather she told stories of her flapper days. Born in 1911, Margaret Boe was a teenager when the twenties roared: she responded to the call and became a flapper. It's no wonder that a generation later I rose to the bait of the sixties and became a hippie. I don't remember her ever reading to me either. She hooked us on stories with a lifetime of spontaneous storytelling at the kitchen table. It was from her that I learned to celebrate life's small disasters. When you have a hell of a day, at least you know that when you get home you'll have a hell of a story to tell.

The day my mother died I was on the West Coast, she was on the East Coast. After getting the phone call, then sitting sad till twilight, my daughter Lily and I admitted to each other we were hungry. My wife didn't want to eat, but she drove off with us. After the burgers, we drove home in darkness. Our house was pitch black, and we figured we hadn't left any lights on. It turned out, though, that the electricity was out, but it was only for our house, not for anyone else on the block. We went up to our bedroom and lay on the big bed by candlelight. In the darkness and stillness the phone rang. The three of us had the same fantasy: It was Mom, calling, as she so often did. I reached to pick up the phone and on the other end I heard deep silence. I hung up the phone and looked at my wife and daughter. Then the lights came on. We felt that it had to have been my mother calling, one last time, to say good-bye and to bring some light to our darkness.

When Mother is dead, certain images of her linger. One image that has stayed with me is my mother in a white slip. My mother came from that generation where women wore white slips (the cinematic flowering of this white-slip generation was Elizabeth Taylor in *Cat on a Hot Tin Roof*). My mother wore white slips under her dresses, but also as her regular sleepwear. If, in my mind, I picture her at bedtime, I picture her in a white slip.

My father often went out of town on business, so when I was young my sisters and I would take turns sleeping with my mother in the big bed. With apologies to Sigmund Freud, I must agree that there are few pleasures that can compare with getting to sleep with Mommy. Ah—warmth, comfort, safety, and the white silky slip, as cool as the underside of the pillow, Mother's bedtime bridal gown, white white white in the night night night.

My mother still regularly appears in my dreams. Just the other night, she was there, having remarried a doctor after my father's death. He was spending her money on his own travel, but she seemed happy, so I was happy for her. In my mind she still exists, is still alive, changing, growing, carrying on with a whole new life. She's still influencing me, surprising me.

For years now, when I'd sit down and be about to play the piano, I'd often get a funny feeling of almost remembering something. I'd try to let it come, to see what my mind had over there hidden in the corner, off to the side, but when I'd try to look, it would be gone; when I'd try to listen, it would fade away. So I'd forget it and begin to play. I was regularly haunted by this lost memory, but I recently discovered what it was.

My mother's mother, my grandma Schneider, once started taking secret piano lessons in order to surprise her husband, who loved music—he sometimes went to German beer gardens in St. Louis and sang with the band or took over the conducting. Grandma knew Grandpa would be pleased if she learned to play the piano, so she started lessons, practicing when he was out of the house, at work. But one day, before she had progressed very far, he came home early and heard her practicing. Her surprise was ruined, so she gave up the lessons and never played again.

Grandma Schneider continued to encourage her children to be musical. She used to give my mother, Margaret Schneider, the choice of cleaning her room or practicing the piano. I guess my mother practiced the piano a lot. She never was very neat.

As a teenager she used to practice the piano and typing on the bus, silently playing Rachmaninoff or "The Quick Brown Fox" on her lap over and over till she got to her stop. The skills of typing and piano playing are related—both develop and require finger coordination and strength. My mother had, as I do, these large piano-player hands (good for basketball and rock climbing too, I've found). As a small child, though, my mother had the tip of the index finger on her left hand cut off when, playing hide-and-go-seek with her father, she caught her finger in the falling top of a rolltop desk. Her sister, a gifted classical pianist, feels that this accident kept Margaret from really developing as a classical musician.

Musically gifted herself, my mother learned the cello in her spare time. But she really took to popular music. Her first marriage was to a jazz drummer, a relatively despicable man as far as I can tell. One of her grown-up granddaughters once asked her why she had married this man. "I was a shithead," my mother explained succinctly.

Part of the attraction, though, was no doubt his drumming: the piano player and the drummer making beautiful music together.

Musicians, like most artists, don't make much money. And so the marriage with the drummer, despite two kids, was soon on the rocks ("When money goes out the door, love goes out the window," Mom used to say). My mother took a night job, playing the piano at a speakeasy. My mother always played great party piano. She knew more songs than anybody, and could fake anything—if you'd hum a few bars, she'd play it. She was also very beautiful, very thin and tall, with savage black hair and strikingly high cheekbones. I can't imagine a better piano player for a speakeasy.

One night at the speakeasy, a World War I vet came in. He had this steel plate in his head. Because of the plate, he wasn't supposed to drink, but being in a speakeasy he knocked back a couple. Then he decided to tear the place apart. It became the classic bar fight, bottles breaking, chairs thrown. My mother hid under the bar. Also under the bar was a salesman, hat in hand, the man who would become my father. Meeting this attractive woman under a bar during a bar fight, he did, I suppose, the natural thing: He grabbed a bottle and poured them both drinks.

Until my mother was an old lady and the doctor suggested it for her high blood pressure, she never drank at all. She'd play the piano through many a party but never have a drink. Maybe she remembered the dramatic changes that could come from a drink, like the time at the speakeasy when she took the first step toward a second marriage and consequent excommunication.

My earliest nighttime memories are the sounds of the party downstairs, the sounds singing around the piano: risqué songs like "Twelve Old Ladies Locked in the Lavatory" ("They were there from Monday to Saturday/Nobody knew they were there"), with the obligatory twelve verses about various old women named Elizabeth, such as Elizabeth Wren (who "got in the wrong door and had to stand in line with the men") and Elizabeth Crandall (who suffered the indignity of sitting on the handle); sad songs about old hometowns (like the poignant "Southie," which some guy from Boston would always request); songs with bawdy lyrics it took me a few years to get ("When roses are red they're ready for pluckin'/And girls of sixteen are ready for high school"); holy roller songs like "The Joy" (first stanza: "I got the Joy Joy Joy Joy down in my heart/Jesus is keepin' me alive"; second stanza: "The holy ghost, the ball of fire, keepin' me alive"; third stanza: "Oh, it's all over (*fill in name*) and it's keepin' him alive"); the popular songs of all eras; the song games, with improvised lyrics; taking people's phone numbers and making them into songs; her trick of taking a well-known song, changing it slightly (playing it real slow, putting it in 3/4, and/or shifting it to a minor key, for example), so that you could almost recognize it, but not quite, then when you did recognize it, you'd feel that "Oh, of course" epiphany. My father, with his astounding memory for lyrics, loud (though not always on key) voice, and large capacity for liquor, was the leader at these song sessions, which would go on and on long after I'd fallen to sleep upstairs, the twelve old ladies dancing in my dreams.

When I was little, my mother used to give me sheets of music paper. I'd sit on the floor and draw in circles, filling some of the circles in, putting staffs on various of the notes, connecting some of the staffs. When I'd finish she would play my compositions—intuiting the divisions between bars. These songs, played with full arrangement, chords and all, were usually beautiful to my ears. If she or I didn't particularly like one of these songs, she'd turn the sheet of music upside down and play it again (John Cage would have been proud). One way or another, either upside down or right side up, I'd have composed a lovely song.

She was a great mother. On cold winter mornings she would warm my socks and underwear on the radiator before waking me up by slipping warm socks on my feet. And she always had new jokes, dirty ones and clean ones. When I was a young boy she made me promise that if I ever heard a dirty joke with the punch line "Not tonight, Josephine," to tell it to her. She had heard the joke once, thought it was tremendously funny, but had uncharacteristically forgotten the setup. This task, of course, gave me maternal encouragement to spend a lifetime listening to dirty jokes, but I am sad to say I never did hear the "Not tonight, Josephine" one.

She didn't force piano lessons on any of her kids, but she exposed us to them. When we'd visit my mother's parents in St. Louis, I'd always end up playing the piano. There was something fascinating about that beautiful black baby grand with the framed picture sitting on it of my mother at nineteen (the same picture now sits on my piano). At age sixteen I really learned to play from a guy who had studied with John Lewis of the Modern Jazz Quartet. After these six months of lessons, my mother was my only teacher. I have hundreds of memories of sitting at the piano, playing something, then hearing her voice from the kitchen, full of pain at my dissonant mistake, but full of love too—"B flat! B flat!"

She used to play for the mental patients at Bergen Pines Hospital. Once a patient snuck up behind her and dropped his false teeth down the back of her dress. Another time a woman started screaming at her when she was playing Mozart. "That's not right! That's not right!" the woman kept shouting, growing more and more upset, till the orderlies dragged her away to sedate her. My mother felt guilty about this, for she knew the complaining woman had been right. My mother had been playing a Mozart sonata from memory, a piece she *had* known years before but was now, in her fashion, faking, playing mostly Mozart, but clearly not playing it right.

In high school, summers and weekends, I got into the habit of sleeping late. When my mother thought I'd slept long enough, she'd start playing the piano, each song louder and faster than the previous one, on into barrelhouse and boogie-woogie, till I'd wake up to the sound of music. When, later in life, I'd visit her, she'd still wake me up with her piano playing (sometimes because it was time for us to go to garage sales). Her piano playing was the best alarm clock ever invented.

Once she showed me this beautiful, slightly dissonant, but full, rich chord. It was at least eight notes, played with both hands, then as you'd descend a half step at a time down the scale, the chord would resonate, hauntingly. I played it for a few weeks when I'd sit down to fiddle at the piano. Then I stopped playing it, forgot about it. One day, years later, I remembered and asked my mother to show me this haunting chord again. "What chord?" she said. "I never showed you such a chord." The Lost Chord died with my mother, indeed died before she did.

My mother frequently gave me two pieces of advice joined into one sentence: "Don't be the first one home from the party and don't worry about your grades." Late in life, she began a variant of "Don't be the first one home from the party," telling any young person who wanted to stay up late and/or had to get up early: "Don't worry, you can always sleep while you're old." But when she was old (in fact throughout her life) she hardly slept at all. She loved life, and I don't think she could ever understand how someone like me could seem to prefer sleep to life. She'd listen to talk radio all night long, not wanting to waste life in silent darkness. When a certain set of young grand-kids would visit, they'd sneak in her bedroom when it was still dark and tickle her feet, and (amazing!) she would wake up laughing.

Occasionally my mother would deny that she was our mother and insist that she was actually Maggie Myers, the cleaning lady. Mop in hand, babushka on head, Maggie would tell us about our elegant, beautiful, but temporarily absent mother. Every so often she'd dress up to go out of town with Dad. She'd sit on the bed, brushing out and putting up her long black hair. Then she'd put on a long dress, perfume, pearls, and jewels and announce, transformation completed, that here at last was our real mother, the beautiful Margaret Boe.

"Maggie Myers" was a running gag in our house. I knew it was just a game, but I also took it seriously: I had learned that my mother had different selves. We all do, I know now (these different selves are what some psychologists call complexes). I find that my mother and her alter ego Maggie Myers gave me an early understanding that people (including me) were complex, had various selves.

One of my mother's selves was the indulgent mommy. She used to tease me about being an overindulgent father to my own children, claiming that I followed the Harry Truman school of child rearing: "Find out what they want and then give it to them." But I learned this style of child rearing from her. She tried to give her kids what they wanted; in fact, she tried to give all kids what they wanted. I've never seen anyone as good as she was at wooing a child, getting down on all fours, giving the kid 100 percent attention, laughing, cooing, joking, touching, singing, doing whatever it took to produce smiles and laughter.

Shortly before she died, we went to her friend Vivian's house for dinner. Vivian was still dressing upstairs, so my mother, my wife, and my kids sat in her luxurious living room while I helped myself to Vivian's piano. I played for a few minutes, till I heard Vivian descending the stairs. "You know," my mother said to me, "you play the piano very well." These words were as sincere as her own mother's compliments had been (and indeed I had become a good piano player). Her praise not only made my night, it made the rest of my life.

One Monday when she was seventy-five she had heart surgery, and I sat on the opposite coast waiting for the phone call and playing the piano. I played out of one of the many fake books she had given me. (Fake books are books full of the melodies and chords for hundreds of songs; when the writers of the songs are given no royalties, such books are illegal, but they are nonetheless invaluable to musicians. My mother bought several of them in the late fifties for $25 each.) I played over and over the sweet sad song "I'll Never Be the Same." When I got the call that she had died on the operating table this became the last song I would associate with her.

And so my mother was dead. But once she was dead, who was she? After death, she was suddenly no longer just the seventy-five-year-old woman who had a heart attack at St. Luke's Hospital in New York City. She was also the child speaking German, the young mother with a house of children, Maggie Myers, the beautiful woman, my mother the storyteller, and Mommy in a white slip. In death my mother became all her ages at once and all her selves at once.

One of my strongest ways of remembering her is by remembering, and playing, the songs she especially liked. Old songs like "Do You Know What It Means to Miss New Orleans" and "Mean to Me," obscure jazz tunes like Russ Freeman's

"Happy Little Sunbeam" and Lennie Niehaus's "Whose Blues," classical music by Brahms. For her, music was a social act. Late in life, when she had arthritis in her fingers, she practiced regularly, not so much for the pleasure of playing, but so that she could continue to play for people. She liked to play for parties, for friends, children, and grandchildren (one set of grandkids always requested her rendition of Mezz Mezrow's "Kitten on the Keys"), for dancing schools, for shows big and little, for churches and for synagogues, for people. And after playing, her music was of course gone forever, a momentary gift that brightened life but couldn't last, a genuine spiritual act.

The painter J. B. Yeats (the poet's father) called art the social act of the solitary man. When I'm at a party and there's a piano, I understand what J. B. Yeats meant, I understand how my mother must have felt, I understand the desirability of getting to hide behind music, to hide behind the piano, to not have to mix and seek people out, but to still be contributing, really contributing to the feeling of the party.

Whenever I see a strange piano I want to touch it, to play it. The piano in any room calls to me, like an attractive and willing woman who wants me to love her, to play with her. Freud would probably say this feeling has something to do with my mother complex, with how I associate my mother (my first image of the feminine) with the piano.

When I recovered my lost memory, the memory that sometimes tried to come up when I sat down in a quiet room at the piano, I was amazed I hadn't figured it out before. I was trying to recall what is undoubtedly my first memory: the sound of piano music. Here I am, *inside* my mother and I hear this wonderful stuff—piano music. There I am, in my cradle, and I hear strange but beautiful sounds. What are they? What is it? It's my mother at the piano.

LILACS

J. Herman Blake

———

The most compelling memory of my mother is that of a warrior.

In the Gullah-speaking communities of coastal South Carolina and Georgia, when women lead services in the Praise House, they often refer to each other as warriors. As one listens to their prayers, supplications, and testimonials, one becomes aware that a warrior is a person in constant struggle with malevolent forces, who always keeps her spirits high, fights a good fight, keeps faith in the Almighty, and ultimately prevails.

Although born and raised in Asheville, North Carolina, my mother married a resident of one of the coastal South Carolina communities. To survive that experience and successfully raise her seven children to adulthood, my mother had to be a warrior.

My memories of her are intense ones, deeply engraved in my consciousness. Only now, as my own years grow long, do I understand how they have shaped many of my actions and attitudes and made me the person I am today.

She was named Lylace—after the lilac flower—and she was always pleased when the awakening spring brought lilacs into bloom. Momma was always happy when my brothers and I would collect bunches for the house. We did not see her happy at many other times.

I remember Momma as a rather short woman, light-skinned, and very obese. Her walk was slow and labored, almost as if she were carrying a heavy weight on her shoulders as she went about her tasks. Everything she wore was castoff or threadbare. She never had adequate clothing, let alone the new or stylish kind that is a source of comfort for so many women.

Her hands were large, her fingers short. They seemed ideal for the way she could make simple meals tasty and rewarding for us. They seemed ideal for the pies and cobblers that were her specialty. Her hands always seemed most attractive when covered with dough.

When I think of the warrior Lylace Elizabeth Blake (née Michael) I remember her as a protector of her children. I do not remember when my father left the household nor why he left. I was much too young. But I remember how much my mother suffered to protect her seven children.

For a while after leaving, my father would bring cash and place it in her hands, with instructions on how it was to be spent. If she said the wrong thing, or did not follow his instructions, he would shed his coat, toss it on the floor, and proceed to pummel her. He would hit her repeatedly about the face and arms. My mother never fought back. She stood silently absorbing the blows, yet never changing her mind about how she spent whatever money was given.

We would cling to each other in fear and panic, crying uncontrollably because our mother was suffering the blows of an abuser and we could do nothing to protect her. It is a searing and painful memory, painful even now more than half a century later. That this warrior suffered so her children could survive is the most compelling memory I have of Lylace Elizabeth Blake.

The years of seeing my mother abused influenced me in ways I have yet to fully understand. This understanding is difficult because unraveling the mystery requires restimulating a pain that is still profound. I do realize that I feel saddened that I could not protect my mother. I do not recall fearing my father. I only recall my inability to protect my mother.

By my early adolescence my father—his pitiful support and his vicious beatings—had completely faded from our life. Our support came from the welfare department through its Aid to Dependent Children program. We now resided in an abandoned store in New York State, which had been partitioned to provide rooms for Momma and her seven children. The front windows were painted green for privacy, with a small unpainted strip at the top to let some light enter.

We lived there more than five years, even though we were told it was only a temporary stopgap until the city built low-income housing. But then Momma was told she could not move into the new projects because they were designed for families with no more than four children. We would have to move to even more substandard housing. Our storefront was to be demolished. Momma refused. We would move only to that apartment that she had been promised.

The city started eviction proceedings and Momma was ordered to appear in court. She did not let us go to school that day. She took us all to the judge's bench and explained to him that when they started construction of the projects she and several others in the neighborhood were told they would have apartments. We had lived patiently in a storefront only to be told that the apartments were too small to accommodate us. Momma told the judge the authorities were wrong in deliberately building apartments too small to meet the apparent need.

To our shock and surprise, he agreed. The authorities were ordered to break through the walls of smaller apartments and combine them into larger ones. We got our apartment, as did several other families. Momma's defense of her children made her one of the most respected people in the community. She was a warrior and we were proud.

Moving day was a joy. It was the only time we lived in a completely new home. It was our first experience having the facilities so many take for granted. Though we had had an indoor toilet before, this was our first real bathroom. And now we had the luxury of two, one with a bathtub, one with a shower! And not just a front room to be used for multiple purposes, but a real living room to gather as a family, to listen to the radio, and enjoy some modicum of togetherness. Even though they were shared, we had real bedrooms with actual closets. To us that apartment with its two bathrooms was the best of modernity and luxury.

The joy was short-lived. The stress of too many demands and too few resources took its toll on Momma. Five years after we moved she became ill. Feeling dizzy, her vision blurred, we rushed her to the hospital. She had suffered a stroke. Only forty-seven years old, she was permanently paralyzed on the right side. Her speech was damaged, she could no longer write, she would never walk again.

My wife at the time was a registered nurse, and with her support and that of my younger siblings, Momma was able to return to the apartment in the projects and live independently for a few more years.

My mother warned against the machinations of the social control agencies involved in our lives, especially the social workers and the ever-present police. They were seen as malevolent forces with feigned friendliness and many questions, but who sought to know us only so they could control our lives and keep us in a lowly status. Those on our side were the visiting nurses who came by without judgment or questions to dispense medicine and advice, helping us combat the diseases we frequently contracted. And the Salvation Army, which supplied us with clothing for the changing seasons and generous food baskets every Thanksgiving and Christmas. Without these two agencies, our lives would have been even more bleak and despairing.

Momma had strong religious beliefs. She saw our church as another bulwark against the malevolent forces that could take us out of her influence. But she was constantly criticized by church members because she did not attend services. With barely enough money to get us nice clothes to wear to church, she rarely spent anything on herself. She lived through our achievements.

She also promoted participation and excellence in school. We were taught to follow the advice and counsel of our teachers and never cause any trouble. She saw education as a path to good jobs and happy lives and all she could give us was confidence in our ability to succeed by taking advantage of any opportunities society offered. And we did succeed.

Church helped us solidify our moral values, her insistence that we avoid the trouble of the streets of our ghetto. In school we learned the academic skills necessary to go beyond the streets and achieve in life. Though she remained in the background because she did not have the knowledge she wanted us to acquire, she was still a strong force in our lives. A warrior.

Momma was a stern disciplinarian. Without the support of a husband she had to make sure that if we broke any of her rules we would suffer the consequences. Discipline was harsh, painful, unpleasant and more. It was always with a switch to the legs. She knew where hedges grew in the neighborhood, and when a whipping was required we would have to bring her a fresh, acceptable switch. Her definition of acceptable was simple: it had to be taller than we were and go around our waist twice without breaking. The journey to obtain a switch was one of the longest walks in the world, the selection was incredibly challenging, and the return home was even longer. I was never persuaded that it hurt her more than it hurt me. That was always her explanation. I am sure she understood but did not feel the pain and agony in the walk, the selection, and the return, and she did not feel the sting on the legs. I was never persuaded.

I was always anxious to please Momma. Underneath this desire was a sense of the hurt and pain she suffered when she was abused and beaten. I wanted to ease that pain by bringing her joy and satisfaction through my achievements. I could not protect her when she was beaten, I could not soothe her soul, I could not give her the comfort she never got from a companion. All I could do was bring her pleasure through achievement.

I excelled in church. Whether in musical groups or in the various organizations for youth, I became a leader. I even became a junior pastor because of my speaking ability. I learned leadership in the church.

I excelled in school. I made every effort to be the top student in every subject. I was an obedient student and never gave a teacher any trouble. I do not recall how well I did, but my memory is that Momma was pleased.

I also brought her lilacs from the woods or other people's gardens every chance I could and she was very pleased.

As I grew into adolescence, continued excellence in church leadership and academic performance were no longer sufficient. I had to do more. At the age of nine I obtained my first job, joining my brothers in working for George Ugelow, who employed us to deliver newspapers in Yonkers, a nearby suburban community. Every morning before school we would be picked up and dropped off in Yonkers with stacks of newspapers left along the route. The papers were all delivered by foot and we were returned home in time for school. On Sundays the papers were larger and the delivery took much longer.

I worked those routes until I was sixteen and never regretted the time spent. For not only did I earn money to help Momma, I learned that the responsible carrying out of the expectations of others would bring just rewards. Each December I would hand out Christmas cards to each home. I was rewarded with generous tips and would use the money to get a very special gift for Momma.

I remember so clearly the year I took my Christmas tips and bought her a pressure cooker. They were all the rage at that time but we could not afford one. I could not have been more than eleven years old at the time, but on Christmas morning I brought a smile to Momma's face and joy to her heart that made me feel like a full adult. Throughout the year as she used that pressure cooker I felt a special pride. It made me work harder, achieve more, so that each year I could bring her the same kind of joy and happiness. Pleasing Momma by meeting her needs and supporting her as much as possible became a strong motivating force in my life.

I entered the Army in 1953. Fifty percent of my monthly salary went directly to Momma. Upon completion of my service two years later, I married and entered New York University with the support of my new wife, my family, and the G.I. Bill. Again it was a period of academic success in the tradition my mother encouraged. I won a spot on the varsity debate team and did well in public speaking contests. I won the first of many engraved plaques and they made my mother proud.

The proudest day, however, was my graduation. My wife drove Momma to a convenient location, where a guard removed her wheelchair from the car and pushed her to a good observing site. The treatment made her feel very special and Momma paid close attention. When my college was called to rise, she pulled herself up by the railing and stood while the degree was conferred. She was proud, as if she was also the recipient, and I was pleased.

Still in my robe and mortarboard, I pushed her among the milling crowd. My professors greeted her warmly and congratulated her on my accomplishments: they in their colorful robes and hoods, I in my black cap and gown. It was rather surreal, this ill-clad, ill-at-ease, poverty-stricken warrior from the ghetto seated in a wheelchair being saluted by university scholars in medieval garb. But in spite of her discomfort she glowed like a queen and savored every moment, particularly when my white-haired French professor, Monsieur Baudin, in his stately robes from the Sorbonne, swept off his hat, bowed deeply and kissed her hand, while congratulating her with his deeply accented English. Only now do I realize how completely I neglected my wife and daughter while sharing this moment of triumph with my mother.

Even though five of her seven children would graduate from college and obtain advanced degrees, mine was the only graduation she was able to attend. It was a glorious moment for her—and a glorious moment for me to see her pride. Her warrior days were ended, but her victories continued to accrue.

Five years later she died. The stroke and other diseases took their toll and she just wasted away. Her death was much too early—she was fifty-four years old—but it took her away from physical pain and misery. For me it was a profound loss and I cried at her funeral even more than I cried as a child when she was abused and beaten by my father. Indeed, when I saw her lifeless and cold body the same childhood sense of panic, the same feeling of helplessness swept over me. She had protected me, she had guided me, she had given me a foundation for a good life, and all I had given her were a few moments of pride and one shining moment of glory. It was unfair. She was taken away much too young to be justifiable and much too soon to be rewarded. It seemed so damned unfair.

As we lowered her in the grave I vowed to dedicate my life to continually serving Momma and returning her gifts to mothers and women, particularly to black women, through my work in the university and my service to communities. I had no idea how much that vow would drive all of my subsequent work. Momma may have died, but the warrior lives on in me and others. I know she is happy and proud.

Had my mother lived a few years longer there are many questions I would have asked, in order to understand her life as well as my own. I am writing my memoirs now and there are many questions to which I have no answers, many experiences where my memory is incomplete. I would like to know more about how she met my father, why she married him. I know little of her various interests and how they developed. Except for her love of music, her enjoyment of Fats Waller and Louis Jordan.

I would ask her why my experience growing up was so different from that of my siblings. Why I alone lived with other families for significant periods of time. Mrs. Maggie Randolph, an elderly member of our church with whom I lived for a period of time, was another extension of Momma for me. But the longest and the most meaningful of these stays was with the Wilson family, in New Rochelle. Thaddeus Wilson was a minister who was soft-spoken and gentle, so unlike my father I did not know what to make of him. He and his wife Charlotte had four children. I lived in their wonderful house like another child. My memories of Mrs. Wilson are like those of Momma, but the family was different. There was no conflict, only love, joy, and good times. There I gained a sense of a comfortable childhood. The love Mrs. Wilson showed to me was generous and the support and encouragement she gave me were very motivating. Like my desire to please Momma, I wanted to please Mrs. Wilson, and the best way was through excellence in school. I loved reading to Mrs. Wilson and she thought I was the smartest and brightest child ever. My ability to read very well at a young age always brought lots of hugs and acclaim.

When the Wilsons were transferred to a pastorate in Buffalo, I found myself journeying every summer by train along the Hudson River to be with them. I have no idea who paid the fare, how the process got started, or why I lived with the Wilsons for so much of my early life.

In my time childhood and adolescence were rehearsals for adult life and all of us went through the period rapidly. The experiences of my children have been very different. They have never lived in poor or dilapidated housing. They have never known the humiliations of grinding poverty: borrowing to survive from week to week, the shame of not being able to dress like your school peers.

Above all, my children have never seen their father strike their mother. Even though social scientists say that children from abusive families are likely to become abusive adults, that has not been the case with any of my siblings. While we have had a range of marital success, failure has not been a result of physical abuse. I suspect that to cause a spouse to suffer the way Momma suffered would be—in the minds of all my brothers—a perpetuation of her humiliation. And myself, I would rather lose my arms and hands than use them against a woman.

When I had my own families, it was hard to move beyond those early experiences. My feelings about family, about the responsibilities of a husband and father, were so controlled by the memories of my mother that I could not view my family in its own right. I treated every wish by my wife as an order that it was my responsibility to fulfill. At the time I did not understand my deeper motivations, that almost paralytic desire to bring comfort, satisfaction, and joy to a spouse or partner. Often I would return to a store to purchase some item that had been admired while window shopping, and then present it as a gift. I

still have regrets about wishes I never fulfilled in my two marriages.

Early in life I determined that my family would never suffer
from a lack of adequate food, clothing, or housing. However, I
did not respond to their emotional and psychological needs,
feeling that if I could meet their physical needs, that would be
sufficient. Understanding the driving force behind my over-
achievement has come only recently, after dramatic failures in
my personal and family life.

I feel Momma's spirit almost like an aura around me, motivating and guiding me. I never gave this much thought until I was
appointed Provost of Oakes College on the Santa Cruz campus of
the University of California and had the opportunity to select the
site for the provost's house. The architects had selected four sites
and ranked them in terms of acceptability. I walked the four sites
on a rainy day and found myself drawn to the one the architects
liked least. They argued against my inclination. However, I
insisted on that site and the house was built there. The first
spring after we occupied the house the canyon behind it was
brilliant with wild lilacs.

The graveside pledge to my mother continues to be a major
driving force in my life. As a college teacher and administrator,
I have the opportunity to touch the lives of many people. In
many I see my mother again, a young adult woman struggling
to meet the needs of her family without the help and support of
a companion. So I strive to help my students become independent through educational achievement. In each success I see a
triumph for my mother, and somewhere Momma must be
pleased, for there are many successes. I do not limit my efforts
to any group, but strive to motivate everyone; I feel most
strongly, however, about those who come from low-income
backgrounds. Sometimes I have to choke back tears when I
address an audience or teach a class and see women before me
who are in situations like those Momma faced, poorly clad,
obese, stressed out—but ever hopeful. The memory of a warrior
propels me to serve those who never knew her. She, I feel,
knows them all.

WHAT AM I: I AM MY MOTHER'S SPIRIT

Gardiner Harris

My brother and I used to play rock-paper-scissors to determine which of us would have to answer our dying mother's call for help.

It's a child's game, simple and fair. We normally used it to decide who got the last french fry or who got first ups in sandlot baseball. But after Dad installed an intercom in the house, Crane and I used the game to choose who had to help Mom.

Sometimes she'd want water or food. Sometimes she'd want to hear about our day in school. Sometimes she probably just wanted someone with her when she'd panic about her impending death.

We knew she was dying. She had told us that. But we wanted to watch TV.

Buzz. Buzz. Buzz. Scissors cut paper, you have to get it.

The memory of this unmerciful insensitivity tortures me. You were too young, they say. You had just turned thirteen. But who ever sees himself as a stupid kid? In my mind's eye, I've always been the way I am. Older people tell me they don't think of themselves as old. We'll all be about twenty-seven in heaven, I think.

But my mother had become unfamiliar. She had lost her distinctive smell, and she looked unkempt—something she'd never been. This upset me. I began having a recurring nightmare that she had been kidnapped and replaced by a kind impostor who was nice but still an impostor. I stopped running up to her room after getting home from school. I took Shadows, my dog, for long walks.

I don't remember my feelings when Mom left the house for her last trip to the hospital, but I was probably relieved. We rarely visited her, and I think I said almost nothing when we were there. I remember one visit near the end. I walked around her bed and, for some reason, glanced at her crotch. She was writhing at the time, and I remember seeing how emaciated her legs and pelvis were. The glimpse horrified me.

A few weeks later, I awoke early in the morning with afternoon clarity. I heard the phone ring, heard it stop, and heard the floor creak as my father walked from his bedroom. I followed the groaning wood as he went to my oldest brother's bedroom, then to Crane's, and then to mine. I lay stiffly in bed as he hugged me and said, "It's over."

I got up, took a shower, and dressed to go to school. Then I thought that perhaps I shouldn't do that. I felt nothing other than a slight worry that I wasn't acting or feeling as a newly motherless child should.

I was reminded of this emptiness recently while watching TV footage of Princes William and Harry. The two boys were looking over some of the thousands of notes and cards left at the gates to the palace. Millions of Brits were looking to the boys for signs of the overwhelming grief that had swept the nation. Uh-uh, I thought. Harry is almost the same age that I was. William is the same age that Crane was. I'm not sure they're capable of genuine tears. I wasn't.

For me, confusion was my dominant emotion during nearly all the ceremonies surrounding my mother's death. The one exception was the viewing, when terror took the lead. I walked into the funeral home, saw a dead body in a casket and walked right out. I remember that I was nearly blinded by the light outside—probably a sign that I was close to passing out.

I finally worked up the courage to go back inside. I approached the casket again, identified the body as having belonged to my mother, and drifted away. I was amazed that my sister, a Down's Syndrome child, was ushering people up to the body and standing with it.

And then, for the only time in my life, I sensed my mother's spirit somewhere else in the room. I looked around and saw nothing. But I knew she was there. And I knew just as strongly that the body lying at one end of the room wasn't her.

A few months later I wrote an essay titled "My Mother's Spirit" for a one-handed ex-Marine who taught a seventh grade creative writing class while tying fishing flies with a stainless steel hook.

I have since seen other men wrap fishing flies. All used needle-nosed pliers. My teacher, an occasional substitute, had no need for such a clumsy tool. His hook clenched the tender threads and spun them quickly, delicately around feathers and barbed metal. And as he wrapped, he would unravel stories about his childhood—stories he hoped would inspire us to write.

The Marine never told the story of how he'd lost his hand. I have heard that losing a limb doesn't really hurt. The shock is so great that the brain blocks the signals from the severed nerves. Maybe if the Marine had told us of his initial numbness, I might have realized mine.

Instead, I was tortured for years by that calm of mine. I tried to forget that I had faked sobs at my own mother's funeral. It didn't work, but I managed to forget almost everything else.

Twenty years later, I still grope to figure out when she died and what grade I was in at the time. The painless, fairy-tale years before her death are gone. I have lost, like a favorite toy, nearly all memory of Mom. But worse than the lost memories was the emptiness.

For ten years after her death, sadness arrived about as often as a Mississippi flood. The first time the water rose was three months after her death. I was sick with the flu and home alone. No one was there to comfort me, fix me toast and soup, or brush my hair. I nearly asphyxiated myself, crying so uncontrollably that I couldn't catch my breath.

My sobs got no response. This was a new and wholly unsatisfying experience. I steeled myself to prevent its repeat.

For years, I avoided sad movies and potentially painful confrontations. I broke up with girlfriends by simply avoiding them. I'd disappear during family arguments. Every two or three years, my floodworks would leak. An essay, a piece of music, or more tragedy, would push through the mortar. But I'd quickly patch the dike and return to business. I started acting in school plays so I could try living in the shoes of people who did feel.

Then in college I took a class that required me to write an essay every day. Working the dikes of my emotions became a huge, daily chore. Finally, I abandoned the works and, to my amazement, survived.

I now live with sadness, allowing mournful regret to wash over me like a warm shower. I think it feels like a phantom pain, but I don't know. The Marine never told us about that, either. This is one of the pieces that I wrote in his class.

WHAT AM I: I AM MY MOTHER'S SPIRIT

I am my mother's slow-moving footsteps as she walks down to the hospital to get her cancer check-up. I am her utter despair as she finds the results, and her trouble in finding the words to tell Dad. I am the slow and reluctant boy who takes a couple of Mom's things to the hospital where she will stay before the operation. And goes home and pretends nothing is happening.

I am Mother's loneliness in her hospital bed as she patiently awaits Father's next visit. I am her joy to find us with him as he walks near her bed. I am her curiosity to learn of the day's events and her sorrow as a very short visiting period ends. I am my mother's frail, ever-weakening body as she slips into a coma. I am the sparkling tear that runs down her stiff face as the words of a friend's letter roll out. I am the disbelief of everyone as the news reaches us that Mom has died.

I am not the pounds of make-up that hide the painful expression on her cold, still face. Just as I am not her whole shell that lies in an open casket. But I am her spirit walking somewhere about the room. I am the sorrow of all as the casket is being lowered into the ground. I was my mother. I am her spirit.

HOLDING AVA

Jess Walter

———

Sometime after midnight, my mother wakes from the dark shallows of morphine sleep and cries out: "Tell Jess not to run around the swing set!"

I lean in close and whisper, "I'm not running anywhere, Mom. I'm right here."

But her hands clutch at the air, causing plastic IV lines to click together. She lifts her head slightly and opens her eyes wide, but unfocused. "Oh good," she says, "you found him. Jess gets hurt so easily."

Morphine sleep isn't really sleep at all, it turns out, but a kind of uneasy dream state, filled with scenes of anxiety and dread, a poor replacement for what we've been told to expect; it is our strife flashing before our eyes.

My mother is fifty-three. She is dying of stomach cancer.

For three months I've come to her house almost every day to help my father nurse her. We work in shifts, spelled by my grandmother, sister and brother. We commune with Mom through a series of tubes: food and water in this one, chemotherapy in that one, medication in a third. We change dressings and bedding, empty bedpans and clean IV ports—wash, flush, repeat. For her pain, I give her a cocktail of drugs that is never quite enough. I also give her the words she whispered so often to me: *"It's going to be OK."*

It feels like some rite we are practicing, the transfer from mother to son of the responsibility for taking care of the other. It has always been the defining theme of our relationship, my mother taking care of a boy who was always in a cast or an eye patch, who suffered from every flu and cold, who collected injuries like other kids collected baseball cards. Trying to take care of the person who took care of me, I find that I am woefully inadequate.

In fairness, it's not all my fault. This is an awful disease, fast and unforgiving. Cancer is a horror made worse by medieval treatment, false hope, and impersonal medicine. Each time I think the pain has peaked, there is some higher anguish.

Tonight it is these morphine-induced visions:

Scenes from my mother's life play on the screen of her subconscious, but they are not what I would wish for her. There are no seven-mile road races, no riotous family dinners, no intimacies from her 37-year love affair with my father. Instead, Mom's eyes race back and forth behind tight lids as she relives busy days as a bookkeeper, forgotten arguments with relatives and—this night—the fear that her accident-prone son is hurt again.

"Jess! Jess!"

"I'm OK, Mom. I'm right here. It's OK."

And then her round eyes drift back from the distant playground and focus finally on the adult Jess. Mom sighs, "OK." We squeeze each other's hands and the noises of her death—her uneven breathing, the grind of an ambulatory infusion pump, the low hum of an oxygen machine—are almost soothing.

I sleep uneasily on a chair next to her, holding her hand. All night, she and I share this dreamy place of comings and goings, this place of life and death, where mother and son swirl around each other like gusts of warm, summer wind.

Seven months before I was born, the doctors told my mother that her baby was dead. Mom had been tossed from a car during a head-on accident and while she suffered only bruises, a blood test confirmed what the doctors feared: she had lost her two-month-old fetus.

I was born on July 20, 1965, the second child of Bruce and Carol Walter and the unlikely survivor of what would be the first of many accidents. Of course, I've heard this story before, but it is different hearing it while I administer pain medication for the tumor that is killing my mother.

I slide the IV tube into the port in her shoulder. "Were you surprised that I lived?" I ask.

"Not really," she says. "I didn't think I'd lost you."

"You weren't scared?"

"Oh sure. But there were worse times."

"When?"

Without hesitation, she says, "Your eye."

In my mind, the stick is huge, two feet long. I was five when it struck my left eye, puncturing the lens, shredding the retina. I bled patiently in the emergency room for two hours while other cases went ahead of us, until the doctors finally informed my parents that I was blind in that eye. I underwent surgery three times, always unsuccessful, and after each, I woke to see my mother's calm hazel eyes and gentle smile.

"It's going to be OK."

I offered plenty of other opportunities for those particular words. I played every sport and was hurt in every sport I played. I broke ribs and fingers, fractured my wrist and tore ligaments in both legs. Twice, I was knocked out by baseball bats, once by boxing gloves. I suffered concussions, contusions and compound fractures. I broke my collarbone *playing golf.* I sprained both ankles in the same basketball game and had my knee surgically reconstructed.

The first time I rode a bicycle, I hit a car. An otherwise tame horse threw me onto my back. I rode my bike off a cliff and, a few months later, flipped my motorcycle in the same place. I wrecked the first three cars I owned. I have collected two dozen stitches in my face—in my chin, my eye and my lips, upper and lower.

As an adult, I continued to rush to my mom for comfort after accidents of the body and spirit. She always listened and hugged me and said that it would be OK.

Being accident prone even informed my early departure from religion. As troubling to me as the question of human suffering was the innate contradiction of a *pattern of accidents*. My first literary hero was the agnostic Vonnegut, who seemed to doubt both science and Christianity in favor of one big, cosmic practical joke.

But what I failed to consider in my self-pitying philosophy was how my accidents were sewn into the fabric of my mother's life too. I watch her now and realize that she suffered my injuries worse than I ever did. I imagine her outside all those hospital rooms, her face in her hands and I wonder how she managed it.

Too late, I've become curious about the patterns of *her* life, which we only began to discuss during these long days of sickness and sleep. Carol was four when her parents divorced, her father dragging her to California to punish her mother, who had been cheating on him. There, he left my mother with her aunt and her grandmother and took an apartment across town.

When Carol was twenty—a year before I was born—her father was killed at work when the crane he was operating fell on him. After that, Mom spent most of her adult life trying to reconcile with her mother, whom she believed had abandoned her. They made an uneasy truce until Carol's mother committed suicide several years ago by shooting herself in the head. Mom found the body, along with a bundle of old letters to her ex-husband, begging to get her baby back.

"I just wish she'd told me," my mom says.

I suppose she had the right to as much bitterness and distance as she could carry. And yet, from this fractured family, she emerged as earnest and self-sacrificing, committed to undoing the things that were done to her. She gave everything for her family and in the hours left over, volunteered for charities and took in foster children.

She passed on to her three kids not just her long fingers and her love for language, but also, hopefully, her empathy and her incredible capacity to love and take care of people.

At fifty-three, she was at her peak, athletic, healthy and happy. So perhaps her doctors didn't take her seriously when she began complaining about heartburn, a sore throat, the inability to keep food down. They put her on antibiotics, told her to reduce the stress in her life. She lost fifteen pounds, went weeks without eating solids and still they told her it was nothing. They scheduled an endoscopy a month down the road. But while Mom was waiting for that test, she began to cough up blood and my father took her to the hospital. I was there when she woke up, frightened and alone.

I said to her, "It's going to be OK."

There is something else. A baby.

My wife is due at the end of May. All spring, Mom and I have talked about this grandchild. It will be her fifth, but there is something different about this one, a clear sense of desperation. She wants to hear everything about this baby and so I squeeze her hand and tell her about Lamaze classes, about the nursery and the gifts we receive. I tell her that when she recovers, she can be the baby's nanny. She smiles at this like someone being lowered into a warm bath.

Of course, I know what she's thinking: Will she even live long enough to see this grandchild?

In May, Mom completes her chemotherapy and radiation and we wait, hopeful that she's somehow beaten eight-to-one odds. While we await an endoscopy to determine whether the tumor is gone, my mother's abdomen begins to swell and she has cramps that are taunting reminders of labor contractions.

My father calls the oncologist but a nurse says the doctor is on vacation. The nurse advises my father to just give her more water, which causes even more swelling of the abdomen and more pain. At night, she curls up on the floor next to her bed and she cries. Helpless, my dad calls the doctor over and over, but the weekend comes before anyone returns his calls.

Finally, the next week, doctors perform the endoscopy and the news is incredible. Unexpected. The tumor is gone. We are shocked. Ecstatic. We cry and laugh and hug. We allow ourselves to imagine the future again.

Mom's pain apparently doesn't hear the good news. Her stomach grows larger and her bowels begin to shut down. The doctors know what this means, but no one tells us until we go in for a CAT scan and find out that the cancer had metastasized and is filling her abdomen with a thick soup made from rogue cells and dying organs. When the doctors tell us that the cancer has spread, Mom turns to me and sobs into my shoulder.

I think of all those times I turned to her and I whisper, "It's going to be OK."

At the end of May, right about the time my baby is due, Mom goes back in the hospital for a last-ditch round of chemo. After a few days, the doctors give up and admit there is nothing more they can do. They advise us to take her home again, so she can die in peace.

They say she has only a few days.

On June 5, clouds curl at the edge of the sky as I drive across town to my parents' house, to prepare their daylight rancher as a place for her to die. We put a hospital bed in the living room, in front of the big picture window overlooking her garden and arrange the flowers and cards in such a way that she might see them.

And then my cell phone rings. It's my wife.

"We're going to have a baby today," she says.

I cry all the way to the hospital, for most of twenty-two miles. That night, my daughter, Ava Caroline Walter, is born by C-section. It shocks me to see her come into life, to gasp those first uncertain breaths.

My brother rushes pictures across town, to my mother's hospital, where she shows them proudly to the nurses and blushes when she realizes we've given the baby her name as a middle name. She holds the pictures in front of her face for several minutes, gasping for her own breath, smiling and taking it all in.

At the other hospital, I cradle Ava in my arms and think about how lonely it must be to die, to know that everyone you love is going on without you. It's almost more than I can bear, this cruel timing. Without Mom, I'm sure that I'll be too weak to raise this baby, to guide her through the accidents and failures that will undoubtedly scar her life.

On June 8, we take my daughter home to begin her life. The same week, my mother goes home to end hers.

I drive from one hospital to the other, raw with fatigue. I doubt that a fiction writer could get away with this contrivance, this overly symbolic, shimmery curtain that has been drawn for me between life and death.

If this were fiction, at least I could create the place I've begun to crave, where a part of my mother would live on forever, where her adult children could go for comfort and advice and to tap into her deep wells of strength and self-sacrifice.

The first time she sees Ava, the timing begins to seem less cruel to me. Mom's face lights up and she won't take her eyes off the baby. I lay Ava on the bed next to her and they nap together that way all afternoon, Mom's hand resting on Ava's back.

The doctors say she could go any time. The morphine is turned up as high as it will go and she is out more than she is in, but in those first few days, while Ava is with her, Mom is revved up, giving my wife and me advice on diaper rash—"Try corn starch"—and asking us for every detail of sleep and poop and eye contact.

She drifts in and out of consciousness, but every time she wakes up, her eyes go right to the baby. "Oh," she says. She makes baby sounds, coos and hums.

Every day, when I leave her house, I tell my mother good-bye and that I love her. I try to disguise this as a normal farewell, but I think she recognizes in my eyes the fear that each day will be her last.

The doctors have stopped trying to feed her or treat the cancer, but my mother will not cooperate with them by dying in a timely fashion. A week passes. And then another. The pain gets worse and the hallucinations more vivid. But there is still the glimmer of her, the empathy in those eyes.

She is only conscious for a couple of hours a day now and she spends much of it holding her new granddaughter tightly against her shoulder, just patting Ava's back and smiling, holding on to life, I guess.

"I'm not ready," she says one day. She talks to each of her children about her death and gives us encouragement and instructions. She tells us she's proud of us and that she will love us forever. She asks me to eulogize her.

I keep trying to give her the chance to talk about her life, expecting to hear how unfair cancer is, or about the things she regrets in life and fears about death. I figure—like any of us— she wants to talk about herself.

Instead, she asks me, "Who's gonna take care of everyone?"

Another week passes. The doctors gave her three *days*, but it's been three *weeks*.

My father is exhausted but he won't leave her side and so my brother and sister and I force him to go to bed. We take turns spending long, sleepless nights with her, trying to provide comfort from the anxious morphine dreams. *"It's going to be OK."*

Being an agnostic doesn't leave much room for hope or prayer and yet I watch her face for some sign that her spirit is moving on and I promise to abandon all my doubts if God will give me even the smallest sign, any indication that she is moving on to *some other place*. But all I see is a dying woman who longs to keep holding babies.

On July 7, almost a month after the doctors said she would die, I tell Mom that I am leaving and that I love her. I ask if she wants me to bring Ava the next day and she smiles and says, weakly, "Yes." It's the only conscious word she speaks that day.

After I leave, my father sits in the chair next to her, holds her hand for a while and then slips off into a nap. When he wakes up, she is gone.

Ava is three months old now and she has the long fingers and gentle eyes of her late grandmother. One day, while I'm at work in the basement, she slips out of my wife's hands and falls face-first on the sidewalk, bloodying her mouth.

My wife sobs and screams for me, but I stand apart for just a moment at the top of the stairs, filled again with the fear that I'm not up to this, that I lack the innate ability to soothe and comfort the way *she* did, that I'm not prepared for the blood and the pain, the disappointment and the awful inevitability of my own death. I imagine again my mother outside all those hospital rooms and I wonder what incredible strength allowed her to go on when she knew full well that there would always be more pain.

This is not the legacy I want for my children, this tendency to split skin and break bones, to tumble and crash and fail.

And yet something profound happens as I cross the room and calm my wife, as I take our crying, bleeding baby in my arms and press her to my shoulder. It is the completion of some circle, I suppose, and there is no greater sound than the softening of Ava's sobs as I whisper, over and over, *"It's OK. It's OK. It's OK."*

The doctor confirms that it is a superficial injury but my wife and I are quiet most of the night, imagining all the things that could have been—brain damage and concussions. Permanent scars. The chance that our child will make it through life intact suddenly seems remote, impossible.

All night, we take turns checking Ava's breathing.

"You know the only person who would make me feel better?" my wife says. "Your mom."

She was terribly camera shy for such a pretty woman, especially at the end. But one day, while she slept with Ava, my dad snuck into the room and snapped a few pictures from a respectful distance. Those photographs are placed carefully in an album, but they exist much more vividly inside of me. I suppose I used to picture my mother holding me in her lap, wiping the blood off my newest wound, whispering to me that I would be OK. But that seems to be my job now.

And so perhaps my mother can finally rest. In my mind, she will lie back forever and press her granddaughter to her shoulder, cover Ava's tiny back with a shaking hand and hold on with everything she has left.

I see now that she drew her strength that way, just as she once drew it from holding my sister, my brother and me, wiping our tears and telling us that everything would be OK. My mother knew something holy—that in the comfort a parent gives a child, life regenerates itself.

That night, unable to sleep, I stand above Ava's bed and place my hand on her back to check her breathing.

Perhaps there is some dreamy place where my mother's spirit lives on. But even if I never find it, there is always *this* place, this tiny back where her hand gripped immortality and where my hand now rests, feeling in every inhale and exhale the gentle rhythm of life.

Nelson Algren was the author of *The Man with the Golden Arm* as well as many other novels. "Childhood" appears in *Conversations with Nelson Algren,* edited by H. E. F. Donohue.

Hilton Als is the author of *The Women.* He lives in New York and writes frequently for the *New Yorker.* He is an advisory editor at *Grand Street.*

Russell Baker is a *New York Times* columnist.

Timothy Beneke is a freelance writer, best known for his *Men on Rape* (1982). His second book, *Proving Manhood: Reflections on Men and Sexism,* was published by the University of California Press in 1997.

Originally trained as a sociologist, **J. Herman Blake** is the vice chancellor for undergraduate education at Indiana University–Purdue University Indianapolis. He was formerly president of Tougaloo College and for many years provost of Oakes College at the University of California, Santa Cruz.

Bob Blauner, the editor of this volume, is professor emeritus of sociology at the University of California, Berkeley. The author of *Black Lives, White Lives: Racial Oppression in America* and *Alienation and Freedom,* he is currently working on a series of autobiographical writings as well as a collection of essays on race relations.

John Boe is a lecturer in English on the Davis campus of the University of California. He is editor of the journal *Writing on the Edge,* a professional storyteller, and an author whose most recent book is *Life Itself: Messiness Is Next to Goddessness and Other Essays.*

Art Buchwald, formerly a columnist for the *Washington Post,* is the author of many books, including *Leaving Home: A Memoir.*

John Cheever's posthumous *Journals* became controversial for their frank discussion of the inner torment brought about by the author's sexual obsessions and bisexuality. They also record his conflicted feelings about his mother, as well as providing a fascinating look at the creative process which produced some of the most important American fiction of the twentieth century.

Nick Davis wrote and directed the upcoming feature film *1999.* He also wrote and directed *Jack* (aka "The Last Kennedy Film") for CBS Television and wrote (with Brooks Hansen) the novel *Boone.*

Kirk Douglas, one of America's leading actors, is also an accomplished writer. Since his autobiography, *The Ragman's Son,* he has written several novels.

Martin Duberman, one of America's leading historians and biographers (*Paul Robeson*), is the founder of the Center for Lesbian and Gay Studies (CLAGS) at the City University of New York Graduate School and the author of sixteen books. He has just published two anthologies, *A Queer World* and *Queer Representation.*

Stephen Dunn has published ten collections of poetry, including *Loosestrife* in 1996. Among his many awards are fellowships from the National Endowment for the Arts and the Guggenheim Foundation. He teaches at Stockton State College in New Jersey.

W. D. Ehrhart is the author of a number of books of prose and poetry, and he is the editor of the Vietnam poetry anthologies *Carrying the Darkness* and *Unaccustomed Mercy*. He lives in Philadelphia with his wife, Anne, and daughter Leela. His mother died in 1990.

Formerly a reporter for the *New York Times,* in recent years **Samuel G. Freedman** has written a number of major works in contemporary American social history, including *Upon This Rock: The Miracles of a Black Church* and *The Inheritance: How Three Families and America Moved from Roosevelt to Reagan and Beyond.*

Henry Louis Gates, Jr., is one of our most prominent men of letters. He is an essayist, scholar, and archivist and Chair of African-American Studies at Harvard University. A recent work is the monumental *Norton Anthology of African-American Literature.*

Rafael Jesús González teaches creative writing and literature at Laney College in Oakland. Widely published in reviews and anthologies in the U.S. and abroad, González was poet in residence at the Oakland Museum and the Oakland Public Library in 1996. A painter, sculptor, and installation artist, he has exhibited his work at museums in Mexico, the U. S., and Europe.

Donald Hall is one of America's leading poets. He has recently published *The Old Life,* a collection of poems about his farmhouse in New Hampshire and his life with the late Jane Kenyon. Hall also writes children's books.

Gardiner Harris is a newspaper reporter who covers Appalachian Kentucky for the *Louisville Courier-Journal.*

Hank Heifetz is a poet, translator, and writer of fiction. His publications include the novel *Where Are the Stars in New York?* and translations of several ancient Indian epics, including Kalidasa's: *The Origin of the Young Lord* from Sanskrit and *The*

Forest Book of the Kambara (with George Hart) from Tamil. He lives in Mexico and most recently has translated Enrique Krauze's monumental *Mexico: Biography of Power.*

Juan Felipe Herrera, "one of America's leading young poets" (*Poetry Flash*), lives in Fresno with his partner, the poet Margarita Luna Robles. Besides teaching at Fresno State University, he is actively involved in theater, and has had leading roles with El Teatro Campesino productions of works by Luis Valdez. He has published seven collections of poems, a children's book, and most recently an account of his return to Chiapas: *Mayan Drifter: Chicano Poet in the Lowlands of America.*

Gus Lee authored the best-selling *China Boy, Honor and Duty,* and *Tiger's Tail.* He attended West Point and the University of California at Davis Law School. A former prosecutor and senior executive, he writes full time and lives with his wife and two children.

Haki R. Madhubuti is the founder, publisher, and director of the Third World Press in Chicago. He is a professor at Chicago State University and director emeritus of its Gwendolyn Brooks Center. His latest books are *Claiming Earth* (1994); *Black Men: Obsolete, Single, and Dangerous?* (1990), and *GroundWork: New and Selected Poems Don L. Lee/Haki R. Madhubuti, 1966–1996.* In 1991 he received the American Book Award for publishing and editing.

Steve Masover was born in Chicago in 1958 and moved to the San Francisco Bay Area in 1970. He studied English literature at the University of California, Berkeley, and is currently working on his first novel.

T. S. Matthews was for many years the editor-in-chief of *Time* magazine. He was also a poet, novelist, and the author of two works of autobiography and biography, *Name and Address* and *Jacks or Better.*

Henry Miller was one of the first American writers to challenge Victorian-era restrictions on candid descriptions of sex. In addition to such well-known (and banned) novels as *Tropic of Cancer* and *Tropic of Capricorn*, his autobiography *My Life and Times* is also a classic.

Fred Moramarco teaches literature at San Diego State University and is the editor of *Poetry International*. His own poetry has appeared in a wide range of periodicals and his books include *Containing Multitudes: Poetry in the U.S. 1950–1990*, *Modern American Poetry*, and *Men of Our Time: An Anthology of Male Poetry in Contemporary America*.

Peter Najarian is a novelist and painter whose books include *Daughters of Memory*, *Wash Me On Home, Mama*, and *Voyages*. "The Artist's Mother" is part of a larger autobiographical work he has just completed.

B. J. Nelson is the author of three novels, *The Last Station*, *Brothers*, and *The Pull*.

Daniel Oberti is a ceramic artist, sculptor, and poet who lives in Sebastopol, California.

Mark O'Brien is a poet and journalist who lives in Berkeley, California. He has published two books of poems, *Breathing* and *The Man in the Iron Lung*. His autobiography, *How I Became a Human Being*, will be published by Kodansha in 1998. His life and work are featured in the film *Breathing Lessons* (directed by Jessica Yu) which won an Academy Award for short documentary in 1997.

Charles Olson taught at Black Mountain College, where, as a leading member of the "Black Mountain Group," he became a major influence on the development of modern American poetry. He wrote his famous *Maximus* poems in his hometown of Gloucester, Massachusetts.

David Ray won the Allen Ginsberg Award for 1997. He lives in Tucson, where he teaches at the University of Arizona. His latest book of poetry is *Kangaroo Paws*.

Kenneth Rexroth was not only a major American poet, he was also a gifted translator of Chinese and Japanese poetry. An anarchist by conviction, he may be best known as a precursor of the Beat poets, whose innovations he supported.

Norman Sasowsky is an artist. He is also professor emeritus of art at the University of Delaware.

A resident of New York and London, **Andrew Solomon** is a contributing writer to the *New York Times Magazine* and a regular contributor to *The New Yorker*. He is the author of the novel *A Stone Boat* as well as *The Irony Tower: Soviet Artists in a Time of Glasnost*. Solomon has been an advisor to the Clinton administration on Russian affairs.

The late **Wallace Stegner** evoked the landscapes of the American West like no other writer in the second half of the twentieth century. The author of *Angle of Repose*, *The Big Rock Candy Mountain*, and *Crossing to Safety*, as well as many other novels and works of nonfiction, he also founded and directed the writing program at Stanford University.

For many decades, **John Updike** has occupied a unique place in American letters. He is a novelist, critic, poet, essayist, and memoirist. A recent book is *Golf Dreams*.

Jess Walter has won regional and national recognition for his writing. He lives in Spokane, Washington, with his wife and two daughters.

Professor of community studies and sociology at the University of California at Santa Cruz, **David Wellman** is the author of

Portraits of White Racism and *The Union Makes Us Strong,* a study of West Coast longshoremen.

Allen Wheelis is a psychiatrist and a novelist. He is the author of many books, including the classic *The Quest for Identity.*

Gary Young's poetry has appeared in magazines such as *Poetry,* the *Kenyon Review* and the *American Poetry Review.* He is the author of *Days, The Dream of a Moral Life,* and several other award-winning collections. Young is also an accomplished designer and illustrator whose prints are represented at the Museum of Modern Art and museums and libraries around the world. He is the publisher of the Greenhouse Review Press.